LITERARY TERMS AND CRITICISM

New Edition

John Peck
and
Martin Coyle

150th YEAR
M
MACMILLAN

First edition 1984
Reprinted 1985, 1986, 1987, 1988, 1989, 1990, 1991
Second edition 1993

Published by
THE MACMILLAN PRESS LTD
Houndmills, Basingstoke, Hampshire RG21 2XS
and London
Companies and representatives
throughout the world

ISBN 0–333–58887–8

A catalogue record for this book is available
from the British Library

Printed in China

HOW TO STUDY LITERATURE
General Editors: John Peck and Martin Coyle

LITERARY TERMS AND CRITICISM

New Edition

IN THE SAME SERIES

How to Study a Novel   *John Peck*
How to Study a Shakespeare Play   *John Peck and Martin Coyle*
How to Begin Studying English Literature   *Nicholas Marsh*
How to Study a Jane Austen Novel   *Vivien Jones*
How to Study a Thomas Hardy Novel   *John Peck*
How to Study a D. H. Lawrence Novel   *Nigel Messenger*
How to Study a Charles Dickens Novel   *Keith Selby*
How to Study a Joseph Conrad Novel   *Brian Spittles*
How to Study a Renaissance Play   *Chris Coles*
How to Study Modern Drama   *Kenneth Pickering*
How to Study a Poet   *John Peck*
How to Study Chaucer   *Robert Pope*
How to Study Romantic Poetry   *Paul O'Flinn*
How to Study an E. M. Forster Novel   *Nigel Messenger*
How to Study Modern Poetry   *Tony Curtis*
How to Study Milton   *David Kearns*

*Freud puts too much emphasis on the controlling
ego being separate from the id. Lacan sees the Ego
as being a carrier of the neurosis:
there is no such thing as a
coherent self.*

Contents

General editors' preface   vii

How to use this guide   viii

1   English, American and post-colonial literature:
    a brief survey   1

2   Poetry   12

3   Drama   78

4   The novel   107

5   Critical concepts   132

6   Critical positions and perspectives   165

Further reading   200

Author index   213

Subject index   217

For Rachel and Pamela

General editors' preface

EVERYBODY who studies literature, either for an examination or simply for pleasure, experiences the same problem: how to understand and respond to the text. As every student of literature knows, it is perfectly possible to read a book over and over again and yet still feel baffled and at a loss as to what to say about it. One answer to this problem, of course, is to accept someone else's view of the text, but how much more rewarding it would be if you could work out your own critical response to any book you choose or are required to study.

The aim of this series is to help you develop your critical skills by offering practical advice about how to read, understand and analyse literature. Each volume provides you with a clear method of study so that you can see how to set about tackling texts on your own. While the authors of each volume approach the problem in a different way, every book in the series attempts to provide you with some broad ideas about the kind of texts you are likely to be studying and some broad ideas about how to think about literature; each volume then shows you how to apply these ideas in a way which should help you construct your own analysis and interpretation. Unlike most critical books, therefore, the books in this series do not simply convey someone else's thinking about a text, but encourage you and show you how to think about a text for yourself.

Each book is written with an awareness that you are likely to be preparing for an examination, and therefore practical advice is given not only on how to understand and analyse literature, but also on how to organise a written response. Our hope is that although these books are intended to serve a practical purpose, they may also enrich your enjoyment of literature by making you a more confident reader, alert to the interest and pleasure to be derived from literary texts.

John Peck
Martin Coyle

How to use this guide

Literary Terms and Criticism is a practical guide to the study of English literature. This revised edition includes a number of new topics and new areas, such as twentieth-century poetry and women's poetry, as well as a number of additional critical terms, such as 'Ideology' and 'Carnival'. Section 6, dealing with critical theory, has been revised to include recent developments in criticism, and we have also now included a section on further reading. Our main intention, however, remains that of offering practical advice on how to come to grips with the texts and authors you are studying.

The guide itself is basically a dictionary of literary terms. It resembles other such dictionaries in that it attempts to provide essential information on a wide range of literary topics. It differs from other dictionaries, however, in that we have tried to produce a book that meets the particular needs of students at school, college and university. This means that the overall structure of the book, the range and kind of terms included, and the approach adopted within the individual entries, are somewhat unorthodox as compared to other guides to literary terms.

First, the overall structure: the standard approach is to provide a straightforward alphabetical listing of terms. This should make things easy to find, but a list of terms is not all that helpful if you are not entirely sure what you are looking for. We have, therefore, divided the book into six sections – a 'survey of literature', 'Poetry', 'Drama', 'The novel', 'Critical concepts', 'Critical positions and perspectives'. If, for example, you are studying a novel, you might find a number of useful ideas simply by browsing through the Novel section. If you know exactly what you are looking for, the quickest way of finding the relevant entry is to consult the Subject index at the back of the book. Our own experience as students was that we were not only puzzled by specific terms, such as 'metaphysical poetry', but also lacked broader ideas about literature.

The Poetry, Drama and Novel sections, therefore, begin with introductory essays that might help you understand the characteristics of the major genres.

These introductory essays, along with the survey and the introductory essay on criticism in the final section, are intended to provide a sense of the broad picture. They are followed by more specific entries, alphabetically arranged. We should point out that this is not an all-inclusive guide: we do not include terms such as 'limerick' which are not in any way central to the academic study of literature. The exclusion of minor terms has allowed us room to include period terms such as 'Renaissance poetry' and 'the eighteenth-century novel'. These are not, strictly speaking, literary terms, but they are descriptive terms that students encounter. It seemed more important to cover the terms and ideas you are likely to meet, even to the extent of including a separate entry on Shakespeare, than to worry too much about maintaining a pure approach. The intention is to provide helpful information which is directly relevant to your studies.

This idea was also uppermost in our minds in determining the approach adopted within each entry. We do not attempt to cover the entire history of any term, nor do we attempt to list all the authors who have chosen to work in a certain mode. In their place we have substituted critical discussion, attempting to provide guidelines for your study of literature. Underlying many of the definitions is the idea that literature attempts to come to terms with, or order, the complexity, or disorder, of experience. You may find this idea limiting, but it should prove useful in helping you to find your critical feet. Our hope is that the definitions will show you how to get started, but really this is a guide to grow out of as you become more confident and learn how to develop and express your own ideas about literature.

Probably the best way to use this book is to browse through it, stopping at whatever catches your attention. But, as we have said, there is a Subject index which should enable you to find a specific term quickly. In addition there is an Author index. Most of the major authors in English are discussed in the guide: by following up the entries in the Author index you should discover some quite useful guidelines about how to approach and discuss an individual author. The major shortcoming of most guides to literary terms is that they so often fail to tell you what you want to know; our hope is that we have gone at least some way towards providing the kind of basic information and critical discussion that you are likely to find useful.

In preparing this new edition of *Literary Terms and Criticism* we have particularly focused our attention on expanding sections 5 and 6 which deal with 'Critical concepts' and 'Critical positions and perspectives'. What we have sought to do is to include as many of the new terms and critical ideas of post-structuralism, feminism, Marxism, New Historicism and modern psychoanalytic criticism as we feel are useful and accessible to students embarking on the serious study of literature. We are conscious of the difficulty of some of this new material but also of its importance to students. Very often you will find that an idea discussed in section 5, under critical concepts, is discussed further in section 6, the critical positions section. The two sections are intended to be complementary and to raise more complex ideas than in the preceding sections of the guide.

We should like to thank those who have helped us in the preparation of this revised edition. In particular, we are grateful to our colleagues Catherine Belsey, who discussed some of the new material with us, and Fred Botting for his comments and ideas. We are also grateful to Cathryn Tanner at Macmillan for offering us the opportunity to prepare this new edition.

University of Wales,   JOHN PECK
Cardiff   MARTIN COYLE

1

English, American and post-colonial literature: a brief survey

LITERARY criticism is primarily concerned with discussing individual works of literature. The most important thing is to read and reread the books you are studying, trying to decide what they are about and how they work. It is also useful, though, to have some broader ideas and information about literature. In particular, an awareness of the larger context into which any work fits can help you understand the individual text you are studying. There are, in fact, two contexts in which any work can be seen: a generic or genre context, and a historical context.

Genre means a type or class of literature. The main generic division today is into poetry, drama and the novel, but in earlier times the major genres were recognised as epic, tragedy, lyric, comedy and satire. The logic behind these divisions is straightforward: all works of a certain kind have a great deal in common and are therefore grouped together under these broad headings. The advantage of knowing about these divisions is that they tell us what sort of text we are dealing with. Many of the definitions in the following sections provide information about the genres and, on a smaller scale, the modes an author might choose to write in. A mode is a recognised type or kind of work within a genre, such as the sonnet or the realistic novel. The way in which the definitions should prove helpful is that if, for example, you have been reading some sonnets but do not know how to start discussing them, the definition of sonnet should indicate the most important characteristics of the mode. The definitions, then, should provide a starting-point in telling you what to expect and what to look for. They should also help you identify what is distinctive about specific works of literature, for much of an author's originality lies in what he or

1

she adds to the established conventions and patterns of the genre and mode within which he or she is working.

Every work of literature has a generic context. In addition, every work has a **historical context**: that is, it belongs to a particular historical period. Writers at a given time tend to have similar concerns and, often, similar values. An awareness of the historical context of a writer, then, should tell you what you can expect to encounter in, say, an eighteenth-century poet as opposed to a romantic poet. This again provides a starting-point for looking at a work; and, once more, seeing what a text has in common with other texts, in this instance texts written at around the same time, should help you see more clearly the ways in which a specific work is distinctive. Many of the definitions in the following sections focus on individual genres at particular times, such as the eighteenth-century novel or modern poetry, but it is also useful to be aware of the broad historical pattern of literature. What follows here, therefore, is a simple historical survey of literature in English.

English literature begins with **Old English** or **Anglo-Saxon** literature, which mainly belongs to the period before the Norman Conquest in 1066. The language in which it is written is more like German than modern English. The greatest single poem is *Beowulf* (probably written around 700), which can be described as either an epic or tragic poem. A king's hall is threatened by a monster called Grendel. Beowulf comes to help, and kills the monster and its mother. Fifty years later a dragon attacks his own kingdom: Beowulf kills it, but dies himself. One way of making sense of this story is to use a simple critical idea that we can apply to a great many literary works: we can say that what the poem is about is Beowulf's attempt to establish and maintain order in a threatening and disordered world. In other words we can look at the poem in terms of its larger meaning and pattern, seeing how it makes use of a tension between the ideas of order and disorder. The same pattern is in evidence in other works from this period, such as the prose Chronicles, Christian poems such as 'The Dream of the Rood', and 'The Battle of Maldon'. This, like *Beowulf*, is a narrative poem, the major mode in Old English literature, and similarly deals with the desire for order in a savage and unruly world.

Middle English or **medieval** literature belongs to the period 1066 to about 1550 (dates for literary periods can only ever be approximate). The outstanding writer is Chaucer. In this period there are narrative poems (such as *Sir Gawain and the Green Knight*, fourteenth century; and Chaucer's works, including *The Canterbury Tales*, around 1400), lyric poetry, and drama (the miracle and morality plays). Perhaps the most distinctive feature of the literature of this period is that it is markedly Christian. It is also often very sophisticated. A familiar pattern is the gap between the Christian ideal and the reality of life in this imperfect world. Chaucer's *Canterbury Tales* can be looked at in this way: the ideal is a devout band of pilgrims on their way to Canterbury, all acknowledging the greatness and authority of God, but the reality is a motley group of characters, with numerous flaws in their personalities, who tell stories that reveal what an untidy and problematic world we live in. An ideal of religious order is thus set against the reality of everyday disorder. It is important to recognise, however, that Chaucer is a comic poet: he is amused by humanity's folly, but not troubled by it. Confident that God's order prevails, he can enjoy the imperfections of fallen man and woman, weighing them against the ideals of Christianity.

The notion of an ideal Christian existence is still in evidence after the medieval period, for example in Spenser's *Faerie Queene* (1596), which presents Christian knights on journeys through life encountering all manner of temptations. This essentially religious view of experience starts to disappear, however, during the period that follows medieval literature. This is the period around the beginning of the seventeenth century and is one of the richest eras in English literature: it is the time of Shakespeare, Marlowe, Donne, Jonson and many other outstanding poets and dramatists. This is often referred to as the **Renaissance** period in English literature (approximate dates are 1550 to 1660), but one can also talk about modern literature starting at this time: from about 1600 onwards the language resembles the language we use today, and this in itself indicates that the works are referring to a world which we can identify with in some way.

The literature of the Renaissance is so rich because society was changing in such a fundamental way: the world was becoming much more complex, with the whole economic and social fabric of society changing. A great gap opens up between those religious ideals which had previously dominated society's thinking and a new sort of dynamic society which no longer found it possible to focus on other-worldly concerns in the same way as had been the case in the past. What we thus find in Renaissance literature is a tension between a traditional order and disruption of this order. It is this tension which is at the heart of such Shakespeare plays as *Hamlet* (1600) and *King Lear* (1605): the old order is dislodged and displaced by the new self-interest of a new sort of worldly-wise person.

The central historical event in the seventeenth century, the Civil War of 1642–51, embodies a similar conflict between old and new, between the king's traditional status and authority and new forces who wish to wrest power from the king. This tension between an old order and disorder is also evident in Milton's choice of theme for his epic poem *Paradise Lost* (1667): the rebellion of Adam and Eve against God. Deceived by Satan, they are expelled from Eden with its ideal order and have to confront the reality of life in our disordered world.

Like medieval writers, seventeenth-century writers still recognise God as the only true source of order, even though so much of their attention is on how people are distracted and tempted by worldly ambition and secular concerns. Towards the end of the century, however, the focus of literature becomes almost entirely secular. Explicitly religious poetry all but disappears and is replaced by social poetry, for example the poetry of Dryden and Pope. The period from about 1660 to 1790 is in addition characterised by the rise of the novel, a genre which concentrates on social life, in particular on the lives of individuals in a complex society. What the poets and novelists (such as Richardson and Fielding) of the **eighteenth century** are interested in is in seeing whether harmony and balance can be created within society. The tension that is in evidence in their works, however, is between this notion of the desirability of social order and their awareness of the inevitability of social disorder. Here again it proves useful to look at the literature of a period in terms of a pattern of the tension between order and disorder, seeing how the writers deal with the gap between how things could or should be in society and how they really are.

Social order, however, is not a very inspiring ideal, although it continues to be at the heart of many subsequent works of literature, particularly at the heart of realistic novels, such as those of Jane Austen, who was writing around 1800, and George Eliot, whose novels were published between 1859 and 1876. The period in which Austen writes is known as the **romantic** period, though Austen herself seems a slightly anomalous figure in the literature of this time (roughly 1790 to 1830), when there was a reaction against the social philosophy of eighteenth-century literature.

The romantic period is one of the great ages of English poetry, with Blake, Wordsworth, Coleridge, Keats, Byron and Shelley all publishing around 1800. Unlike earlier writers, the romantics do not turn to God as the source of order, nor is order sought in society: what the romantics seek is to find a harmony in life which is at one with a pattern that can be found in the natural world. At the same time there is a great stress on the imagination: the source of order becomes internal, as in the work of Wordsworth, where there is a stress on how his mind interacts with what he sees in the natural world, so that some pattern and harmony is created in life. Wordsworth is aware, however, that this vision is a rare thing, that it might be illusory, and that life for the most part is disordered, puzzling and fragmented.

Victorian literature develops from, rather than reacting against, romantic literature, and the poets of this age (1830 to the end of the century), such as Tennyson and Browning, are the heirs of the romantics. They cannot, however, sustain the romantics' confidence in the autonomy of their own imaginations. There is no longer the same ability to create a vision of order and unity. Instead, there is a far more dominant impression of the world as fragmented, of life being too complicated and painful for any real sense of order to be found. The feeling of confusion and despair that characterises a lot of Victorian poetry has much to do with the religious doubts and uncertainties of the period. Literature might have been explicitly secular from the late seventeenth century onwards, but it is only in the Victorian period that a certain traditional religious confidence disappears, and, with the disappearance of this confident faith in a controlling deity, the world begins to seem much more confusing, depressing, and even chaotic.

In addition, society itself was becoming increasingly complex, something that is reflected in the Victorian novel. The Victorian period is the great age of the novel, possibly because the novel was the only form that could expand enough to cope with the scale and complexity of Victorian society as it, too, expanded and changed with the growth of industrialisation. The great novelists of the age are Dickens and Eliot, both of whom seek to create a full and intricate picture of a complex social world. They are fully aware of the disorder, injustices and hardships of the world they live in, yet at the same time there is a confidence in their writing that the novel can confront the whole of life.

It is a confidence that subsequent novelists cannot sustain. As we move towards the **twentieth century** we find an increasing sense that life is overwhelmingly confusing and complicated. In late nineteenth- and twentieth-century literature, for example in the novels of Hardy, Conrad, Joyce, Woolf and Lawrence and in the poetry of T. S. Eliot and Yeats, there is a feeling that the world has become so baffling that it is impossible to make sense of it, particularly as the decline, and in many cases the total eclipse, of religious faith robs writers of any secure perspective or framework of shared values from which they can interpret and make sense of experience. The central historical event of the early years of the twentieth century is the First World War (1914–18), a war so terrifying and tragic that it seems to sum up a world that is closer to chaos than to any sane order.

Yet the early twentieth century is a period of extraordinary creativity in all the arts – not only in poetry and the novel, but also in music and painting, and even drama is revitalised after many years of stagnation. What this points to again is the fact that rapid social change, an alteration in the whole structure of society, almost always stimulates the production of great art. The text which perhaps best exemplifies the age is T. S. Eliot's poem *The Waste Land* (1922), which presents a vision of a fractured society where the poet can find no order or consolation. As with so many works of the period it is innovative and experimental in form: it seems to be built out of fragments of poetry, reflecting a world where the artist can no longer impose confident and comprehensive control over the facts he encounters. A term often applied to the formally innovative works of this period is **modernist:** modernist works, such as Eliot's, Woolf's or Joyce's, are often difficult to read, but they become less difficult if we see that the difficulty simply enacts the problems the artist is having in making sense of the world.

T. S. Eliot was an American, and at this time it makes sense to start looking at British and American literature together. We could trace a lengthy history for **American literature**, but as far as most readers are concerned American literature really comes to life around 1850. Significant works are the essays of Emerson and the poems of Walt Whitman and Emily Dickinson, but it is perhaps most rewarding to focus on the development of the American novel from about 1850. The most important texts in this context are Hawthorne's *The Scarlet Letter* (1850), Melville's *Moby-Dick* (1851) and Twain's *The Adventures of Huckleberry Finn* (1884). Unlike the English novel, which emerges from and comments on a long-established society, the American novel is not immersed in society in the same sort of way. Instead it often takes the form of a symbolic journey, which can be a journey into the unknown territories of the mind. American novels are often referred to as 'romances', for the writers, unlike their English counterparts, tend to turn their backs on society and go off into conjecture, dream and myth.

What we witness in the second half of the nineteenth century, then, is the development of a distinctively American novel. As American literature moves into the twentieth century, however, it establishes a closer link with European culture. This is first evident in the novels of Henry James, published between 1875 and 1904, which present the lives of young American idealists and their experiences in the English social world. Later novelists such as Fitzgerald and Faulkner, while having distinctively American qualities, are heavily indebted to the example of Joyce, but it is a two-way exchange, for the American poets T. S. Eliot and Ezra Pound are domiciled in London and help shape the whole course of English poetry at this time.

After the modernist era, however, which can be said to come to an end in the twenties, American literature is by and large far more adventurous than British literature. It is as if British writers do not know how to advance from the experiments of the twenties, and so retreat into safer waters. W. H. Auden and Graham Greene are the two best-known names from the thirties and forties, yet neither is a writer of the first order. Throughout the fifties, sixties and seventies, the English novel, with the exception of the works of William Golding, settles down into a fairly conventional realistic pattern. Similarly, the poetry of this time, apart from the interesting work of Philip Larkin and Seamus Heaney, remains unexcitingly modest.

In a relatively unambitious period of British literature the one exception has been in drama; the last forty years have been an exciting period for the English theatre. There are both established dramatists such as John Osborne, Harold Pinter and Tom Stoppard, and newer writers such as David Hare, Caryl Churchill and Trevor Griffiths who together offer an important discussion of the state of contemporary Britain. Here again the pattern that is in evidence is one of writers trying to order their impressions of a complex society undergoing change, and in Britain since the Second World War (1939–45) it seems to be the theatre that has provided the most suitable forum for discussing these changes. This is possibly because the questions that have had to be faced are political questions about the way society orders itself, and drama is the form that lends itself best to this sort of political or social debate.

America has also produced impressive drama in the period from 1930 to the present day, for example the works of Eugene O'Neill and Arthur Miller. In America though, unlike in Britain, the same period has been an equally strong one for poetry and the novel. There is the poetry of Wallace Stevens and William Carlos Williams, and America continues to be the source of the most energetic and original poetry in English, for example in the works of Robert Lowell, John Berryman, Adrienne Rich and John Ashbery. Even in the realistic novel a writer such as Saul Bellow offers us the impression of an author who is exploring new territory while so many British novelists seem to be retracing familiar ground. America has also set the pace in experimental fiction, as in the novels of Thomas Pynchon. Pynchon can be described as a **post-modernist** writer: the term suggests an experimental form of writing, which can be found in poetry and drama as well as in fiction, which moves beyond the methods of the modernists in finding a new way of writing about the experience of living in a very confusing world. It is not until the late seventies that English fiction begins to catch up with these developments, when, as in the works of Ian McEwan, D. M. Thomas and Salman Rushdie the English novel moves out of its realistic rut and begins to find fresh confidence.

Salman Rushdie is an Indian who lives in England. This leads us on to the fact that alongside British and American literature there is also what has come to be called **post-colonial literature**. The term post-colonial is used to refer to all those literatures and cultures affected by the experience of colonization. Countries affected include the African nations, Australia, Canada, the Caribbean states, India, Pakistan and New Zealand, as well as the islands of the Pacific and Malaysia. (This entry concentrates on texts written in English; if we looked beyond English we would, for example, have to include the literature of South America, which has a complex, and very productive, relationship with the languages, literatures and cultures of Spain and Portugal – see p. 129) What the literatures of the Commonwealth, or in some cases former Commonwealth, countries often share is the idea of a mythic search for a new order that is distinctive and different from that of their imperial British colonizers. This can be seen, for example, in the novels of Patrick White, such as *The Eye of the Storm* (1973). As well as a search for a new kind of order, however, what is also evident in a great deal of post-colonial literature is an awareness of a complex relationship with Britain, and the need to wrest control away from the colonizer by using language in new ways. For example, the New Zealander Keri Hume's *The Bone People* (1983) is a striking novel which tells the story of how three figures – a woman, a man, and a child who cannot speak – come to create new relationships through the recognition of the importance of Maori spiritual values which are conveyed to the reader by the use of the Maori language in the novel.

If there is one theme that could be said to dominate post-colonial literature it is perhaps the meeting of two cultures, and in particular the way in which an indigenous order has been usurped by alien and intrusive values. This theme is evident in Hume's novel, and is also at the heart of much African literature. The Nigerian novelist Chinua Achebe in *Things Fall Apart* (1958) focuses on the disruption of tribal life and traditional culture, while the Nigerian dramatist Wole Soyinka (who was awarded the Nobel Prize for Literature in 1986), in a play such as *The Lion and the Jewel* (1963), examines the way in which modern civilisation threatens the traditional society and culture. Such texts reveal a clash between traditional values and new ideas which is as far-reaching as, and in various ways similar to, that experienced in the English Renaissance, a fact which is borne out in the extraordinary flood of literature from Africa in recent years.

The gap between two cultures, between black and white, is also something that is inevitably at the heart of South African literature; indeed, it would seem impossible in the context of the political regime that dominated South Africa up to the present decade to write about anything other than that country's apartheid policy. It is at the centre of such novels as *The Grass is Singing* (1950) by Doris Lessing, and also at the heart of the work of the radical dramatist Athol Fugard in plays such as *Sizwe Bansi is Dead* (1972). Other post-colonial writers, such as the Trinidadian novelist V. S. Naipaul, author of *A House for Mr Biswas* (1961), also deal with the conflict between black and white cultures, but in Naipaul there is also an awareness of being in a sort of limbo where he has lost his cultural identity because of his extended associations with Britain. And, indeed, it is argued by some that there has often been too much of a Eurocentric orientation in African creative writing. Perhaps the outstanding example of a writer who has attempted to resist such an outside influence is Ngugi wa Thiong'o, who, after completing *Petals in Blood* (1977), with its emphasis on the peasantry and the land as a source of cultural strength, stopped writing in English, arguing that while the bullet of the colonizer 'was the means of physical subjugation, language was the means of spiritual subjugation'.

African-American literature also stands in a complex relationship to a dual African and European cultural heritage: every American writer of African descent works within and against the dual tradition – oral and literary, African and European, male and female – that each inherits as part of his or her North American cultural legacy. Frequently, novels by twentieth-century writers such as Richard Wright, Zora Neale Hurston, Ralph Ellison, James Baldwin, Toni Morrison and Alice Walker explore the disparity between Euro-American myths and Afro-American reality. In the novels of Toni Morrison and Alice Walker, in particular, there is also an exploration of the whole issue of women's place in society, and especially the place of women who are poor and black. In *The Color Purple* (1983), Alice Walker explores the plight of the fourteen-year-old Celie in the harsh world of the American deep south; in *Sula* (1973), Toni Morrison focuses on the friendship between two black women, Sula Peace and Nel Wright, as they mature during the 1920s and 1930s. Their friendship is based on a shared sense of alienation from community and family values, and a similar experience of emptiness in their other relationships – especially with men.

Both *The Color Purple* and *Sula* are extremely powerful novels which foreground issues previously skirted over by literary texts. They are clearly novels which indicate the prominence and importance of women writers in the twentieth century. But in addition, they are part of a radical questioning in the late twentieth century of the way in which traditional order, especially white male order, has been constructed at the expense of ethnic groups, women, the poor, indeed anyone who did not fit readily into the British or American middle classes. What we see happening in post-colonial literature is the challenge to that old order and an exposure of its values. In the place of that old order, we can see, comes a new set of values as writers seek to articulate an alternative and more just sense of things. Art is sometimes defined as the attempt to bring order out of chaos, but in the writings of the second half of the twentieth century it is often order itself that is the problem in the way it is seen to construct and constrict people.

2

Poetry

THERE are a lot of people who read poetry frequently and derive a great deal of pleasure from it, but there are far more who find it difficult to read and hard to understand. Indeed, it is possible to read a poem over and over again and yet still remain at a loss as to what it means. One way of overcoming such problems is to give some consideration to the question of what poetry as a whole is about. If we have a simple but clear idea of how poetry usually works and what sort of topics it normally deals with, then we should be in a better position to understand individual poems.

There are, broadly speaking, two main ways of thinking about poetry. One approach is to concentrate on the poet. Underlying this approach very often is the idea that poetry is primarily an expression of the poet's emotions. The clearest statement of this viewpoint is a comment by Wordsworth that 'poetry is the spontaneous overflow of powerful feelings'. The focus of our attention as critics in this approach is on what the poem can tell us about the poet's innermost being as revealed in the work: we read the poem in order to learn about the figure behind it. Although this is a popular approach to poetry, it is not a very practical one for the reader who is simply baffled by a poem or who cannot see what the 'feelings' are that the poet is expressing and therefore cannot appreciate them. The other shortcoming of this way of looking at poetry is that it is more concerned with the mind and personality behind the poem than with the text itself. It is, then, an unsatisfactory approach, not least because it bypasses the real problem we all experience: reading the poem and trying to understand it.

The second approach, and the one we shall be following throughout this section, concentrates on discussing the poem itself. The focus of our attention here is on the words on the page. Such an approach involves a very different conception of poetry from that outlined above: there the poet is regarded as an elusive, mysterious figure behind the text; here the emphasis is on the poet as 'a maker', a maker of meanings with words. The moment we stress this element of craftsmanship it becomes possible to talk about both the content and form of poetry in much more tangible terms.

Content is what a poem says, what it is about, its subject matter. Form is the way in which it says it, how it is written, the language it uses, the patterns it employs. If we are to come to grips with poetry it does seem essential that we try to account for its most obvious feature, its use of patterned language. (Most poems are written in lines of the same length; usually these lines are arranged into the symmetrical groups we call stanzas; often the poem has a repeated rhyme pattern running through each stanza which is usually fairly conspicuous.) One reason why we find poetry difficult is that all these patterns serve to concentrate and compress the words into much more meaningful relationships with each other than in prose. This does not mean, however, that the poet is therefore dealing with much more complicated issues than we find in prose. The most common misunderstanding of poetry is the assumption that it is concerned with esoteric, abstract matters remote from everyday experience. This is not the case. While poetry itself is a complicated way of writing about experience, its basic subject matter is usually far from complicated.

In theory a poem can be about anything. There are, however, certain topics that concern us all and these are the recurrent themes of poetry. Love is a central experience in life, and it is not surprising that love poems outnumber all others. Death is also a major concern to us all, and this can be linked with religion: most people at some time wonder whether life ends with death or if they are part of some greater pattern. Poets need not, however, concern themselves with such weighty topics: they might wish to write about nature, or their families or some other domestic matter. Poetry becomes less frightening if we realise that it is always concerned with ordinary human concerns, with the daily matters of everybody's life.

It is at this point that we can start to see how the poet is a maker. The central themes of poetry are familiar topics from everyday experience: love, death, nature, religion. What the poet does is take one of these familiar themes and write about it in a striking way. Often he or she will be saying something fairly obvious: for example, that being in love is preferable to not being in love. Our interest as critics is in seeing how the writer takes this sort of ordinary idea and makes it new by the way he or she orders his or her language. Just as a designer might make a beautiful piece of furniture out of something as common as wood, so the poet makes something original out of the ordinary materials of life and words.

Poets, however, can never be totally original. Like any artist they have to work within the limits of their chosen art. In the case of poetry these limits are surprisingly narrow. We can, in fact, reduce poetry to two basic types: narrative and lyric. A narrative poem is a poem that tells a story: the main kinds are the epic, the ballad and the romance. The vast majority of poems, however, are lyrics. A lyric is a poem in which the poet offers a direct response to some aspect of experience, for example the death of a friend. There are poems that are actually called lyrics, but the term 'lyric' is the general label we use to describe most non-narrative poems, including such specific forms as the sonnet, the ode and the elegy, which are all types of lyric.

This division of poetry into two basic types is enormously helpful to us. First, it means that we can readily identify and label the sort of poem we are reading. Second, it enables us to approach a poem – and most often it will be a lyric – with certain expectations about how it will work. This is because of the way in which lyric poetry is usually structured. A conventional love poem will contrast the unhappiness of not being in love with the happiness caused by love. A poem about war will present war as terrifying, but then set against this an impression of the attractiveness of peace. The general rule we can extrapolate from these examples is that lyric poetry works upon the basis of a contrast between some problem or some unattractive or disorderly aspect of life, and an idea of a better, more attractive, order. This disorder/order structure is inherent in the very nature of poetry, which deals with something as diffuse and complicated as life but imposes on life the orderly pattern of the poem itself. The easiest way of thinking about poetry in general is to see it in terms of this broad structural opposition between order and disorder, and this in turn can help us structure our response to an individual poem.

Reading a poem for the first time we might well be baffled. It seems reasonable to assume, however, that the poem must be dealing with some sort of problem: the poet might feel that life is pointless, or he or she might be grieving over the death of a loved one, or be shocked at the awful state of society. What we have to do is look through the, perhaps confusing, surface detail of the poem and identify the nature of the writer's discontent: even if the poem appears cheerful it is likely at some point to hint at unhappiness. The poet is writing about some aspect of the disordered nature of life. He or she is, however, essentially a maker, a maker of order. The poem might start by, say, grieving over a death, but by the end it will probably come to terms with the problem by creating an ordered response. It helps when reading poems to recognise that they will probably contain a number of lines reflecting on some aspect of the disorder of things in the world, but that we shall probably also be able to identify an opposing, more positive, view in the poem. The details of the poem, which can initially appear puzzling, will begin to make sense when we have got hold of this broad structural opposition. Studying poetry becomes much easier if we know that we can always start by looking for this sort of pattern in the text, for a fairly obvious and straightforward opposition: for example, the unhappiness of doubt set against the joy of confident religious faith.

Such a structure is in evidence in all lyric poetry and provides us with a simple way of getting hold of what any poem is about. This will be the case even with those poems where we may feel that very complex ideas are being advanced. Reading poets such as Donne, Wordsworth or T. S. Eliot, for example, we might feel that they are making some kind of large statement about life, that they are putting forward a philosophy about life. This raises the possibility of another way of thinking about poetry, that it explores ideas and that, in order to come to terms with the poet, we need to grasp the informing philosophy. It is this approach to major writers that is taught most often in schools.

The attraction of such an approach is that it offers us some-thing tangible – the poet's ideas – to hold on to. It also makes poetry seem useful, in that the poet is represented as having a valuable philosophy to offer. The limitation of such an approach, however, is that it makes too much of the idea that poetry has a 'message' to convey at the expense of the words on the page. It is really the same kind of approach as that discussed at the beginning of this introduction, the approach that concentrates on the figure of the poet. There is nothing inherently wrong with being inter-ested in the poet's personality or in his or her thinking, it is just that if we do follow these approaches, if we do try to pinpoint the person or ideas behind the text, we can easily lose sight of the important thing, the poetry itself. Such approaches often go hand in hand with studying the author's life, with the result that the poetry can come to be seen as merely an echo of the poet's life or views instead of the main subject of interest.

This is why we have stressed the idea that the poet is a 'maker', for this idea does help us concentrate on looking at the text. It also provides us with a simple critical method for tackling even the most complicated and ambitious poetry: even with major authors we can always make use of, and rely on, the simple critical strategy outlined above of looking for a broad opposition between order and disorder. Even if the poet does have a philosophy, it is always going to be the case that he or she will devote much of the poem's space to creating a sense of life's problems before introducing his or her positive response, before putting forward his or her own theories about what makes life bearable or how it should be ordered. Rather than try to unravel the poet's ideas, it is much more practical to approach even the most philosophically complex poem in a fairly naïve way: looking at how the poet uses language to create an impression of some of the woes of the world, and then looking at how he or she presents the idea of a more desirable order.

So far our stress has been on how the poet looks at life and offers an ordered response. Our interest as readers lies in seeing the way in which he or she establishes a sense of something negative and something positive in the text. Most students, it is true, begin to feel a lot more secure when studying a major poet such as Keats or Wordsworth once they have grasped a sense of what the writer's positive values are, the answers the poet gives to the problems he or she sees. One view of poetry, however, would argue that many poems, rather than providing answers, simply ask questions. Keats's 'Ode to a Nightingale', for example, presents a cruel world where people die young, but sets against this the ideal world of the nightingale. Keats examines the idea of a disordered world and an alternative ideal world, but the poem does not provide any answers: all it does is set the facts of disorder against a desire for order.

There are many such poems where the meaning is found not in the poet's ideas but rather in the gap between the patterns the writer creates and life's lack of pattern, in the gap between the dream of order and the reality of life's lack of order. Although this might seem a difficult idea to grasp, it is not really so, because it takes us back to the main characteristic of poetry: that it is a patterned response to that unpatterned thing life. In this view of poetry, the poet does not seek to impose his or her ideas upon us but merely enacts the human need to try constantly to make sense of the world. This is why poetry so often seems more complicated than any message or meaning we can extract from it, for the poet is as much caught up in life's problems as we are. Indeed, reading poets such as Donne, Shakespeare or Wordsworth, we might well feel that they are far less concerned to order life than to suggest, in the complex texture of their verse, that the world is more complicated than our ability to understand it. We may well be able to find positive ideas in their poetry, but we do scant justice to such poets if we do not also recognise the extent to which they create a very complicated sense of the world we live in and how, in the end, their sense of disorder is often greater than their sense of order.

Obviously, however, no one expects you to deal with this level of complication in poetry when you are still finding your critical feet. Indeed, what we want to stress most here are the initial moves you can make with a poem. It is helpful if you remind yourself of two simple points: first, that all poetry (with the exception of a few modes such as the verse epistle) can be divided into two basic types – that is, lyric and narrative; second, that all poetry deals with familiar issues. A way of approaching narrative poetry is outlined on p. 52, but with lyric poetry, at the outset ignore the details of the poem and instead look for a clear structural opposition in the text. The details will then begin to make sense in relation to this broad pattern you have established. In the entries that follow, both on the different kinds of lyric and narrative poetry as well as on such important matters as imagery, we have attempted to provide further ideas about how to approach and discuss poetry. In every entry we have also sought to talk about the language of poetry, the words on the page, both how to make sense of them and how to discuss the ways in which the words serve to create the meaning and effect of a poem.

Alliteration. Repetition of the same letter (or, more precisely, sound) at the beginning of two or more words in a line of poetry. For example, describing a river in 'Kubla Khan' (1816) Coleridge writes, 'Five *m*iles *m*eandering with a *m*azy *m*otion'.

Alliteration is easy to spot in a poem, but you will receive no credit at all for merely noting that the poet has made use of the device. It is the same with any feature that you notice in a text: far too often students point to a detail but fail to justify its presence.

The rule is, when you spot something of interest, go on to discuss how it functions in the poem. In the line from Coleridge, for example, the use of alliteration serves to reinforce the meaning of the words which are intended to create a vivid impression of a meandering river. In discussing alliteration, resist the temptation of investing letters with some special sound quality: it is not the repetition of the 'm' sound that suggests the meandering, dreamlike movement of the river but the meaning of the words themselves. The alliteration simply serves to link the words together at the level of sound. The 'm' sound in itself suggests nothing: it is the meaning of the words that is important.

A poet who makes extensive use of alliteration is Spenser: a Cave of Despair is described as 'Darke, dolefull, drearie, like a greedie grave'. Depressing and frightening words are clustered together; the impression that the words convey is made more forceful because the use of alliteration establishes a link between them. It is the same when he writes 'So faire and fresh, as freshest flower in May': the 'f' sound in itself suggests nothing; it is the clustering of attractive words that is important. Spenser was writing in the late sixteenth century and alliteration is a central feature of his poetry: his epic poem *The Faerie Queene* (1596) tells the stories of knights on quests encountering temptations, and his bold use of alliteration helps make clear the nature of the people and things encountered on the journeys.

Subsequent poets, perhaps because their intentions are not so straightforward, are far more sparing in their use of the device, using it only occasionally to create a special effect. An exception is Hopkins, a late-nineteenth-century poet. The main theme of his poetry is the wonder he finds in God's world. In order to stress this wonder Hopkins employs both unusual language and an unusual degree of alliteration. In 'Pied Beauty' (written about 1880, published 1918) he writes,

> Whatever is fickle, freckled (who knows how?)
> With swift, slow; sweet, sour; adazzle, dim;
> He fathers-forth. . . .

The words and ideas, all of which are in praise of God, acquire additional force because they are linked together through the alliteration. This is the main purpose of alliteration, to lend ideas and images additional emphasis and force.

Archaism. The use of old or antiquated words in poetry. The device is mainly associated with Spenser's *Faerie Queene* (1596). Spenser was writing in the late sixteenth century but used and also invented words which struck him as Chaucerian or from the Middle Ages. In this example, a knight is watching some ladies dance; they are the Graces, the representatives of perfect beauty, chastity and love:

> He nigher drew, to weete what mote it be;
> There he a troupe of Ladies dauncing found
> Full merrily, and making gladfull glee.

The archaic words are 'nigher', 'weete' and 'mote'. Spenser uses them to help create an impression of a make-believe world, an unreal world far removed from everyday experience, and indeed the poem as a whole presents a vision of how things might be ordered in an ideal world.

Archaism is used in a similar way in the poets that Spenser influenced most. Milton in *Paradise Lost* (1667) uses archaic words to help create his picture of the Garden of Eden: language that is distanced from everyday speech creates an impression of a place that is distanced from everyday experience. It is the same with Keats, who often, as in 'The Eve of St Agnes' (1820), presents a vision of an ideal world. One difference between these poets and Spenser is that, whereas Spenser is primarily concerned to present an impression of an ideal world, Milton and Keats show how the disorder of real life intrudes into and disrupts the order of their ideal worlds. In all these writers, though, archaic words both help to create the picture and signal to the reader that we are in a world removed from ordinary experience and ordinary speech.

Archaic words are examples of **poetic diction:** this means, words found in poetry which are not used in everyday speech or prose. The most commonly used of such words is 'O'. Addressing a river in 'Tintern Abbey' (1798) Wordsworth writes, 'O sylvan Wye! thou wanderer through the woods'. He is struck by the ideal beauty of the river. 'Sylvan' and 'thou' help create the desired impression, but it is 'O' that first signals to the reader that Wordsworth is entering a realm of heightened feeling. 'O' is usually used in this way in poetry, to indicate that the poet is leaving dull reality in pursuit of something perfect. The artificiality of 'O', however, alerts us to the fact that there is something suspect in this flight from reality. In a poem as a whole, sections employing the word 'O', which signal to us that the poet is in an ideal world of poetry, will usually be set against more uncomfortable lines where the poet is aware of the gap between any ideal world and the disorder of the real world.

Assonance. Repetition of the same vowel sound in two or more words in a line of poetry. When Wordsworth writes of 'A host of golden daffodils' there is a repeated 'o' sound. This reinforces the meaning of the words and gives them emphasis.

A common mistake by students is to exaggerate the importance of sound effects in poetry, spotting assonance (and alliteration, *see* p. 17) everywhere and arguing that certain repeated sounds are crucial in creating the effect of a poem. It is, however, the meaning of the words that is important, and sound has only a minor role in underlining that meaning. Most poets use assonance sparingly and always in a very straightforward way. For example, Keats's 'Ode on a Grecian Urn' (1820) begins,

> Thou still unravished br*i*de of qu*i*etness,
> Thou foster-ch*i*ld of S*i*lence and slow T*i*me.

What attracts Keats to the urn is its ideal innocence and stillness: it is words such as 'bride', 'quietness', 'child' and 'silence' that principally suggest this, but the assonance on 'i' helps reinforce the impression because it links and emphasises these words. There is a slight jarring note with the one important word in the first line that does not fit into this pattern: 'unravished' carries within it a hint of its opposite, the idea of aggressive assault. Something less harmonious and peaceful is thus hinted at in the word itself, and this idea is underlined by the slight discordance of this word amidst a sequence of words employing the same 'i' sound. In itself, however, the repetition of the 'i' sound does not convey anything: it only becomes significant in the context of these specific words. The thing to avoid is the idea that certain sounds have inherent significance: they do not. If you comment on assonance try to see how it is used to support the meaning of the words.

A related device is **consonance:** the repetition of the same consonant sound before and after different vowels in two words: for example, '*live*' and '*love*'. Wilfred Owen, a First World War

poet, often uses consonance instead of rhyme, as in this extract
from 'Strange Meeting' (1920):

> It seemed that out of battle I e*scap*ed
> Down some profound dull tunnel, long since *scoop*ed
> Through granites which titanic wars had *groin*ed.
> Yet also there encumbered sleepers *groan*ed.

The subject matter is the nightmare of war. It is principally the
imagery that creates a terrifying impression, but the half-rhymes
(when consonance replaces rhyme it is called **half-rhyme**) are
important as well. Whereas rhyme in such a poem would seem far
too neat and orderly, the half-rhymes add to the shock of the
language, which is deliberately clumsy and unlyrical or
unharmonious. They also stress the brutal ugliness of the meaning
of the words. Half-rhyme is a central device in Owen's poetry,
which always concentrates on the pain and suffering of war, and is
also used by other poets, particularly twentieth-century poets, when
they want to suggest a world in fragments, a world where things will
not hold together in an ordered way.

Ballad. The traditional ballad is a song that tells a story. The theme
is often tragic, such as a tale of personal misfortune, or it can recall
a public event such as a battle. Supernatural themes are also common. It is an oral form, dating back to the later Middle Ages, and
simple in structure: the story is central, and is usually related in
fairly plain four-line stanzas.

Ballads usually deal with a personal or public disaster, as in
'Mary Hamilton':

> A sad tale through the town is gaen,
> A sad tale on the morrow:
> Oh Mary Hamilton has born a babe
> And slain it in her sorrow.

An unhappy event is put in the form of a story and, with the
addition of music, some form of harmony is imposed on unharmonious events; the ballad thus represents an attempt to come
to terms with the catastrophe. Ballads usually begin abruptly at the
point where the tragic event is about to occur. The tale is told with
little comment, the meaning being apparent in the description of

the action itself. The simple conventions employed (an uncomplicated stanza pattern, simple language, and stock phrases) might lead us to expect a tedious poem, but such features add to the impact of the story: this is particularly true of **incremental repetition**, where lines are repeated from stanza to stanza, but with some small but crucial alteration as the line is repeated. The extent to which ballads present the characters speaking also adds to their dramatic immediacy.

Traditional ballads are relatively simple poems: the dialect used in so many might prove difficult to understand, but if we can follow the story we should be able to see its significance: that is, how the ballad confronts a disaster. **Literary ballads**, however, are more difficult: at the end of the eighteenth century poets took the form and typical subject matter of the ballad, but, as in Wordsworth's contributions to *Lyrical Ballads* (*see* p. 43), Keats's 'La Belle Dame sans Merci' (1820), and Coleridge's 'Ancient Mariner' (1798; *see also* p. 53), produced complex poems. Coleridge's poem deals with a mariner who shoots an albatross and the punishment he receives. In a traditional ballad the same story would suggest a simple moral meaning: here, that the mariner is punished for his sin. Coleridge's poem, however, is more puzzling: the poem contains complex and cryptic details which we might find difficult to reconcile with a neat overall moral reading of its significance. This is a form of complexity that we often encounter in great poetry, where we see a poet facing up to the baffling nature of experience. The traditional ballad presents a tragic tale, but deals with it directly; the author of a literary ballad writes from a stance of being rather more puzzled at life's misfortunes, and, presenting a story that defies a simple interpretation, offers a more troubling impression of the disorders of the world.

Blank verse. Unrhymed poetry, but a very disciplined verse form in that each line is an iambic pentameter (a ten-syllable line with five stresses; *see* Metre, p. 46). It is close to the rhythm of speech, but stylised enough in its regularity to be quite distinct from speech or prose. A poem in blank verse appears less formally contrived than a poem that rhymes, and therefore our attention is not so forcibly drawn to the way in which the poet is creating a pattern. As such it is a good medium for the sort of long narrative poem that tells a complicated story or explores experience in a fairly comprehensive way. It is also well suited to the sort of lyric poem where the poet is thinking in a discursive way rather than fitting his or her thoughts into received stanza and rhyme patterns (as is the case in, for example, a sonnet). Blank verse is also used extensively by Shakespeare and other Renaissance dramatists.

Milton's epic poem *Paradise Lost* (1667) is written in blank verse, while Spenser's epic *The Faerie Queene* (1596) employs a regular rhymed stanza throughout. The choice of verse form tells us something about each poem. Implicit in Spenser's method is the idea that there is an informing pattern, a divine order, which is easy to grasp. *Paradise Lost* is also a religious poem, but it is a far more troubled faith that is in evidence. It begins,

> Of man's first disobedience, and the fruit
> Of that forbidden tree, whose mortal taste
> Brought death into the world, and all our woe
> With loss of Eden. . . .

The way the lines expand, a fresh complication being added in each clause, suggests the complexity of the problem Milton hopes to deal with: nothing less than justifying God's ways to man. Rhyme might suggest that God's plan is easy to grasp, but blank verse suggests a more troubled, wide-ranging enquiry: the regularity of the lines, however, keeps an idea of order in the background.

Blank verse is also appropriate in poems such as Wordsworth's 'Tintern Abbey' (1798) and *The Prelude* (there are two, slightly different versions, the 1805 and the 1850), where he explores his complex ideas about nature. When we analyse blank verse, we can look at how the poet maintains variety by shifting the pause in the line and by using run-on lines in the verse paragraph (the separate sections in a blank-verse poem are called **verse paragraphs** rather than stanzas). Our real analysis, however, involves moving beyond the verse pattern as such and looking at what the poet says and how he or she says it. One thing we should be aware of is that in reading blank verse we follow the sense from verse to verse, while in a shorter poem we might linger longer over each line. We need to grasp the argument or story that is being developed, appreciating how the form permits the poet to create a very full impression of life's complexity. We then have to look at how the language of the poem, both the complex structure of sentences and the imagery employed, creates this complicated impression, and yet at the same time we should be aware that the regularity of the verse form implies a search for some order and significance in the diffuseness and difficulty of what is being presented.

Conceit. A metaphor describes one thing in terms of another: for example, 'a granite jaw'. A conceit is a far-fetched metaphor in which a very unlikely connection between two things is established. A famous example is Donne's description of lovers' souls as being like the two legs of a pair of compasses (*see* 'A Valediction Forbidding Mourning', *c.* 1600):

> If they be two, they are two so
> As stiff twin compasses are two;
> Thy soul, the fixed foot, makes no show
> To move, but doth, if the other do.

Donne is saying that if one leg (soul) moves, the other inevitably moves as well.

Many metaphors in poems from different periods might be described as conceits (e.g. T. S. Eliot in 'The Love Song of J. Alfred Prufrock', 1917, compares the evening sky to 'a patient etherised upon a table'), but conceits are most common in seventeenth-century metaphysical poetry. The wider implications of the use of metaphor and conceits in poetry are discussed on p. 151, but the rest of this entry is concerned with the role of conceits in metaphysical poetry, which is itself discussed separately on p. 44. A common, but misguided, response to conceits is to say that the comparison seems odd, but on reflection seems valid. Conceits, however, are not meant to strike us as apposite. They are meant to strike us as ingenious.

It is, however, not only the conceits that present problems in metaphysical poetry. The complicated arguments, convoluted syntax and rapid jumps from idea to idea also baffle many readers. To come to terms with such poetry we have to decide why anyone would want to write in such a manner. The answer must be that the methods employed reflect an awareness of just how difficult experience is to understand. Of course, many poets acknowledge life's complexity, but metaphysical poetry represents a very rational, intellectual attempt to confront experience through an ordered argument. The argument gets tied up in knots, however, because the poet gets tied up in knots in trying to understand an increasingly complicated world. When Donne compares lovers and compasses, one thing that is implicit is his awareness that the world is changing: the compasses suggest a new age of exploration and scientific enquiry. Donne is trying to order and understand this early-seventeenth-century world that contains such a baffling variety of things. He establishes a link between two areas of experience, but it is a precarious link, and the conceit has to strike us as ingenious: we are meant to feel that it takes considerable invention and imagination to forge a connection.

Donne's use of conceits, therefore, suggests life's complexity, and suggests that connections can only be made in a desperately fanciful way. In a bewildering world the poet finds likeness between the apparently unlike. In 'The Canonization' (written about 1600, published 1633) two lovers are compared to saints: the comparison is simultaneously comic and serious, as Donne attempts to link the secular and the divine, seeking to connect the separate components of his experience. One way of regarding conceits is to see them as the last desperate expression of a medieval view of life, in which every component of experience is part of a grander religious order. The metaphysical poets are driven to the limits of ingenuity to achieve this synthesis. At the same time as Donne was writing, Ben Jonson and others were writing a new kind of social poetry, which no longer sought to reconcile all aspects of experience, but limited its attentions to the secular world alone. Even while the metaphysical poets were writing, then, other poets no longer shared their desire and need to try to confront and order the whole of experience.

Courtly-love poetry. Courtly-love poetry is generally concerned with an idealised view of love. The lover is a knight who worships his lady from afar; he sighs, weeps, and prays for her with a burning desire, pledging eternal faithfulness. She, however, is remote, representing everything good in life. The language used to convey these ideas is elevated and passionate, and religious imagery is usually in evidence. Chaucer's narrative poem *Troilus and Criseyde* is a fine example, but courtly love is also a common theme in Elizabethan sonnets.

There is, however, more to such poems than just the 'courtly love code', a phrase that conveniently sums up these ideas. For the most part, poets who exploit the convention contrast ideal love and the more complicated reality of emotional relationships. *Troilus and Criseyde* (about 1386) tells the story of Troilus's idealised love for Criseyde, how he wins her with the help of Pandarus and how she betrays him. It is a tragedy and yet Chaucer's narrative stance is comic and quizzical. Often we are unclear about how we are meant to respond, whether we are meant to be moved or amused. Troilus's love seems both heroic and pitiable. What has happened is that Chaucer has used an idea of perfect, uncomplicated love to high-light the fact that the realities of experience are far more com-plicated. The poem sets an ideal of perfect love against the baffling nature of genuine experience.

The pattern is similar in Sidney's sonnet sequence *Astrophel and Stella* (1581–2), which started a vogue of sonnet sequences in the Elizabethan period. The ideas, imagery and language used are the same as in any other courtly-love poem, and again the intention is to show what real relationships are like by contrasting them with a simple idea of an ideal relationship. We are conscious of the gap between the pleasant fiction and how things really are. Shake-speare too, in his sonnets (1609), is fond of mocking idealised views of woman and love. All the sonnet-writers, however, have their individual characteristics: Sidney, for example, often seems more concerned with writing about the fact that he is writing about love than with actually writing about love itself. Spenser's sonnet sequence *The Amoretti* (1595) is much simpler, with an emphasis on beauty as a moral quality. Donne in his love lyrics is extravagant in his praise of love, but then is just as extreme in his questioning of love. All these writers, though, use the courtly-love idea as a simple fiction of love: what we are concerned with in looking at any individual poet is the distinctive way in which he or she complicates the idea, demonstrating that love in the real world is a far more complicated matter.

Dramatic monologue. A poem in which an imaginary speaker addresses an audience. The poem usually takes place at a critical moment in the speaker's life and offers an indirect revelation of his or her temperament and personality.

Monologues are common in plays and longer poems (e.g. Satan talks at length about himself and God in Milton's *Paradise Lost*), but the development of the dramatic monologue as a distinct kind of poem is associated with the Victorian poet Robert Brown-ing. 'My Last Duchess' (1842) illustrates the characteristics of the mode: there is an imagined speaker, the Duke, who is addressing a representative of the girl he hopes to marry. The Duke talks about his deceased wife. As we read the poem we assess his character: he inadvertently reveals himself as a tyrant who could not tolerate his wife's independence. The monologue is colloquial, following the patterns of the speaker's voice.

All dramatic monologues present one person's response to life. Many poets offer us their personal view, but Browning is not presenting his own view, rather the way in which an imagined character orders the world. The Duke is despotic, wishing to limit the freedom of others, as if the whole world must conform to his pattern. It is a good poem, but fairly simple. In his subsequent poems, such as 'Fra Lippo Lippi' and 'Andrea del Sarto' (both published in 1855), Browning continues to present characters talking, but our assessment of the speakers is often far more ambivalent. They come across as complex personalities with bad points and good points. Our response to the protagonists is usually a mixture of sympathy and judgement. Browning's ability to present a complex impression depends upon developments in the sophistication of his technique. Two things in particular are noteworthy. The first is his use of imagery, especially the many images that suggest movement and freedom as against images suggesting restraint and confinement. Such images are appropriate as all his characters are trapped within the limits of their own thinking and personalities. Second, there is the quickness and flexibility of his verse, suggesting the quick movement of thought and the difficulty any speaker has in trying to pin down and comprehend existence.

Other poets, such as Tennyson in 'Ulysses' (1842), Kipling, T. S. Eliot in 'The Love Song of J. Alfred Prufrock' (1917) and Robert Frost, exploit the mode in different ways, but the point all dramatic monologues have in common is that they do not present the poet's direct view of life, but take one step back and examine how imagined characters try to impose a shape and interpretation on the world they encounter. As in so much literature, we are concerned with the world's lack of pattern and people's attempt to pattern, understand, and find some meaning in experience.

Dream poetry. A poem that tells of a dream. Also known as dream visions and dream allegories, dream poems were popular in the Middle Ages. Most of Chaucer's early poems are dream poems.

In Chaucer's *Book of the Duchess* (1369) the poet describes how he fell asleep while reading. He awakes and follows a dog to a black knight who tells him of his grief for his dead wife. This should be moving but the tone is comic, with the narrator failing to understand the knight's grief. The effect is puzzling, and we remain puzzled until the very end of the story. Up until this point the imagery has been pleasant, and there is the reassuring regularity of Chaucer's couplets, but then come the blunt words 'She is dead'. It is here that reality breaks through. The dream vision allows Chaucer to make the widest possible contrast between the world of the dream and its attractiveness and the painful fact of death.

A similar dream-and-reality structure is also in evidence in Chaucer's other narrative poems, *The Parliament of Fowles* (1380) and *The House of Fame* (1384). He also makes use again of a naïve imagined narrator, as does Langland in *Piers Plowman* (*c.* 1360–90). This, however, is also an allegory. Allegory (*see* p. 133) is a way of telling a story so that it makes sense on a literal level, but implicit in the story is also a more general moral meaning and applicability. In *Piers Plowman* the dreamer sees a 'field full of folk': it is a field, but also the world, and the poem also includes abstract figures such as Truth to signal the fact that there is a broader significance to the story. Langland uses the dream to present a vision of a corrupt society while also emphasising his Christian faith.

This idea of a visionary dream, in which something profound is perceived, re-emerges in poetry in the romantic period, for example in Coleridge's 'Kubla Khan' (1816) or in the reverie that Keats drifts off into in 'Ode to a Nightingale' (1820). Again, as in Chaucer, there is a contrast between the dream and the realities of everyday life, but there is a far greater emphasis on the special sort of truth that is revealed in the dream. 'Kubla Khan' seems to probe the depths of the unconscious mind, and the vision in Keats's poem, although it dissolves, for a moment comes in contact with a perfect world. In both poets it is more than day-dreaming: the emphasis is on the value of what is revealed in the unconscious or semi-conscious mind. As a whole, then, dream poems contrast dreams and reality, but something significant can be discovered, revealed or explored in the dream.

Eighteenth-century poetry. This is, generally, social poetry concerned with manners and morals. The most representative poet is Pope. The kind of lyric poem which is typical of the seventeenth century, dealing mainly with love or religion, fell out of favour. A new attitude does not, however, spring into existence overnight, and this kind of social poetry can be traced back as far as Ben

Jonson. Two other terms are also frequently employed to describe the poetry of this period: **Augustan**, usually applied to the period 1700–45, and the broader **neoclassic**, covering the period from 1660 to the end of the eighteenth century.

In the finest eighteenth-century poetry the writer looks at a corrupt society, and offers his or her corrective thinking, with an emphasis on decorum and moderation: the heroic couplet (*see* p. 35) is the favoured verse form, because it suggests an idea of balance and order. Writers look back to those classical authors who were felt to have established the enduring models; form and content coincide here: value exists in existing structures.

A problem with eighteenth-century poetry is that the topical references can prove puzzling. Do not, however, spend too much time consulting footnotes: look at the poetry itself. The basic meaning is transparent – the writers are for moderation and against excess – so we need to look at how well they put across these ideas. The poetry is usually satiric, mocking the errant, the poet writing from a position of ironic superiority. Identify what is being attacked, and see where and how the writer states his or her positive values. Much of the appeal of the poetry depends upon the poet's ability to create a vivid picture of a disorderly society, as in these lines from Johnson's 'London' (1738):

Here Malice, Rapine, Accident, conspire,
And now a Rabble rages, now a Fire;
Their Ambush here relentless Ruffians lay,
And here the fell Attorney prowls for Prey;
Here falling Houses thunder on your Head,
And here a female Atheist talks you dead.

The intention is to suggest the chaos and corruption of the city: the lines are full of images of disorder and dangerous movement, something that becomes frightening when lawyers are compared to voracious animals. The city begins to fall apart as buildings collapse. It is a world in disarray, where atheism prevails and true values have gone, and there is a repeated insistence on destruction and death. Yet the tone is superior and comic, and the balance of the couplets suggests how Johnson can stand aloof from this shambles.

Similar effects are evident in many eighteenth-century poems, but always seen at their best in Pope, where, particularly in *The Dunciad* (1742), his vision of a society in disarray is sometimes so powerful that it can seem as if anarchy is going to overwhelm his own balanced values. (*See also* Verse epistle, p. 73; Irony, p. 147; *and* Satire, p. 158.)

Elegy. A poem written on the death of a friend of the poet. The ostensible purpose is to praise the friend, but death prompts the writer to ask, 'If death can intervene so cruelly in life, what is the point of living?' By the end of the poem, however, we can expect that the poet will have come to terms with his or her grief.

In Milton's 'Lycidas' (1637) his friend has drowned: life has been overwhelmed by the uncontrollable chaos of the sea. Milton uses the poem to try to find a purpose in living and writing, for what truth or value can there be in poetry's ordered response to experience if untimely death mocks all our endeavours? It is such thinking that always informs elegy. By the end, Milton has found his answer: a traditional Christian one, that God has ordained this, and his friend has been absorbed into a greater pattern. The argument in the poem, however, is less important than the way in which Milton uses the poem itself to confront the problem. At first Milton and his friend are young shepherds, as in pastoral (*see* p. 55), but by the end he has found the true significance of the shepherd image: his friend has joined Christ, the shepherd of humankind. The imagery of the poem expresses the dilemma, yet it is also through the imagery that an answer is found. This is just one image thread in the poem: initially the range of imagery in the poem can confuse the reader, but it is vital to see that the poet must explore poetic language, especially imagery, to discover if there is any point in writing poetry.

In Tennyson's *In Memoriam* (1850) the dilemma is the same: a friend has died, and life seems futile. Again it is the poetic working-out of the problem that is important. One sustained image is that of a hand, a hand he can no longer clasp but yearns to touch. The poem also makes effective use of darkness: it starts in a black and morbid mood, but light gradually breaks in as he comes to terms with his grief. Other image patterns can be traced, but another thing that is impressive in Tennyson's poem is its overall structure. Consisting of over a hundred fragmentary lyrics, the form seems to enact the way the poet's mind has disintegrated into fragments: he is searching for a purpose, but the structure makes us feel that life might perhaps consist of scraps of feeling which cannot be mar-shalled into any grander pattern. Whereas Milton's poem works as a whole, in Tennyson's the expression of grief is more impressive than the answer he eventually finds. As in all elegies, though, we are offered an extended poetic consideration of the problem of death.

Epic. The most ambitious kind of poem. An epic presents the great deeds of an heroic figure or group of figures. The classical models are Homer's *Odyssey* and *Iliad*, and Virgil's *Aeneid*: they are massive narrative poems, focusing on a crisis in the history of a race or culture.

There are two major English epic poems. Spenser's *The Faerie Queene* (1596) tells the stories of knights on quests and the adventures and temptations they encounter. Milton's *Paradise Lost* (1667) tells the story of Satan's expulsion from Heaven, his tempting of Eve, and Adam and Eve's expulsion from Eden. The stories seem dissimilar, but what they have in common is that they both deal with major challenges and disruptions: Spenser deals with the whole range of temptations that can threaten human beings and Milton deals with the events that led to the fact that we live in a fallen world. Evil and disorder are thus central in both poems. The other side of the issue is the heroic response to this. Spenser's knights cope with all the challenges they meet. In Milton the issue is more complicated: there is some dispute about whether Christ or Adam is the hero of the poem. Christ is obviously the counterforce to Satan's wickedness, but some would argue that Adam in the poem, by his decision that he would rather stay loyal to Eve than accept the opportunity to remain in Eden, is the true hero. In both poems, though, we have the idea of heroic resistance to extreme threats, and the style is suitably elevated.

There is, however, more to epic than just the story. The scope of epic is encyclopaedic: it is the big poem that seeks to explain everything. The poet does not just focus on telling the story but attempts to include all knowledge and the whole of human experience. The poems are made all-inclusive in various ways. Vast areas of learning are reflected in the use of imagery and allusion. Both poems are packed with classical references, reflecting the classical origins of epic. Such knowledge must be incorporated, for the epic is the poem which examines everything, and which intends to demonstrate that all of experience can be assimilated into a pattern, that everything makes sense and interconnects. **Epic simile** contributes to this: the poet makes long digressions, comparing events in the story to events that we are familiar with or events in other stories or history. This contributes to the inclusiveness of epic, that it embraces all of life, and makes for coherence, suggesting that everything is part of a grand pattern.

Spenser's use of allegory (*see* p. 133) works in a similar way. To take just one example: in the first book, one of the knights sees a vision of a city. It is, simultaneously, Jerusalem, Athens and London. Spenser connects the three most important things in his life: his Christian faith, his classical education, and his identity as an Englishman. All his learning and experience are thus brought together in the allegory. And brought together very neatly: *The Faerie Queene* is a melodious, untroubled poem. The threats exist, but are easily overcome. Spenser's use of a regular nine-line stanza pattern throughout adds to the sense that there is a pattern behind the diffuseness of life. He repeatedly stresses, both in his stanzas and in his stories, his sense of a religious order that can be perceived in experience.

Milton's poem, however, is far more unsettled and unsettling. It sets out to justify God's ways to humankind, and we can argue that it does, through Christ, find an answer to the problems Milton deals with. Some critics, however, suggest that it ends up justifying people's ways to God, in that Adam, who is rebellious yet loyal to Eve, can be seen as the hero. This is not a shortcoming: indeed, the problems Milton experiences in trying to match the disorder of the biblical events with an orderly interpretation of them may be said to create much of the poem's power. Satan, for example, is an evil figure, but his human qualities of energy and drive are impressive.

When you are reading an epic, initially you should succumb to and enjoy the story. Then, when it comes to forming a critical response, think first about the significance of the story you have read. After that you can move on to the manner in which it is narrated, noting, for example, the ways in which the style is elevated to suit the author's ambitious intention. In the case of Milton it is important to look at the presentation of Satan and Adam and Eve, seeing how the impression created to some extent resists the overall purpose of justifying God's ways.

Epithalamion. A song or poem in honour of a marriage. By tradition it would have been sung outside the bride's room on her wedding-night. This might seem a very minor mode and, indeed, most students will only ever come across Spenser's 'Epithalamion' (1595), but Sidney, Donne, Jonson, Herrick, Marvell, Crashaw, Dryden and Shelley also wrote such poems, and Tennyson's *In Memoriam* (1850) ends with an epithalamion. In addition, many plays (particularly Shakespeare's comedies) and many novels end with marriage. In every instance, marriage is representative of the settled order that can be established in society, as well as being sanctioned by God. This is especially so in the marriage poem where marriage is used as a symbol of perfect order.

The pattern of such poems can be found in Spenser's 'Epithalamion': the poem is organised around the events of the entire day. The central characters are the bride and groom, and the poet is the public celebrator of the private experience (Spenser's poem is addressed to his own bride). It is a joyful, celebratory mode, and the poet is not likely to make many references to any of the darker aspects of life beyond saying that a wedding banishes all problems for a day. Spenser in his opening stanza asks the muses to forget what is sad in life:

> Now lay those sorrowfull complaints aside,
> And having all your heads with girland crownd,
> Helpe me mine owne loves prayses to resound

In the course of the poem nature imagery is employed to equate his future wife with everything that is fresh and fertile. He uses simple description, along with a fair number of classical references, to evoke her innocent beauty. It is a very straightforward poem: the reward for us as readers is simply an appreciation of how effectively he uses language and the structure of the poem to celebrate the event.

There are just hints of more problematic levels of experience:

> Now al is done; bring home the bride againe,
> Bring home the triumph of our victory.

The military images remind us that there are areas of conflict and tension in life, but here such images are not disruptive. On the contrary, military imagery is subsumed into the controlling idea of the importance of this wedding. Throughout the poem there are images that hint at life's problems, but for this one day all such difficulties are forgotten: everybody stops work, everybody stops fighting, to watch the bride. A poet laureate might well produce an epithalamion on the occasion of a royal wedding.

Free verse. Poetry written in irregular lines and without any regular metre. To grasp the significance of this we need to know that other forms of verse are based upon a regular metrical pattern.

Most commonly in English poetry poets write in ten-syllable lines, with five stresses in each line, called iambic pentameters (*see* p. 46). Free verse, however, abandons any such regular pattern, and usually also abandons rhyme. Widespread use of free verse is a fairly recent innovation, beginning with Walt Whitman's *Leaves of Grass* (1855). In the twentieth century it has become very common. T. S. Eliot, Ezra Pound, William Carlos Williams, Wallace Stevens and D. H. Lawrence are just some of the modern writers who have used it. It is possibly the case that modern poets, confronting a very disorganised world, distrust any notion of a regular pattern and so prefer free verse, which seems to acknowledge the untidiness of life and of the mind.

Eliot's 'Ash Wednesday' (1930) is in free verse:

Because these wings are no longer wings to fly
But merely vans to beat the air
The air which is now thoroughly small and dry
Smaller and dryer than the will
Teach us to care and not to care
Teach us to sit still.

This is difficult to understand out of context, but what Eliot is writing about are his feelings of uselessness coupled with his desire to accept God's guidance. As in all poetry, the poet is seeking order in an often bewildering world. Rather than using a traditional poetic frame to organise his thoughts, though, Eliot opts for the much looser form of free verse which allows him to trace out the pattern of his thinking in all its disorder and confusion. Free verse is well suited to this sort of excursion of the mind. Repetition of word and phrase is important in introducing some element of organisation: Eliot alights on a word and it becomes a touchstone as he advances to his next proposition. The technique suggests both the untidiness of a bewildered response and the desire to try and establish some degree of coherence and continuity of thinking. A free-verse poem is irregular, but the poet seeks the occasional moment of symmetry: Eliot, in fact, employs rhyme here to suggest that search for order. The effect is that we gain a sense of how bewildering the overall picture is, but equally sense the poet searching for even a fragment of order.

In most free-verse poems we are struck by the impression of a poet struggling to make even a little sense out of a very confusing world. Whitman, however, is a system-maker. His poetry celebrates the diversity of America, but he also offers us his personal credo.

His beliefs, though, are very individual, even quirky, as they are not developed in a context of traditional poetic frames. Yet, as with all successful free verse, Whitman's poetry presents a vivid impression of a complex mind grappling with the world.

Heroic couplet. A pair of ten-syllable lines (i.e. iambic pentameters, *see* p. 46) that rhyme: a poem as a whole can be written in a sequence of heroic couplets. First used by Chaucer, and later by Spenser, Shakespeare, Donne, Byron and Browning amongst others, the form is, however, always most associated with the poetry of Dryden and Pope. It was the most popular verse form in the eighteenth century.

When couplets are used in narrative poetry (e.g. in *The Canterbury Tales*, about 1400, or Keats's 'Lamia', 1820) we are not all that conscious of the rhymes, as the writers keep the couplets open, allowing the thought to run on rather than the pattern of the verse being allowed to dominate. In such poetry, heroic couplets are almost as flexible as blank verse, letting the story progress with only a gentle reminder of the organising presence of the poet. Dryden and Pope, however, usually write in closed couplets (with a semi-colon or full stop at the end of the second line), and this serves to draw attention to the rhyme. This suits their intention as writers: both are satirists, mocking folly, and the balance of the couplet serves as a repeated reminder of the sort of simple balance and order that should prevail in society. An idea of balance is implicit in the couplet form, but they accentuate this – so successfully, indeed, that we now always think of heroic couplets as the appropriate verse form for satire.

When the couplets are closed the thought in each couplet often inclines towards a kind of epigrammatic neatness, as if an issue is wrapped up in the neat form of the two lines. One way of approaching Pope's couplets in particular is to regard them as something like miniature stanzas in which he confronts a problem but exerts his poetic control over the material presented. For example:

> Some have at first for wits, then poets pass'd
> Turn'd critics next, and prov'd plain fools at last.

Pope writes of things getting out of hand: there is instability, people chopping and changing, but the anarchy that almost takes over in the illustrations is always dominated by Pope exerting his own authority in the couplet as a whole. It is often the case that the themes of the whole poem (here *Essay on Criticism*, 1711) are crystallised in every couplet. Pope also uses couplets effectively to state his own principles directly: on these occasions the whole progress and organisation of the lines suggest order and good sense. From the same poem:

> True wit is nature to advantage dress'd,
> What oft was thought, but ne'er so well express'd.

The lines themselves, in their structure and expression, are a perfect illustration of the sentiment they contain.

Imagery. When we read a poem there are several things we respond to. Initially we follow the argument or story, trying to decide what the poem is 'about'. If we cannot immediately see, it helps, as explained in the introduction to the Poetry section (*see* p. 12), to look for some structural opposition. Once we have got hold of the poem's theme we can then start to examine some of its subtleties and how it creates its effect upon the reader. One aspect of this is how the poet orders the poem (his or her use of stanza, rhyme and syntax to create certain effects), but the most important thing we have to look at is what the poet does with language. Terms such as 'alliteration' and 'assonance' cover the effects of the sounds in a sequence of words, but much more important is the choice of individual words. The most convenient way of describing the key words in a poem is to use the term 'imagery': imagery covers every concrete object, action and feeling in a poem and also the use of metaphors and similes.

Much of this might become clearer if we look at the first line of Hardy's 'The Voice' (1914): 'Woman much missed, how you call to me, call to me'. We can see that the poem promises to be about a woman, possibly a sweetheart, who is no longer a physical presence in the poet's life. The poem will probably contrast past happiness and present misery. The syntactic organisation of the line, the repetition of 'call to me', creates a specific effect: a wistful longing for the woman. Play with sound, as in the alliteration of 'much missed', helps emphasise the idea of how much he misses her. None of this, however, would make any impact without the con-

crete image of the woman and the concrete image of her calling:
the poet is not talking in abstract terms about his feelings but
describing a particular experience in a specific context.

So, in analysing a poem, we have to report on the basic images
used, how they ground the poem in a particular experience and
context. There should be no difficulty at all in considering these
basic images which simply serve to create the picture (though not
necessarily a visual picture). Take these opening lines from W. B.
Yeats's 'The Lake Isle of Innisfree' (1893):

> I will arise and go now, and go to Innisfree
> And a small cabin build there, of clay and wattles made. . . .

The poem opens with a simple image of a small cabin which creates
an idea of escape to an ideal, innocent world in tune with nature.

If the matter stopped here there would be no problems at all
in discussing imagery in poetry. The difficulty is, however, that the
term imagery covers not only these basic elements of presenting
the situation but also the **figurative** use of language in poetry:
'figurative' means language being used in a non-literal way: most
commonly the poet uses either a metaphor or a simile to extend
the significance of what he or she is saying (*see* p. 151). As Yeats's
poem continues his use of language becomes figurative: 'There
midnight's all a glimmer, and noon a purple glow'. This is not
literally true: in trying to describe the scene he has chosen two
words associated with forms of light and applied them to evoke the
atmosphere at Innisfree. We can see how effective this is, but, if we
are to tackle imagery as a concept, we cannot just praise individual
examples but need a theory about why figurative imagery is so
common in poetry.

It helps if we start from a general theory about poetry: as
imagery is a component of poetry it possibly does on a small scale
what poetry does as a whole. An easy way of thinking about poetry
is to say that poets confront the disorder of the world but try to
offer some sort of ordered response in their verse. It might, then,
be the case that figurative imagery can add either to the sense of
disorder or to the sense of order. Here are some lines by Sidney:

> With how sad steps, O Moon, thou climb'st the skies!
> How silently, and with how wan a face!

The meaning of the lines is that the moon is sad. Having said that, there would be little left to say unless we commented on the imagery: here the movement of the moon is compared to the laboured ascent of stairs and the moon has a wan face like an unhappy person. All of this works in various ways: the personification of the moon, as capable of suffering human woes, makes the idea vivid. There is also the attraction of the poet finding a clever, indirect way of writing about unhappiness. The lines, however, mainly create a very forceful sense of unhappiness by associating sad things from various areas of life with the moon. Imagery thus complicates and makes an idea more forceful, because associated ideas of sadness are clustered together.

In some lines by Keats he imagines himself to be a star gazing down on 'the new soft-fallen mask/Of snow upon the mountains and the moors'. Keats could have said that he felt lonely and cold, but, by finding images from various areas of life that suggest the same thing, he not only makes his point more vividly but complicates the impression by associating his mood with cold, stark images from other areas of experience. Later in the same poem he says that he would like to be a star shining down and 'Pillow'd upon my fair love's ripening breast'. There are two figurative images here: 'pillow'd' and 'ripening'. At this point a positive ideal is put forward, but made more complex because it is not simply stated. 'Pillow'd' with all its associations of softness and sensuality is applied to the experience, and 'ripening' associates his lover with ideas of growth and fecundity in nature. Imagery thus works in two ways: an association of something negative with negative images creates a more forceful sense of what is unpleasant in life. The association of something positive with positive images creates a forceful impression of the preferred alternative. In both instances the idea is made richer, more complex and more interesting through association.

It is possible to list some of the areas of experience from which poets most frequently select their images. Objects in the poem can be associated with religious or cosmic concepts. They are also frequently associated with things in nature, such as flowers, animals or the weather. Often there are well-established opposites which usually operate in the same way in poems, so bad weather can add to a sense of things being wrong, while good weather can add to a sense of something positive. Darkness (negative) and light (positive) are often seen in opposition in a poem. Apart from religious, cosmic and natural imagery, images can be drawn either from daily life (images of money, business, war – all of which usually contribute to a sense of something disorderly in a poem), or from the body (images of sickness, disease, health and death). It is, therefore, possible to have some idea in advance of what sort of images one is likely to encounter in a poem.

The images are something that we have to comment on when discussing a poem: if we are looking at the disorderly side of things, we can comment on how the idea is made more disturbing by the association with other unpleasant things in life. Similarly, the poet does not simply state his or her positives, but conveys them through appropriate imagery. It is important to grasp that imagery is not decorative ornament: there are informing ideas in poems, but those ideas are realised and find expression largely through the poet's use of imagery. What we are really talking about is the fact that poetry is an art of indirect statement, and, in order to appreciate poetry, we have to appreciate the logic of imagery, how it allows a poem to suggest things a bald statement might not. The thing to avoid, however, is the idea that there is some level of hidden meaning in imagery: because a poem may be saying something in terms of other things, it can encourage the belief that there is some concealed message in the poem. There is, however, nothing cryptic about imagery: it is central to poetry because it is a device that enables the poet to achieve complexity and force in his or her verse through associating an object or idea with other areas of life.

Imagism. Around 1914, Ezra Pound (who coined the term) and others, produced economical poems, mainly characterised by their use of a few, hard, clear images. Pound's two-line poem 'In a Station of the Metro' is one of the finest:

> The apparition of these faces in the crowd;
> Petals on a wet, black bough.

The principle behind the poem is that Pound wants to represent his impression of the scene in a very concentrated manner. It is a terse poem, presenting just the scene and a poetic response, and avoiding any comment or development of an argument. Pound insists both on direct treatment of 'the thing' and that every word must count. It is in free verse, as if it is an untainted response. The major feature, however, is the juxtaposition of one impression with another, so that the figurative image in the second line interacts with the observed image in the first. Imagist poems are as simple in structure as this: a hard, precise description of the scene, then a metaphoric comparison. Imagist techniques are a significant aspect of the work of Pound and William Carlos Williams.

Imagism represents, in part, a reaction against the weakest sort of romantic poetry where the poet might indulge his or her imagination in a verbose expression of personal fantasies. It reveals a desire to get back to the object which is there in the world. The real significance of imagism, however, is that it represents the start of modern poetry finding ways of expressing a sense of a puzzling and fragmented world. Whereas most earlier poetry seeks to organise experience, modern poetry tends to hold back and concede that understanding is impossible. The deliberate small scale of an imagist poem suggests that reality can only be apprehended in isolated glimpses, and then only indirectly through an image as opposed to any sort of logical analysis.

In addition, imagism marks a new self-consciousness about poetry, an insistence that the methods of writing need reforming. A high degree of formal innovation is something that is characteristic of much modern literature: often we stop short at the surface, struck mainly by the experimental or difficult quality of the writing. In Pound's poem we do not merely accept the content: we stop at the surface, asking why the poet is writing in this strange way. The kind of question such a poem implicitly asks is how can or should a poet write about life, and unusual and difficult modern poetry often forces us to consider this sort of question. Such self-consciousness is not just experiment for its own sake: on the contrary, the problems the poet is having in finding a technique adequate to describing the world force us to reconsider what reality is like.

Lyric. A poem in which the poet writes about his or her thoughts and feelings. The basic type is the song, but we use the term to cover all poems that present the poet's immediate response to life, including sonnets, odes, and elegies. Lyric poems can deal with any facet of experience, such as love, death, nature or religion, or some domestic, social or political issue, but we are always offered the poet's direct response. Most poems are like this: indeed, the only other approaches a poet can take are to write a narrative poem, in

which ideas are explored through the medium of a story, or to opt
for a form borrowed from prose, such as the verse essay or epistle.

   In essence the lyric is an attempt to confront and understand
some aspect of our complex experience of life. The poet tries to
order and organise his or her feelings and impressions. We can
begin by looking at seventeenth-century lyric poetry. For example,
in 'To Celia' (1616) Ben Jonson is writing about his love for a
woman:

> Drink to me only with thine eyes,
> And I will pledge with mine;
> Or leave a kiss but in the cup
> And I'll not look for wine.

What he desires is a perfect relationship, but the wine imagery
suggests how a sensual thirst and desire is something that has to be
taken account of in his feelings. A repeated pattern in lyric poetry
is that a sense of something ideal (here, perfect love) is set against
the complexity of feelings and experience. The attractive quality of
Jonson's lines suggests that he is managing to order his potentially
problematic emotions. The same pattern is found in most religious
poems: the poet writes about the disorder of experience but sets
against this the perfection of God. In these lines from Herbert's
'Virtue' (1633) he describes the sensuous but transient beauty of
life:

> Sweet day, so cool, so calm, so bright,
> The bridal of the earth and sky,
> The dew shall weep thy fall tonight,
>   For thou must die.

The attractive images are undercut by the reminder that all this will
die; we thus seem to be confronted by the painful disorder of life,
but the regularity of the lines and the attractiveness of the images
suggest that Herbert can make sense of this, that he can see how it
is part of a divinely ordered universe. Both of these poems tackle
problems but manage to create a sense of order.

   Most of Donne's love lyrics are at an opposite extreme. The
jagged nature of his lines, with leaps from idea to idea, make it
clear that he is pursuing thoughts and feelings in all their disorder.
Donne might have an ideal of secular or religious love, but his
poetry forces us to notice the complex and disordered nature of

experience. While Herbert stresses the order that can be found through religious faith, Donne acknowledges that life can be almost overwhelmingly confusing. Secular or divine love is the theme of most seventeenth-century lyric poems. The most attractive are often those that create a sense of order, but the most impressive are often those, such as the poems of Donne or Shakespeare, that present a sense of how difficult it is to understand and get the measure of experience. (*See also* Metaphysical poetry, p. 44; *and* Renaissance poetry, p. 56).

Lyric poetry fell out of fashion in the eighteenth century. A social poet such as Pope preferred to explore his ideas through narrative verse or a social form such as the epistle. It is not until the romantic period that lyric poetry again becomes popular, but with a shift in subject and approach. The great subject now is nature and the poet's attempt to construct from it some order and harmony. Thus Keats in 'To Autumn' (1820) describes the perfect beauty of the season. But autumn is followed by winter: perfection is transient, and so the disorder of life intrudes into the poem. It is the familiar pattern of lyric poetry: a sense of something ideal is set against the world's disorder. As is so often the case, the poetry is at its most attractive when it creates a sense of harmony – in romantic poetry, a harmony in the natural world – but what eventually impresses us is the poet's awareness that life itself is more complicated than the ideal. In Wordsworth's *Lucy* poem 'She dwelt among the untrodden ways' (1800), that opening line alone suggests a wonderful impression of the girl in harmony with nature, but the poem ends with her death and the poet's distress: the pain of experience disrupts the ordered picture (*see also* Romantic poetry, p. 62).

This gap between an ideal order – the order of love or order in nature – and the disorder of reality gets wider after the romantic period. For Victorian poets, such as Tennyson and Arnold, the search for some stability gets increasingly desperate. Arnold's 'Dover Beach' (1867) ends,

> And we are here as on a darkling plain
> Swept with confused alarms of struggle and flight,
> Where ignorant armies clash by night.

It is a frightening picture: the sweetness that we might expect to find in lyric poetry has gone. 'Dover Beach', like 'To Celia', is a love poem, but, instead of idealising love, Arnold sees only the problems that stand in its way.

Looking back, we can see that a lyric will lean in one of two directions: it can lean towards a harmonious, ordered picture, or it can lay more stress on the disorder that experience offers. It is the same in the twentieth century. In 'Sailing to Byzantium' (1928) Yeats creates a dream world where he can avoid the problems of age and death, but in his 'Second Coming' (1920) there is a greater stress on things falling apart. What makes 'Sailing to Byzantium' impressive, however, is that Yeats's beautiful evocation of the dream world is coupled with an awareness that escape is impossible. Philip Larkin, a post-war poet, in 'Church Going' (1955) juxtaposes a traditional order, associated with churches, and a sense of the aimlessness and emptiness of life today. It is this tension or gap between the ideal and the real that provides us with a focus for our critical discussion of any lyric poem. We can look at how the poem suggests an ideal of harmony or order, but then we should always be able to spot some note of complication conflicting with the simple ideal. Attractive but straightforward poets tend to master the complications. Other poets set up a far more complex tension between the ideal and the real.

Lyrical ballad. Wordsworth and Coleridge's *Lyrical Ballads* appeared in 1798 and is accepted as the real starting-point of romantic poetry (*see* p. 62). The importance of the volume is that it turns away from the social and intellectual sophistication of so much seventeenth- and eighteenth-century poetry, and turns to nature. It thus introduces a central concept of romanticism, that there is a natural existence people have lost sight of because they have become too rational and worldly.

Most of the poems are by Wordsworth, with 'The Ancient Mariner' as Coleridge's only substantial contribution. Wordsworth subsequently (in 1800) added more poems and a famous preface outlining the new aims of romantic poetry. The very title of the volume is significant: 'ballad' suggests a desire to get back to a consideration of the simple misfortunes that befall ordinary people. This is a conscious reaction against the witty, urbane style of eighteenth-century poetry, which concerns itself with the morals and manners of the town. The addition of the word 'lyrical' suggests a greater degree of authorial involvement than might be found in the traditional ballad: the poet offers his response to the experience presented. At the same time the term 'lyrical ballad' seems deliberately to break the mould of previous poetic forms, combining both narrative and lyric modes.

The typical Wordsworth contribution is a story of rustic life. It is an unsentimental picture, stressing the hard life of the characters, yet he finds something inspiring in a tale of humble fortitude. Two of Wordsworth's positive values are readily apparent: the importance of love between parents and children, and the naturalness of family affection. In 'We Are Seven' he talks to a child who insists that she is one of seven children, even though two are dead. Wordsworth tries to persuade her to be more rational, but she will not give way. The poem confronts us with both family affection and a way of thinking at odds with rational thought: the girl, and other characters in the other poems, seem to possess innocent knowledge and values that rebuke the poet.

The style of the poems suits their content, Wordsworth deliberately writing in a simple manner:

> 'How many are you, then,' said I,
> 'If they two are in heaven?'
> Quick was the little Maid's reply,
> 'O Master! we are seven.'

It is an attempt to discard the artifice of previous poetry and treat the subject directly. Although this works well in some poems, and others contain striking lines, it must be added that the style can appear too contrived in its simplicity. A lot of the poems from the first edition might strike you as too deliberately naïve: the sentiment is genuine, but an excessively simple style can make the informing idea seem trite. This is, however, early work by Wordsworth: he establishes his positive values, but, starting with 'Tintern Abbey', the last poem in the first edition, he changes to a more complicated style and begins to examine and even question his beliefs, his perception of a valuable pattern in the natural world. (*See also* Romantic poetry, p. 62.)

Metaphysical poetry. A term used to refer to the poetry of Donne and other seventeenth-century poets such as Herbert, Crashaw, Vaughan and Marvell, who all employ a similar poetic manner. The poems are often written in knotted sentences in which it is hard to trace the line of argument, and the argument itself is often involved, with wild leaps from idea to idea. The imagery is extraordinary, making the most unexpected comparisons between things.

Donne in particular seems to delight in witty paradoxes and ingenious ideas.

It is, therefore, not surprising that many students find metaphysical poetry difficult, but some of the problems disappear when we realise that it is only Donne who is really difficult. Metaphysical poets write about conventional subjects, especially secular and divine love, and, as with most poets who write on these themes, they set the disorder of experience against the redeeming quality of love. Where metaphysical poetry differs from a lot of other poetry, however, is that it places a rather greater emphasis on how difficult it is to make sense of experience. For example, in Herbert's poem 'The Collar' (1633) he writes of his urge to rebel against the restrictions of religion. The poem is crowded with images suggesting freedom and restraint. It is disorderly, leaping from one image to the next. At one point Herbert describes himself as tied up by 'a rope of sands': this conceit (see p. 23) or witty image suggests a labyrinth-like rope, but one that is very weak. It is such images that convey his predicament, how he is knotted up in confusion. The complicated syntax and images are designed to suggest the turmoil of his mind. The last four lines of the poem, however, are calm, and it ends with a simple declaration of faith: 'My Lord.' It is as if he has untied the knot and found an answer, an order that can discipline his turbulent mind.

In Donne's poetry, however, the sense of life's bewildering complexity is far more extreme. He ends one of his Holy Sonnets by telling God that he will never be chaste 'unless you ravish me' – that is to say, unless he is raped by divine love. This sort of outrageous paradox is one of the things that makes Donne altogether more complex than other metaphysical poets, for they do resolve the complicated experience they describe by using love as a solution. But Donne questions everything, refusing to untie the knots he has created. Throughout his poems there is a puzzled, argumentative attitude to experience: he is never looking for easy answers or final solutions to the mystery of love.

At the same time Donne's poetry is very confident. The rhythms are those of the speaking voice and the language is colloquial, but the real sign of confidence lies in the ingenuity of the poetry, the delight in making connections through conceits between things which have little in common. His most famous conceit is where he compares two lovers to a pair of compasses. In 'The Flea' (written about 1600, published 1633) he argues that because the lovers have both been bitten by a flea they now share the same blood and ought to consummate their love. What these conceits have in common is that they are witty: **wit** here means self-consciously clever, surprising, extravagant and outrageous. It is such wit that makes Donne so much more difficult than the other metaphysicals: he takes more chances and risks, endlessly complicating the issue, even to the point of totally confusing us. The others pull everything together into a pattern, but Donne always asks another question, or sets up another paradox (a self-contradictory statement, containing two facts which cannot be reconciled in any logical way; *see* p. 154). He is forever puzzling over the paradoxes of experience rather than reaching for an answer and a resolution.

When reading Donne, begin by identifying his topic – religious or secular love: look through the difficulties to identify the familiar theme. Secondly, look at the way in which the poem is written, its complicated syntax and startling images. Do not worry if you cannot understand everything: work on the clearer bits. See how he creates an impression of how we live in a puzzling and complicated world. Then look at how he constantly juxtaposes different ideas and concepts in order to demonstrate his ingenuity and wit, his delight in the world's complexity. Finally, do not try to 'solve' the poem: do not expect to find a neat sense of order emerging. Donne leaves his poems in knots, and our main task in discussing him is to see how he creates an impression of the knotted complexity of experience.

Metre. Metre means the pattern of stressed and unstressed syllables in a line of poetry. The most widely used line in English poetry is the iambic pentameter: this is a ten-syllable line with five stresses or emphases.

For example, the following line from Gray's *Elegy* (1750) has ten syllables:

> 1   2   3   4   5   6   7   8   9   10
> The plowman homeward plods his weary way.

When we read the line our voice goes up and down because of the different stresses we naturally give the different syllables. In poetry we mark these differences by using signs: ˘ for an unstressed syllable, ´ for a stressed one, and this reveals the metrical pattern:

The plówmăn hómewărd plóds hĭs wéarў wáy.

As you can see, an unstressed syllable is followed by a stressed one. Each little unit or group of syllables is called a foot: in this case each foot is an iambic foot because it has the pattern unstressed – stressed syllable. The conventional way of marking off the feet from each other is the sign ' : thus, Gray's line has five iambic feet:

Thĕ plów-mărn hóme-wărd plóds' hĭs weá-rў wáy.'

Do not worry if you cannot hear this pattern: nobody actually reads poetry in this broken, halting way. What we are doing is scanning the line, looking to see what its metrical pattern is. Instead of saying that the metre is five iambic feet we can use the technical term iambic pentameter ('penta' means five).

Metre seems a frighteningly technical topic, but it becomes less frightening as soon as we realise that the bulk of English poetry, both rhymed and unrhymed (unrhymed lines in iambic pentameter are called blank verse, *see* p. 22), is written in iambic pentameter, with the same pattern as that illustrated above. A pattern is created in the verse, but it is a fairly natural pattern as the speaking voice does rise and fall in this way. Indeed, the easiest way of thinking about metre is as a regular rise and fall pattern.

Often, however, poets will disrupt this regular pattern or rhythm to produce certain effects in their verse. The reason for this is that a poem written in a totally predictable and regular pattern would become very mechanical. The regular metre of Gray's line suits its sense: it describes the laboured, tired journey of the plowman. Not every line, however, will have five clear stresses in this way. Often, indeed, we may only hear four, as in this first line from Milton's *Paradise Lost* (1667):

Ŏf mán's fĭrst dĭsōbédĭēnce ănd thĕ fruít.

Milton is writing about troublesome concepts: the fall of Adam and Eve and the relationship of humankind to God. A totally regular metrical pattern would suggest this was an easy thing to do, that some simple order can be found, whereas this is not so.

The pattern of verse, then, can vary to suit the subject. The metre, however, still remains iambic pentameter because metre describes the most frequently occurring pattern in the poem. This is the case even when a poet introduces variations into the poem by using a different sort of foot. Variation stresses different words and emphasises them unexpectedly. The most common way of varying the iambic pattern is to start the line with a strong stress instead of a weak one. When Pope writes,

Óft shĕ rĕjécts, bŭt névĕr ónce óffénds

the word 'Oft' is unexpectedly emphasised and so its meaning is stressed. This sort of reversed foot, with the stressed syllable appearing first, is known as a trochaic foot or trochee. The only other significant variation is the spondee: this is a two-syllable foot where both are stressed, as in this line from Keats:

Thŏu fóstĕr-chíld ŏf Sílĕnce ănd slów Tíme

Once again the effect is to emphasise the meaning of the words. This is true of metre as a whole. Metre is one way in which the poet orders language to make it more meaningful than ordinary language, compressing it into a pattern.

We have called this pattern both metre and rhythm. The difference between these, strictly speaking, is that metre is something the poet imposes on the words, arranging them into a pattern. Rhythm, however, is something that comes with the language itself because of the way we speak. In reading a poem it is the rhythm of the language we hear, its movement and flow (*see* p. 60). Indeed, the only way to spot the stresses in a line of poetry is to read it as you would normal prose, noticing which syllables you emphasise. Most of the time the pattern of syllables will be straightforward. When it is not, then the poet will be varying the metre to suit his or her theme.

Not all poetry is written in five-feet lines. There are names for every length of line (length means how many syllables and feet in a line): the most significant are the tetrameter, which has eight syllables divided into four feet, and the hexameter, which has twelve syllables divided into six feet. If the feet in a hexameter line are iambic it is called an alexandrine. Such conventions do not apply to Old English poetry and medieval alliterative poetry, where syllables do not matter, only stress. The name for this is pure-stress or strong-stress metre, and there are always four stresses to every line, regardless of length.

A form of pure-stress metre is found in the work of the late-nineteenth-century poet Gerard Manley Hopkins. He experimented with his verse a great deal but essentially he works in free verse (*see* p. 33) with strong stresses in each line. Hopkins called this 'sprung' rhythm because he felt we had to spring from one strong syllable to the next without any pause between. This is a line from 'The Wreck of the Deutschland' (1875, published 1918):

> Our héarts' charity's héarth's fire, our thóughts' chivalry's thróng's Lórd.

It has six strong stresses according to Hopkins, though the reader has nó way of knowing this. What Hopkins is getting away from is the discipline of the traditional iambic pentameter. He is writing in free verse; there is no regular metre or line length, but the verse is still patterned, most often by the repetition of words or by parallel sentences. In other words, such verse is rhetorical rather than metrical – its effect is that of speech, not of organised rhythms.

There are three other technical terms related to prosody (prosody is the study of versification, especially metre, rhyme, stanzas) which it can prove useful to know. (a) **Caesura:** a pause in a line of poetry, often marked by punctuation. (b) **End-stopped lines:** a pause at the end of a line of poetry, marked by punctuation. (c) **Run-on lines:** there is no pause at the end of a line. This running-over of the sense of one line into the next is also called **enjambement**, meaning a striding-over.

Mock-heroic: A mock-heroic (or mock-epic) poem imitates the elaborate form and elevated style of epic poetry, but applies it to some trivial subject matter. Epic is the most ambitious form of poetry, presenting its protagonists in heroic encounters which can affect the whole destiny of the world. When the style and conventions of epic are used to describe petty incidents the effect is comic and satiric.

There are three major mock-heroic poems in English: two by Pope and one by Dryden. Pope's *The Rape of the Lock* (1714) concerns the theft of a lady's curl: by presenting this action, and the consequences, in grandiose terms, Pope ridicules the foolishness of people in society. Social affectation and pride are made to seem absurd.

Dryden's *MacFlecknoe* (1682) presents a notoriously bad poet, Flecknoe, choosing his successor, Shadwell. Here Dryden describes the two of them:

The hoary prince in majesty appeared,
High on a throne of his own labours reared.
At his right hand our young Ascanius sate,
Rome's other hope, and pillar of the state.
His brows thick fogs, instead of glories, grace,
And lambent dulness played around his face.

The knowledgeable reader might notice an allusion to Satan in *Paradise Lost* here, but the passage is effective even if we do not notice this. The initial impression is elevated, but then we notice the undercutting: Flecknoe has made his own throne, and the flickering on Shadwell's face is dulness. The concepts are grand – the imagery is of monarchs and Rome, and Dryden uses dignified words such as 'glories' and 'grace' – but it is all being subverted to ridicule the characters. *MacFlecknoe* as a total structure mocks the protagonists, but there is an additional barb in virtually every line.

Such effects are always present in mock-heroic poetry, but the poems do have an individual character. *The Rape of the Lock* is light and playful, *MacFlecknoe* savagely ironic, while Pope's *The Dunciad* (1742) is by far the most powerful and denunciatory. It presents the dunces who are taking over English culture. It ends with a great yawn and a nation reduced to sleep: the light is eclipsed and everything subsides into barbarism. It is a tremendously powerful poem, Pope transforming our ideas about mock-heroic as he presents this terrifying and terrible vision. As is so often the case in poetry, the more substantial the picture of disorder that the writer presents (provided, of course, that a language can be found adequate to presenting the picture), the more substantial his or her verse is likely to appear. A poem such as *The Dunciad* presents us with poetry's familiar confrontation between disorder and order in an extreme form, with Pope's desperate desire for balance almost overwhelmed by his despairing awareness of how close society is to chaos.

Modern poetry. The most common problem students experience with a lot of modern poetry, from Ezra Pound and T. S. Eliot onwards, is its difficulty: it can appear baffling. Consider these lines from Eliot's *The Waste Land* (1922):

Summer surprised us, coming over the Starnbergersee
With a shower of rain; we stopped in the colonnade,
And went on in sunlight, into the Hofgarten,
And drank coffee, and talked for an hour.
Bin gar keine Russin, stamm' aus Litauen, echt deutsch.

Any attempt to understand this is likely to falter as Eliot unexpectedly switches to a foreign language. This is not an isolated example:
the whole poem can appear to be an odd jumble of confusing lines.
The same is true of the overall design, the poem shifting from
scene to scene without any apparent logic. We are bewildered, and
the foreign names add to our confusion, our sense of being lost.
The intention, however, could be to create a sense of being lost in
a confusing world. In these lines, a sense of home and security is
absent: we are in a foreign setting hearing a foreign voice. Even the
weather is all awry. Eliot's images suggest his impression of contemporary disorder.

What we find here is not uncommon in modern literature.
There are writers who continue to produce fairly traditional
poems, but there are other writers who seek appropriate images
and an appropriate style to suggest their sense of a very confusing
world: in this instance, Europe immediately after the First World
War, when it must have seemed that all existing structures had
collapsed. The thing to look at first in baffling modern poems is
the way in which the images and structure suggest a complicated or
puzzling world. Yet, as in all poems, there are likely to be threads of
order. Eliot often uses phrases from earlier literature: it is as if he
is aware of how generations of writers have all sought an order in
life, but, although he shares their desire, he is left with only their
example. In fact, Eliot eventually turned back to the traditional
order of Christianity, and a desire for religious conviction can be
traced in *The Waste Land*, but what mainly impresses us is the
manner in which he creates a picture of a sick world.

Yeats is another difficult modern poet troubled by a sense of
life's complexity, though again there is also some sense of order in
his verse. One of his favourite tactics is to juxtapose the messiness
of life and the neatness of art, as in his creation of the mythical
ideal world of Byzantium. It is not, however, a poetry of escape, but
rather a poetry that acknowledges the gap between reality and the
artist's dreams of order. Many modern writers, such as Wallace
Stevens, put this question of the relationship between life and art at
the centre of their poems, and, indeed, in reading difficult modern
poems it often helps to look for a life (disorder)/art (order)
division in the work, simply because so many writers in this century
concentrate on the nature of the relationship between the two.

This does not mean that the ideas in modern poetry are
necessarily difficult: the difficulty resides in the technique: the
poets want to find a style adequate to a sense of a confusing world,

and also want to present and look at some of the devices we use to help us structure our experience.

Narrative poetry. A poem that tells a story. The two basic types are epic and ballad, but a varied tradition has grown from these roots: poems such as *Beowulf* (around 700), *Sir Gawain and the Green Knight* (fourteenth century), Chaucer's *Canterbury Tales* (about 1400), Pope's *The Rape of the Lock* (1714), Wordsworth's 'Michael' (1800), Coleridge's 'Ancient Mariner' (1798), Keats's 'The Eve of St Agnes' (1820), Byron's *Don Juan* (1819–24), Tennyson's *Idylls of the King* (1859), Browning's *The Ring and the Book* (1868–9), and many poems by Robert Frost. Poetry as a whole can be split into two broad groups: lyric and narrative. Poets do not always want to offer their immediate response to life, as is the case in lyric poetry, so might prefer to explore their ideas through the medium of a story. The stories, then, are not told for their own sake: they have implications. The basic plot might carry some significance, but what principally interests us is what the poet brings to the story.

For example, in *The Canterbury Tales* pilgrims tell stories. The Pardoner tells a tale and draws his own moral: 'The love of money is the root of all evil'. A poet is, however, unlikely to tell a story simply to get across a simple message. Usually the intention is more complex, and this is certainly the case here. The author of the poem is not the Pardoner but the poet, and Chaucer makes the Pardoner speak to us in a lengthy prologue and in asides in his story, where we get a clear impression of his addiction to money. His personality is, therefore, at odds with the morally instructive tale he tells. The nature of the complication is a familiar one. Poetry looks at life, and poets seek a meaning in what they see, but good poets are ready to admit that life itself is untidier than any order we might establish. Chaucer, coupling the prologue and the tale, reminds us of the gap between moral ideals and how things are in this imperfect world: reality is always more complex than the stories we might trace in it, or the interpretations we might place upon it. Many of the finest narrative poems are open to the complexity of experience in this sort of way. Chaucer's most characteristic method of suggesting this is his use of a morally suspect imagined narrator. A variation of this is used in Browning's *The Ring and the Book*, where several characters tell the same story, all seeing things differently: we are confronted with interpretations of reality rather than with reality itself.

A similar challenge to the neatness of story-making can be achieved in other ways. One is to introduce awkward details that do not fit in with the point the story seems to wish to make. In Wordsworth's 'Michael' a shepherd's son falls into dissolute ways in London, while his father, saddened by this, continues his hard life. The poet might seem to be commenting on the importance of family ties and the quiet heroism of the shepherd, and the poem is often read as if Wordsworth has a message to teach us. The disaster that befalls the family is, however, so total that it seems at odds with any desire to read something positive into the events: life is so problematic that any scheme of values sought by the poet seems suspect. By the end Wordsworth's narrative voice seems almost as suspect as the Pardoner's, as if there will always be a gap between fine poetic phrases and the hard realities of experience. Yet this is the strength of the poem: Wordsworth has searched for order and significance, but he finally acknowledges the disorder of life.

Coleridge's 'Ancient Mariner' also challenges the desire for a simple interpretation of experience. A mariner shoots an albatross and is punished for his sin. We might read into the poem a simple moral about the need to respect all life, but the details of the poem, in particular the strangeness of the events that occur, suggest that a moral reading is too reductive. Again we are forced back onto the complexities of experience. It might seem hard to see what value there is in a story that does not have a moral point, but the value is that we see the poet looking at life and also indulging in the most characteristic human activity – thinking, thinking about what it all might amount to. And the finest thinkers are always ready to admit that experience is more complex than their theories about experience.

This level of complication is not present in all narrative poetry. Keats's 'Lamia' (1820) does little more than tell a story, but his 'Eve of St Agnes' includes all kinds of elements at odds with any simple message we might try to extract from the poem. A simple way of describing what happens in the best narrative poems is to talk about the difference between the 'story' and the 'discourse'. The story in outline is a sort of parable, an anecdote with a point, but good poets introduce all sorts of complications in their telling of the story – the discourse – that undermine this simple moral significance. One of the finest illustrations of this is Wordsworth's long autobiographical narrative poem, *The Prelude* (there are two versions, the 1805 and 1850), which confuses and loses many readers simply because the material is so diverse and becomes so complicated in the telling that it will not accord with any simple ideas about Wordsworth's beliefs that we might try to extract from the text.

Looking at a narrative poem, you might find yourself going through three stages: first, reading it simply as a story; second, looking for the simple idea the story seems to put across; third, looking at the complicated details the poet introduces which suggest that life is always more complicated than any story or moral pattern we might trace in it.

Ode. An elaborate and elevated lyric poem, extending over quite a few stanzas, and addressed to a person or thing or to an abstraction (e.g. 'Melancholy'). In its more straightforward form it simply praises the subject, but as it developed in the romantic period the typical ode became more hesitant and philosophical.

The opening of Milton's 'Hymn on the Morning of Christ's Nativity' (1629) illustrates the central idea that characterises the mode:

> It was the winter wild,
> While the Heaven-born Child
>   All meanly wrapped in the rude manger lies;
> Nature in awe to him
> Had doffed her gaudy trim,
>   With her great Master so to sympathise.

Christ is the embodiment of order, overshadowing all things: even nature acknowledges this greater power. An ode is always addressed to somebody (or something) who seems to transcend the problems of life, and thus stands as a symbol of perfection. Milton's poem continues by juxtaposing Christ and the confusions of the world. An ode becomes more complicated, however, if the poet begins to question the status of the object addressed. Marvell's 'Horatian Ode upon Cromwell's Return from Ireland' (1650) appears to be a straightforward eulogy, but as we look more closely we might sense that the poet's attitude is ambivalent: possibly we are meant to see that Cromwell has been ruthless in his treatment of those who oppose him. As in many poems, it is this level of complication, the way in which the writer suggests that reality is more complicated than the ideal, that impresses us.

Such hesitancy becomes far more extreme in the romantic ode. Keats's 'Ode on a Grecian Urn' and 'Ode to a Nightingale' (1820) both focus on images of perfection, but there is far more stress on the fact that we live in an imperfect world. The object of the address is principally a device, a remote and attractive symbol of order that enables Keats to write about the gap between any ideal and how life really is. Similarly, Wordsworth's 'Ode: Intimations of Immortality' (1807) eulogises childhood, but the poem is more concerned with present feelings of unhappiness and loss. The direction in which the ode has moved is away from the positive celebration of the traditional ode towards a greater emphasis on negative feelings. The length of the ode provides room for a discursive enquiry into life's problems.

In analysing an ode, look first at how elevated language is used to create a sense of something that transcends the mundane. Then look for the opposing images that create a sense of the harsher realities of life. The poem is likely to become complicated – with difficult ideas, an involved argument and a variety of images in each stanza – as the poet attempts to convey his or her awareness of being trapped in everyday difficulties, an awareness of the gap between the ideal and the reality of life.

Pastoral. Pastoral means dealing with the life of shepherds and shepherdesses. Pastoral poetry presents a peaceful, rural world far removed from the corruption of contemporary life.

Poetry often deals with the contrast between an ideal world and the hardships of the real world: pastoral poetry, though, might seem rather suspect in that it appears to offer us simply a nostalgic image of escape into a world of Arcadian innocence (Arcadia is the idealised country celebrated in classical pastoral poems). Pastoral poetry, however, does not evade reality: what it does is present an artificial picture of an innocent world which reflects back on the corrupt realities of the world the poet lives in. This is certainly the case in Spenser's *Shepheardes Calendar* (1579), the finest English pastoral poem. Much of the pastoral poetry produced in the late sixteenth century was written in imitation of Spenser. *The Shepheardes Calendar* consists of twelve poems, one for each month of the year, the main themes being religion, love, and poetry. The language of the poem, like its form, is consciously artificial, signalling to the reader that it is not to be taken at its face value: the poem has wider, contemporary reference, satirising the moral, political and religious state of society.

Pastoral in *The Shepheardes Calendar* is thus a form of allegory (*see* p. 133): it presents an ideal world which we are meant to interpret as referring to the real world even though the real world is not explicitly referred to or presented. This essentially medieval allegorical way of thinking all but disappears with Spenser so that what we find in later pastoral poetry is that pastoral is used in a different way. Thus in Milton's pastoral elegy 'Lycidas' (1637) pastoral is used as a vehicle whereby the poet can confront the problem of death: his friend has died, but through pastoral Milton is able to come to terms with this painful fact, seeing his friend as a good shepherd ordained by God to die. In 'L'Allegro' (1632) and 'Il Penseroso' (1632), on the other hand, Milton associates the pastoral with the ideal world of art, affording him escape from experience.

The differences between Milton's use of pastoral imagery and Spenser's point to a shift of thinking that took place in the seventeenth century: the medieval allegorical way of thinking was replaced by a more empirical (relying on observation) response to experience. This meant that writers confronted the real world rather than just holding up an imagined world as a contrast. In Milton there is a more explicit focus on the gap between the ideal and the real than is the case in Spenser.

Wordsworth takes the whole process a stage further: when he focuses on the realities of rural life his poetry can include an implicit attack on the unreality of the pastoral mode. 'Michael' (1800), for example, begins with the poet escaping from 'the public way' to 'a hidden valley', suggesting it will follow the conventional pattern of pastoral poetry by presenting an idyllic landscape of carefree shepherds. What follows, though, is a disturbing story of a family tragedy which undercuts and rejects the pastoral gestures of the opening.

Nobody, however, ever really believed in that simple world of pastoral innocence: it was no more than a device for writing about what the world could be like as opposed to how it really is.

Renaissance poetry. In England the term 'Renaissance' (the word means rebirth) can be applied to the century following the accession of Elizabeth I in 1558. The great Renaissance poets are Spenser, Shakespeare, Donne and Milton. Their favoured modes are the epic and the short lyric poem, and their central subject is love, both secular love and divine love.

The difference between Chaucer and Spenser helps define the poetry of the period. Both write narrative poems – the tragic *Troilus and Criseyde* (about 1386) and the epic *Faerie Queene* (1596) – and both write from a standpoint of absolute belief in a Christian, ordered universe. In addition, Spenser has much in common with medieval poets in his use of allegory and romance, but there are the first slight signs of the strain that marks Renaissance poetry. Chaucer can take a comic view of the disorder of love and experience, but in Spenser there is a need to impose order on everything. He is not quite as secure and confident as Chaucer, and each subsequent poet is less secure. If we compare Spenser's and Shakespeare's sonnet sequences, Spenser's *Amoretti* (1595) presents a reassuring impression of idealised love, but Shakespeare's sonnets (1609) admit far more of the bitter reality of existence – the reality of ageing and death, those things that disrupt love.

In Donne's poetry (written about 1600 and published in 1633) a coherent sense of an ordered universe is pushed further into the background and the stress is very much on the disorder of experience. There is a dramatic difference between Donne's knotted syntax and the smooth lines of Spenser. Yet Donne's awareness of strains and tensions does not lead him in the direction of despair; on the contrary, he delights in puzzling over the paradoxes of experience, essentially because his ultimate faith in God is still very secure. He knows very well that God can reconcile the contradictions and problems of earthly existence. It is only when we come on to Milton that we encounter a poet who is really deeply troubled about the apparent gap between God and man. For Donne poetry is largely an intellectual game, but Milton writes in a far more serious and worried way. There is a real sense of bafflement that God's pattern is at such a remove from the lack of pattern of life in the world. The very purpose of *Paradise Lost* (1667), an attempt to justify the ways of God to man, indicates that there is a real problem: just a few years earlier God's order could be taken for granted, nobody would have felt the need to justify God's actions. A major factor that influenced such a change was the experience of the Civil War of 1642–51, which must have emphasised the difference between society's disorder and God's order.

Yet, whereas *Paradise Lost* is a complete epic, *The Faerie Queene* was left unfinished: possibly Spenser's more traditional faith and values would not sustain an entire work of this length at a time when the medieval world picture was breaking up. At the end of the Renaissance period is the social poetry of Dryden and Pope and the birth of the novel: art has shifted almost entirely to a focus on the problems of the secular world. Renaissance poets pay increasing attention to such problems, but the characteristic strength of Renaissance poetry probably lies in the fact that it represents the final attempt to hold everything together, an attempt to reconcile human experience and an all-embracing world picture, as in Milton's completed epic.

Rhyme. Identity of sound between two words, extending from the last fully stressed vowel to the end of the word: for example, 'hill' and 'still', 'follow' and 'hollow'. Rhyme is usually employed at the end of lines, but poets can make use of internal rhyme. Rhyme suggests harmony and order: the poet finds connections between words, if only at the level of sound, but the connection made suggests a broader idea of finding an order in things. This search for order will be most apparent in what the words of the poem say, but the verse form, including rhyme, helps realise the idea.

In these lines from Yeats's 'Sailing to Byzantium' (1928) he makes a plea to priest-like figures:

> O sages standing in God's holy fire,
> As in the gold mosaic of a wall,
> Come from the holy fire, perne in a gyre,
> And be the singing-masters of my soul.
> Consume my heart away; sick with desire
> And fastened to a dying animal
> It knows not what it is; and gather me
> Into the artifice of eternity.

In this instance the actual sense of the words might be difficult to grasp, but the use of rhyme (including the internal rhyme of 'fire'/ 'gyre' in line three) helps create a pattern in the verse which actually helps us grasp what is being said: that he wants to escape to a rarefied, ritual-like life outside time.

Rhyme can link problematic words. Marvell's 'To his Coy Mistress' (written about 1650, published 1681) begins,

> Had we but world enough, and time,
> This coyness, Lady, were no crime.

'Time' and 'crime' are troublesome ideas, but here they are absorbed into a couplet: we feel that the poet has got control of the concepts. So rhyme has an ability to unify and connect disparate entities, finding similarity in dissimilarity. It is never enough to point out that a poem rhymes: you have to construct a case about how the use of rhyme contributes to the overall meaning and effect of the poem. The answer, however, will always be that rhyme contributes to a sense of order.

What is also worth looking out for are the occasions on which the rhyme pattern falters. In Yeats's poem, we might expect line six to rhyme with line two or line four, but they do not quite rhyme. The idea in the line is a painful one, that of the heart 'fastened to a dying animal', and serves to remind us of the impossibility of escape for the poet, but the poem's failure to rhyme perfectly also contributes to the sense that the disorder of the real world is breaking up the pattern of the poem. There is a similar effect in Marvell's poem. Suddenly the rhyming-pattern falters:

> And yonder all before us lie
> Deserts of vast eternity.

It only just fails to rhyme, but the break in the poem's orderly pattern is sufficient to underline the idea of the vastness of eternity, an idea too big to absorb into Marvell's ordered response to life.

There are technical terms for the different kinds of rhyme, which it can prove useful to know. (a) **End rhyme** occurs at the end of lines. (b) **Internal rhyme** occurs within lines. (c) **Masculine** or **strong rhymes:** a single stressed syllable – 'hill' and 'still'. (d) **Feminine** or **weak rhymes:** two rhyming syllables, a stressed one followed by an unstressed one – 'hollow' and 'follow'. (e) **Eye rhyme** or **courtesy rhymes:** words spelt alike but not actually rhyming – 'love' and 'prove'. (f) **Imperfect rhymes** (also called **partial, near, slant** or **off-rhymes**): words which do not quite rhyme and so produce a sense of discordance – 'soul' and 'wall'. (g) **Half-rhymes** (also called 'consonance', see p. 20): repetition of the same consonant sounds before and after different vowels – 'groaned' and 'groined'. The conventional method of referring to the rhyme scheme of a poem is to work through the alphabet, assigning the same letter to the lines that rhyme: a poem in rhyming couplets could be said to rhyme *aa bb cc dd ee*, etc.; a four-line stanza might often rhyme *abab*. This, however, does not tell us anything impor-

tant about the poem; we always have to go further and talk about
the rhyme words themselves. For example, in Yeats's lines above,
the rhyme between 'me' and 'eternity' reinforces the idea of the
poet's yearning for an ideal world by connecting the two words
through sound.

Rhythm. Rhythm means the flow or movement of a line, whether
it goes fast or slow, is calm or troubled. But how do we know
whether a line is fast or slow? The answer is that the meaning of the
words tells us: rhythm and meaning cannot be separated.

For example, in the closing stanza from Hardy's 'The Voice'
(1914) he is haunted by a woman's voice, a woman he still loves
even though she has gone:

> Thus I: faltering forward,
> Leaves around me falling,
> Wind oozing thin through the thorn from norward,
> And the woman calling.

Cold images of falling leaves and the north wind suggest his mood
of despair. Turning to the rhythm, the first line is about the poet
faltering: the idea is suggested by the break after 'Thus I'. The
rhythm falters, but the meaning of the words has told us what to
expect in the rhythm. Similarly, the second line mentions the
falling leaves, and the rhythm itself is falling – as we read the last
word our voice trails away. The rhythm thus matches and reinforces the sense of the words. It is the same in the third line: it is
tempting here to say that the line imitates the noise of the wind,
but it does not. The description of the wind is an image that
expresses the poet's feelings of pain. So the depressing, lifeless
rhythm of the line matches the speaker's feelings. As always, the
rhythm supports the real meaning of the line.

The way in which rhythm supports meaning can be seen again
in Donne's 'The Sun Rising' (written about 1600, published 1633):

> Busy old fool, unruly Sun,
> Why dost thou thus,
> Through windows and through curtains call on us?

The language is colloquial, the rhythm almost chatty but also
angry. We can set the lively, questioning manner of this against
these lines from Tennyson's 'The Lotos-Eaters' (1832):

> There is sweet music here that softer falls
> Than petals from blown roses on the grass.

The scene is attractive – the words make that clear – so Tennyson opts for a contented, rather dreamy rhythm. Rhythmic effects are always as simple as this. If the speaker seems troubled then the rhythm will be troubled. If the speaker is happy and excited, so too will the rhythm be. If he or she is calm and contented the rhythm will be relaxed. It is always best to work from meaning back to the devices of the poem, such as rhythm, rather than trying to guess the meaning from the rhythm.

Romance. A narrative poem that tells a story of adventure, love and chivalry. The typical hero is a knight on a quest: it is a symbolic journey during which moral and spiritual qualities are tested. Supernatural events and the use of a fairy land are common.

Romances were popular in the Middle Ages. *Sir Gawain and the Green Knight* (fourteenth century), which tells of the testing of Gawain's honour and chastity by a magical green knight, is the finest example from this period. Gawain is held up as the ideal example of a courtly knight. The text is elaborately patterned to reinforce this sense of something ideal and remote from ordinary life, but there is a further complication in the playful, teasing manner of a narrator, who hints at the baffling nature of experience. There is thus a gap between the simple view of Gawain as a perfect knight and the complications of the actual telling of the story which remind us of the gap between the ideal and how things really are. Spenser also uses the romance motif of knights on quests in his epic poem *The Faerie Queene* (1596), but Spenser is didactic (i.e. morally instructive), intent on demonstrating the ideal order and harmony he can perceive in the world and so uses the stories of his knights to illustrate this. Allegory (*see* p. 133) in the poem works in the same way. The hero of the first book is the Red Cross knight, who is at once St George, Holiness and the Church of England. The impression is that all of experience does interconnect to form a coherent pattern.

Romance fell out of fashion in the eighteenth century but was revived in the romantic period by poets such as Keats. His 'Eve of St Agnes' (1820) tells the story of Madeleine's escape from her parents' castle with her lover. It presents a vision of an ideal world where death and hatred are left behind, but as in *Sir Gawain* there

is a firm sense of the gap between how things might be in a perfect
world and how they are in the everyday world. There is obviously a
connection between the words 'romance' and 'romantic', but 'romantic', rather than signifying just the creation of a make-believe
world of knights and ladies, has more to do with ideas of the
imagination. The romantics turned to the stories of the Middle
Ages because they involved a flight of the imagination whereby a
vision of a harmonious world could be created in the mind. The
strength of the finest romantic poetry, however, is that it is always
fully aware of the gap between the vision of an ideal world where
everything integrates and makes sense and the far less comfortable
reality of life.

Romantic poetry. A major change in thinking occurred in the late
eighteenth century. A new feeling came into existence, a sense that
people had become separated from nature. This is most evident in
the publication in 1798 of the *Lyrical Ballads* by Wordsworth and
Coleridge, which provides the effective starting-point for romantic
poetry. The romantic poets repeatedly turn to nature, finding
there a truth and value which had been lost sight of by rational
philosophers (romanticism is in many ways a reaction against the
prevailing rational mentality of the eighteenth century). Romantic
poets also attribute a tremendous importance to childhood, feeling that the child possesses an innocent wisdom which disappears
as maturity approaches. This emphasis on what is natural and
uncorrupted leads to a new emphasis on the importance of the
emotions and feelings. Such thinking finds expression in an extraordinary flood of great poetry from Blake, Wordsworth, Coleridge,
Keats, Byron and Shelley. Their work is very popular, but it is a
common failing to underestimate the poetic sophistication of these
writers. It is often assumed that a romantic poet has a positive
philosophy centring on simple, natural values, but, for the most
part, the major poets are very hesitant romantics, fully aware that
there can be no simple scheme of values.

We can begin with Blake, whose most celebrated poems were
in fact published before the *Lyrical Ballads*. His *Songs of Innocence*
(1789) and *Songs of Experience* (1794) are short poems presenting
an innocent and contrasting experienced view of a topic. Most
readers encountering Blake for the first time begin to extract a
philosophy from his work: that he is for innocence and freedom,
and against authority, discipline and restraint. The poems, how-

ever, are more complex than this: an innocent view is often too naïve. In addition, we only appreciate innocence because we are experienced. If the poems of Innocence and Experience are seen as complementary, we can see how they deal with the conflict there will always be between these two states. Rather than providing a philosophy or message, the poems ask questions about the relationship between innocence and experience, between the (perhaps too simple) ideal and the real.

The danger of assuming that the poet's works offer a philosophy is most damaging in the case of Wordsworth. 'Tintern Abbey' (1798) opens with a description of a rural landscape. Here we have the poet turning to nature, and Wordsworth continues by writing about the effect of the scene: it enables him to see a pattern in the world ('We see into the life of things'). Here we do have a romantic expression of the perception of truth and order in the natural world, just as in the other poems in the first edition of the *Lyrical Ballads* (*see* p. 43). Wordsworth finds truth and value in the close-to-nature lives of the characters he describes.

Wordsworth's poetry is often appreciated for his perception of this natural order. The problem, however, is that in 'Tintern Abbey' Wordsworth is sufficiently sceptical to realise that this order might not exist, that it might be simply an invention of his imagination. In fact, this is the point the poem eventually arrives at: Wordsworth realises that it is nature and his mind working together that create this deeper harmony. This concept of the imagination is central in romantic thought, for it is the creative insight of the poet that allows him both to perceive and create an order in the natural world. At this point some readers start talking about Wordsworth's great gift, as if he has an imaginative capacity that most people lack, and which can never be fully explained. If one looks closely at 'Tintern Abbey', however, it becomes clear that Wordsworth is less concerned to present his imaginative perception than to talk about, examine and even question his imagination. Thus, instead of being a relatively straightforward poem in which Wordsworth is concerned to present his almost religious insight into 'the life of things', 'Tintern Abbey' is in fact a much more complex and hesitant work which begins by setting up the idea that an order can be found in nature, but then questions the imaginative process that creates that idea.

Many of Wordsworth's finest poems follow a similar pattern. He presents us with a picture of something natural (either land-

scape or a character) on which he imposes an imaginative interpretation, but then questions whether the order he creates can be
trusted. In an encounter with a leech-gatherer in 'Resolution and
Independence' (1807) we have a typical Wordsworth character:
pathetic but also courageous. He inspires the poet. What we might
feel in reading the poem as a whole, though, is that there is a gap
between the reality of the leech-gatherer's lot and the rather too
confident uplifting sentiments Wordsworth draws from the encounter. Again we are confronted with a hesitant romantic, dis-
trusting and questioning his own imaginative interpretation of
experience. The poem does not have a message: on the contrary, it
makes us feel that any interpretation the poet might impose on life
cannot be totally trusted.

The point being made here is that romantic poets do not have
a simple philosophy to offer. In the end, their good poems, like all
good poems, show us that reality is more complex and confusing
than any order that the poet might create. Wordsworth's poems
only work so well, however, because he does give such serious
consideration to his own imaginative search for order: the self-
doubts and hesitations of his poems are so effective only because
they are played off against his ability to create a sense of an almost
mystical insight into the life of things.

Coleridge is another poet who often turns to nature, and then
writes of how the imagination can perceive a harmony and order in
the natural world. In his 'conversation poems', however, such as
'Frost at Midnight' (1802), his theme is most commonly the failure
of his imagination to detect this pattern. He has an ideal, and the
poems hint at this ideal, so we are offered a concept of order.
Indeed, there are numerous lines in Coleridge where a vision of
harmony is offered to us, but the main stress of the poems is on
how he cannot shift from the problems of the real world to how he
would like things to be. If Wordsworth's most repeated theme
could be said to be his distrust of his own imagination, Coleridge's
is the failure of his imagination.

Coleridge is also relevant to another aspect of romantic
poetry: the emphasis on the imagination suggests how the mind
is central in romanticism, and the awareness of how the poet
creates ideas in the imagination puts a new importance on the
fantasies that can be created in the mind. The imagination need
not relate to the everyday world but can create its own make-believe
world. This is important in Coleridge, especially in 'Kubla Khan'

(1816), where he creates a sort of fairy-tale kingdom. Coleridge does not, however, just drift off into fantasy: the poem works so well partly because there is always an implicit tension between the dream and the reality. The other important aspect of the poem, however, is the vividness of its imaginative picture: as with Wordsworth, Coleridge can create an intense imaginative vision, even if the poem as a whole undercuts and questions it. Keats is another poet who uses his imagination to create make-believe worlds – a world of romance in his narrative poems, the world of the nightingale or the Grecian urn in his odes – and again the vividness of the imaginative picture is important. The make-believe world he creates in his mind is, however, always put in conflict with the real world. We see again poetry's familiar tension between dreams of order and the world's lack of order. In the case of Shelley, though, the pattern varies. Shelley has never been as highly regarded as the other romantic poets mainly because he did tend to believe in his own imagination, so that his ideas and ideals are not sufficiently measured against things as they really are.

The romantic period runs from the end of the eighteenth century to about 1830, yet to a large extent we are still living in the wake of romantic thinking. One effect, seen in the poetry of Yeats, Wallace Stevens and others, is the frequency with which poets write about art itself, setting life against the orders that can be created in the artistic imagination. There is also, in this century, a great emphasis on the mind: writers are fond of exploring the unconscious and contrasting what is found there with what we might perceive in the everyday world.

When studying a romantic poem, initially you should try to see how the poet has used the power of the imagination to create something positive in the poem (either a vivid picture or a strong statement of positive beliefs), but then try to see how the poem as a whole might be offering more than this: that it might well be alert to the disorder and problems that are always present in experience, for the great poet is always ready to acknowledge that reality is more complex than any order he or she can create.

Sonnet. A fourteen-line poem. There are two basic types: the Italian or Petrarchan has an octave (eight lines) and a sestet (six lines) and rhymes *abba abba cde cde*. The English or Shakespearean sonnet is made up of three quatrains and a couplet and rhymes *abab cdcd* *efef gg.* The metre is iambic pentameter (*see* p. 46). A sonnet sequence is a series of sonnets on the same theme by the same poet: there are three major sequences in English, by Shakespeare, Spenser and Sidney. All are about love. The sonnet form, however, has been used by many poets to treat all manner of themes.

The sonnet appeals to poets because it is such a disciplined form: there is a challenge in confronting the diffuseness of experience within such an ordered mould. The sonnet's rigidity of form really forces the poet to concentrate very directly on questions of the disorder and problems of life and on the possibility of creating an ordered response. This is clear in Milton's Petrarchan sonnet 'When I consider how my light is spent' (1652). It deals with his blindness and his concern that, being blind, he will no longer be able to serve God. The first eight lines are immensely troubled, but the last six are calm as Patience replies that God only requires faith. The typical pattern of the Petrarchan sonnet is in evidence here: the octave sets out a problem, the sestet is used to resolve it.

The English sonnet, however, usually conforms to a different pattern. Shakespeare in 'Let me not to the marriage of true minds' (1609) is trying to define the nature of love. There is a contrast between love's constancy and ideas of change which is repeated and developed in each quatrain, but the couplet introduces a new idea:

> If this be error and upon me prov'd,
> I never writ, nor no man ever lov'd.

Shakespeare is saying that his love is as obvious as his writing of poetry, but his claim that he is stating something simple and obvious is suspect, for the couplet itself is an ingenious ending to the poem: it ties the poem up neatly but is far from simple. And sonnets are not simple poems. The elaborate rhyme scheme signals to the reader that the poet is trying to reconcile or harmonise opposite or contradictory feelings. Most often in the Elizabethan sonnet an ordered notion of ideal love is set against a sense of love's problems. Another favourite ploy is to write about writing itself even when the professed subject is love: this acknowledges the artificiality of the sonnet form and stresses the difference between life and trying to organise life in something as contrived as a poem.

The sonnet form, then, can be used in two ways: it can be used to express a logical argument, in which the poet imposes an ord-

ered answer on a problem. Or the poet can play against the rigidity
of the sonnet suggesting that life itself burgeons beyond the restraints of poetic form. Shakespeare's sonnets in particular convey
a very complex sense of the difficulty of resolving any issue. In
reading sonnets, first identify the theme. Then decide whether it is
English or Petrarchan. Third, see if the language is calm or violent.
If the overall impression is calm then the poet will be using the
sonnet to get on top of difficult ideas; if the poem is disorderly then
there will be a tension between the sonnet's ordered form and an
awareness that life itself will not fit neatly into such a poetic mould.

Stanza. A sixteen-line poem might be divided into four equal units
of four lines: these units of verse, separated by a space in the
printed text, are called stanzas. Four-line units (quatrains) are the
most common, but the term refers to any such group of lines. Each
unit normally contains the same number of lines, and usually the
same rhyme scheme is employed. In long poems, where there are
divisions at irregular intervals, each unit of verse is referred to as a
verse paragraph.

Later in this entry we list some of the great number of English
stanza forms, but such technical description is less important than
understanding the role of stanzas in poetry. There must be some
reason, connected to the overall meaning of the poem, why a writer
might choose to organise a poem in this way. A stanza from George
Herbert's 'Jordan I' (1633) provides a clue:

> Who says that fictions only and false hair
> Becomes a verse? Is there in truth no beauty?
> Is all good structure in a winding stair?
> May no lines pass, except they do their duty
>   Not to a true, but painted chair?

Herbert is criticising the elaborate images and ideas that poets are
so fond of. One thing he criticises is a structure like a winding stair
– that is, a poem that ties itself up in knots in pursuit of its idea. The
verse states this, but Herbert's point is supported by his use of a
regular five-line stanza (rhyming *ababa*), which stands as a counter-
weight to the convolutions of writing he is so much against.

Stanza patterns usually operate in this way. By employing a
regular pattern the poet offers an idea of order within the work.
Within the stanza all kinds of complications can occur, but this is
held in tension with the overall desire for a pattern. We can see this

in Browning's 'Two in the Campagna' (1855): he is trying to define the essence of love, but it is difficult, as the chopped syntax of the poem indicates:

> No. I yearn upward, touch you close,
>   Then stand away. I kiss your cheek,
> Catch your soul's warmth – I pluck the rose
>   And love it more than tongue can speak –
> Then the good minute goes.

The rapid move from idea to idea suggests the intangibility of what Browning is trying to define, but the overall stanza pattern stands as a testimony to his desire to understand and order experience.

The logic informing the use of stanzas is simple, but always worth commenting on, particularly if you feel that the stanza pattern falters at any stage in a poem, as this is an effective way of enacting the difficulty the poet is having in ordering his or her view. Many stanzas have no special name and often a poet will invent a stanza form for a particular poem. But there are some patterns that are widely used. (a) **Couplet:** a pair of rhymed lines. (b) **Heroic couplet:** rhymed lines in iambic pentameter (*see* p. 35). (c) **Tercet** or **triplet:** three lines with a single rhyme. (d) **Quatrain:** a four-line stanza. (e) **Rhyme royal:** a seven-line stanza in iambic pentameter rhyming *ababbcc*. (f) **Octava rima:** an eight-line stanza rhyming *abababcc*. (g) **Spenserian stanza:** a nine-line stanza rhyming *ababbcbcc*; the first eight lines are iambic pentameter, the ninth an alexandrine. (h) **Sonnet:** a fourteen-line poem in iambic pentameter (*see* p. 65). There are variations on the sonnet, such as a shortened form invented by Hopkins called the curtal sonnet. This has two separated stanzas, one of six lines, the other of four – with a half-line tail-piece. (i) **Canto:** a sub-division of a narrative poem.

Symbol. An object which stands for something else (e.g. a dove symbolises peace). In a poem it is a word which, while signifying something specific, also signifies something beyond itself.

Students are often unclear about the difference between an image and a symbol. The difference is that what an image is associated with is stated in the poem, but with a symbol we have to infer the meaning and associations. An example might make this clearer. A poet who compares his or her lover to a rose is using a figurative image, associating the lover with something from a different realm of experience. In this poem by Blake, however, published in 1794,

a rose is used as a symbol: we suspect that he is not only talking
about a rose, but what the rose stands for or is associated with is not
stated:

> O Rose, thou art sick!
> The invisible worm
> That flies in the night,
> In the howling storm,
>
> Has found out thy bed
> Of crimson joy,
> And his dark secret love
> Does thy life destroy.

Reading the poem we might work out that Blake is talking about
something evil destroying something beautiful, possibly corrupt
passion destroying a young woman's innocence and beauty. The
poem does not, however, state this, yet is effective because it is so
indirect.

Students often make the mistake of thinking that symbols are
rampant in poetry, and sometimes read poems in a silly way in
which everything is assumed to have a hidden meaning. The truth
is that most poems are far more direct, stating an idea and usually
using imagery to add associations and complexity to the idea.
Symbols are only used when a writer wants to express an apprehension of something which is not directly observable in the everyday
world. The writer has to use a symbol because he or she can only
convey this non-rational apprehension of something by using objects and words from the familiar world. Symbols are first used a lot
in romantic poetry, where the poets often want to express their
sense of an unseen world in the imagination. Coleridge's 'Kubla
Khan' (1816), with its creation of a mythical world which does not
have an obvious meaning but seems somehow to reflect the fantasies of the unconscious, is a good example of a symbolic poem. A
poet can, however, start with an object in the real world and make
it symbolic by loading it with meaning which is not explicitly stated:
for example, the solitary figures Wordsworth encounters become
symbolic, and Keats's nightingale, in 'Ode to a Nightingale' (1820),
is something he sees but then invests with a tantalising significance.

The danger with symbolism is that the poet can lose all touch
with the ordinary world. This happens in some of Blake's longer
poems where he explores the inner mind, using symbols, but the

symbolism has become so private that we can see no meaning in it. Successful symbolism – as in 'Kubla Khan', or 'Ode to a Nightingale', or when Yeats creates Byzantium in his *Byzantium* poems (1928 and 1933) – is rather more of a compromise, in that we can fairly confidently infer a meaning, and see how the imaginings of the mind relate to ordinary experience.

Twentieth-century poetry. Twentieth-century poetry covers a vast number of writers who offer very different responses to the chaos of a world torn apart by two world wars. Obviously, in this entry we cannot consider all the poets you might come across; all we can attempt to do is consider the broad picture.

We start with the **Georgian** poets, writing at the beginning of the century before the Great War; writers such as Rupert Brooke, A. E. Housman, Walter de la Mare and John Masefield. Much of their poetry is very traditional, celebrating the order of rural England. It is solid, uncomplicated poetry. The contrast with the poetry that follows – the war poetry of Wilfred Owen and Siegfried Sassoon, and the modernist poetry of T. S. Eliot and Ezra Pound – could hardly be greater. Where the Georgians create a sense of simple harmony and order, the poets that follow insistently offer us a sense of a world without links or coherence. What separates the poets is the cataclysmic shock of the First World War (1914–18). The sense of shock is registered in the often bitter, grimly ironic verse of the trenches, with its use of dream and nightmare imagery, and, above all, its language of violence and slaughter. Often we get a sense of a language only just coping with the desperate world it depicts. It is as if a terrible reality intrudes into poetry for the first time. And yet, at the same time, we are often struck by the echoes of order in such verse, for example in the use of half-rhyme and in references to love. There is, then, an intense awareness of disorder in war poetry, but also a recollection of, and clinging on to, the idea of order.

By contrast, the initial experience of reading **modernist** poetry, such as that of Pound or Eliot, can leave us with the impression that all order has gone; they might seem to be writing in a language without grammar or syntax, a language without rhyme or rhythm. The baffling experience of Eliot's poetry in particular conveys a sense of people alienated from each other and living broken, fragmented lives in a world without values. It is not simply that the poetry seems to be in revolt against traditional forms of verse but, rather, that it seems to register the extent to which language itself is in crisis as it confronts a world in decay which no longer has any role for poetry. The difficulty presented by modern poetry is discussed elsewhere in this guide (*see* p. 50), as are the ideas of imagism and symbolism which influenced Pound and Eliot and also W. B. Yeats (*see* pp. 39, 68). In each case what we notice is how intense, condensed and self-conscious the poetry is: it is a poetry that refuses to give us access to a tangible, solid world but instead draws attention to itself, as if there is no longer any meaning to be found in the world.

     With the poetry of the 1930s there is a shift away from this position with the political poetry of W. H. Auden, Stephen Spender, Louis MacNeice and C. Day Lewis. This is not to suggest, however, that the poetry of Eliot or Pound is apolitical. Modern critics who have reservations about T. S. Eliot do not criticise him on the grounds of his obscurity or the disorder of his verse; indeed, it is just the opposite, as attention is drawn to the right-wing notions of order that underlie his writings, the way in which his symptomatic analysis of a sick society is often tainted with anti-semitism and bigotry. Ezra Pound is even more clearly an extreme right-wing writer; with both writers, it is as if their sense of the disorder of twentieth-century society is so extreme that they seek the security of the most conservative myths of order. With the writers of the 1930s, by contrast, the attraction was to left-wing politics: poetry and language come to have a purpose, a role to play in a world beset by social issues and drifting towards war again. The difference can be seen in a poem such as Auden's 'Musée des Beaux Arts' (Museum of Fine Arts):

> About suffering, they were never wrong,
> The Old Masters, how well they understood
> Its human position: how it takes place
> While someone else is eating or opening a window or just walking
>   dully along.

The topic is the place of human suffering in the universe and how the tragic is always set next to life's ordinary untidiness. The tone is detached, but sympathetic; we are asked to think about the gap between the heroic and the ordinary, and consider further the plight of human beings caught between such poles. But what is also noticeable is the language Auden uses: where Eliot is allusive and difficult, Auden uses everyday words and images. It is a split that recurs time and time again in twentieth-century poetry, between poems that acknowledge the ordinary, the popular, and poetry that seems dense, communicating more by images than by ideas.

Auden went on writing after the Second World War (1939–45) and, like Eliot, was an important influence on later poets. The difficulty we meet at this point, however, is the sheer diversity of poetry that follows the thirties. There is, for example, the war poetry of Keith Douglas, the exuberant poetry of Dylan Thomas, the bleak pastoral poetry of R. S. Thomas, the intense psychological poetry of Sylvia Plath. The list could go on and on, but one other point we have to take into account is the way poetry after the Second World War turned more and more away from the large issue of order in the world towards a more restricted sense of life. This point might become clearer if we consider '**The Movement**' poets of the 1950s, in particular Philip Larkin. His poetry is rational, dealing with the world of everyday reality in a pessimistic manner without a touch of romantic excess or the wilful obscurity of modernist verse. It is, in the narrowest sense, orderly poetry, as if life after the war is being re-established on a reduced scale. Yet for all Larkin's emphasis on clear-eyed endurance, there is, particularly in the 1964 collection *The Whitsun Weddings,* a guarded celebratory tone, and even in his last collection, *High Windows* (1974), with its emphasis on ageing, illness and death, there is still an affirmative note.

The '**New Poetry**' of the 1960s reacted against the suburban gentility of 'The Movement' poets: there is a move away from sobriety and tidiness towards the kind of innovativeness we associate with modernism, with energetic poems prepared to consider the violence and cruelty of life, and also the recesses of the human mind. It is a disturbing, anguished vision that we find in the poetry of such writers as Sylvia Plath, Thom Gunn, Ted Hughes, Robert Lowell, John Berryman and Anne Sexton. Where 'The Movement', with its air of post-war austerity, sought to confine and give order to poetry, the 'New Poetry', written in the shadow of nuclear weapons and the Vietnam War (1957–75), gave voice to a sense of disintegration and darkness that characterises the post-modern period.

The term **post-modern** is used very loosely to cover all literature written since the Second World War (the more precise use of the term limits it to works characterised by fragmentation, discontinuity, indeterminacy, dislocation and self-consciousness). In poetry, it includes the poets named above and also contemporary poets such as Tony Harrison and Seamus Heaney. Their poetry is deeply influenced by, in the case of Heaney, the political problems in Ireland, and, in the case of Harrison, issues of class and a sense of alienation in society. Other significant figures in contemporary poetry include John Ashbery (sceptical, self-referential, self-enclosed poems), Craig Raine (clever poems, with original, startling metaphors), Charles Tomlinson (cold poetry, with a continuing commitment to modernism), and Adrienne Rich (increasingly innovative forms, used to explore feminist themes). Ashbery and Rich are Americans, as were Eliot and Pound, and, later, Plath, Lowell and Berryman: something that needs to be borne in mind when studying contemporary American poets is that Robert Frost, William Carlos Williams and Wallace Stevens are as significant as influences as Eliot and Pound.

Looking back, we can see that twentieth-century poets tend to lean in one of two directions, either towards writing in a traditional form (Thomas Hardy stands out as perhaps the leading example of this kind of poet in the twentieth century), or towards writing dense and often disjointed verse. Of course, there are plenty of poets who call upon both these ways of writing, and a poet, as is the case with Yeats, may begin his or her career by writing traditional, romantic, nature poetry and then move on to a more complex style, using symbolism and new stanza forms. And it is also the case that a contemporary poet might employ a very traditional stanza pattern to express radical or disturbing ideas. But if you take as your starting-point the fact that a modern poem is likely to appear either relatively 'conventional' or deliberately 'unconventional', this should give you an initial purchase on the poem. The unconventional poem, you can assume, will be using its dislocated, disorientating form to create a sense of a world where all security has disappeared. But sometimes you might be surprised by the force of the quietly disturbing and unnerving picture of modern life that can be created within the seeming order of an apparently conventional poem. As always with poetry, we need to feel that a precarious balance is established within the work, between, on the one hand, a sense of order, and, on the other, a sense of life's unpatterned and unpatternable confusion.

Verse epistle. A kind of letter in verse, dealing with moral and philosophical themes. The finest examples in English are Pope's

Moral Essays (1731–5) and his 'Epistle to Dr Arbuthnot' (1735). It is a mode well-suited to Pope's poetry of social comment: the short lyric can be used to this end (as in Blake's 'London', 1794), but the verse epistle gave Pope space and freedom for wide-ranging comment.

'Arbuthnot' is typical: Pope begins by complaining about how would-be authors pester him. He goes on to explain why he writes and criticises some other writers. Stating that no honest man need fear his lash, he then becomes more vicious, attacking a character called Sporus whose lack of principles contrasts with Pope's own high standards. The difficulty some readers experience is seeing what all this amounts to: it might appear to be little more than a mixture of sniping and self-congratulation. The point is, however, that if Pope wrote in abstract terms his poetry would be uninteresting. It is serious moral poetry, but the method is indirect.

By presenting a satiric picture of those who annoy him he creates a vivid impression of folly: the opening list of people who solicit his favour dramatises the idea of a society dominated by the mad pursuit of fame and fortune. Pope often presents a picture of mad movement, or, as in his reference to a drunken parson, a picture of people losing sight of their true roles in life. It is a topsy-turvy society, but we only feel this because the method of using appropriate illustrations allows us to feel it. In looking at Pope's poetry, look first at how he uses snapshots of characters to create an impression of a society where disorder prevails. The second thing to look at is his opposing standard: for example, how his respect for balance makes itself felt in his use of heroic couplets. Pope also usually states his principles, though always in a calculated manner, sometimes playing the part of naïve victim, or, at the other extreme, the part of morally outraged patriot.

It is, however, when one looks more closely, particularly at Pope's use of imagery, that the full force of his sense of social corruption becomes clear. He says of Sporus,

> Yet let me flap this bug with gilded wings,
> This painted child of dirt, that stinks and stings.

We do not need to know that Sporus was Lord Hervey: the picture works because of the viciousness of the imagery, which associates him with insect life, dirt, and effeminacy (in that he wears make-up). It is a disturbing impression of social corruption: Sporus is more like an insect than a man. The method is comic but there is no mistaking the seriousness of the picture presented. (*See also* Heroic couplet, p. 35; *and* Satire, p. 158.)

Women's poetry. Only gradually is it becoming clear just how much, and what a variety of, poetry there is by women writing in the seventeenth and eighteenth centuries. In addition, nineteenth-century poets such as Elizabeth Barrett Browning, Emily Dickinson, Emily Brontë and Christina Rossetti have in recent years begun to receive serious critical attention (and been republished in greatly improved editions), while twentieth-century poets such as Sylvia Plath, Adrienne Rich, Stevie Smith and Margaret Atwood are now seen as major figures who alter our sense of the whole map of English poetry. This also applies to poets such as Fleur Adcock and Carol Ann Duffy who write on specifically feminist issues.

When they start to consider women's poetry, students are often unsure what moves to make: should they try to locate the poems in the historical and social contexts in which women were writing, usually a context which excluded them from education and politics? Or should they try to identify feminist issues in the poems, such as the idea of woman's experience or the relationship of women to language? There are, too, other topics you might want to consider: how women's poetry challenges stereotypes, how it uses conventions and conventional forms, how it can often be humorous as well as moving, how poetry can be used to create a space where women can seek to define their own identities.

As ever, the best place to start is with the text itself. Begin by getting a broad sense of the way in which the writer is handling her theme; use an order/disorder contrast to help you establish a firm sense of the poem. For example, here is the opening stanza of a poem by an anonymous eighteenth-century poet who calls herself simply 'A Lady'. The poem is called 'Woman's Hard Fate':

> How wretched is a woman's fate.
> No happy change her fortune knows;
> Subject to man in every state,
> How can she then be free from woes?

You should be able to see how the poem is a protest at the way women are constrained by men: it is a protest at the way in which a woman's life is ordered by man, and made wretched by male order or patriarchy. Notice how conventional the verse form is, as if that, too, is part of the restraint on women, that there is no freedom even in poetry with its binding rhymes. And the fact that the woman dare not name herself adds to our impression of a stifling order that treats women as slaves. Yet the very act of writing the poem, you might conclude, suggests a defiant stance or questioning of the social structure. A similar point emerges in the following short poem by Emily Dickinson:

> I never hear the word 'escape'
> Without a quicker blood,
> A sudden expectation,
> A flying attitude.
>
> I never hear of prisons broad
> By soldiers battered down
> But I tug childish at my bars
> Only to fail again.

Once again, we are aware of a sense of how order imprisons the speaker: she is immediately heartened by the word 'escape' and longs to break down the 'bars' that hold her. The poem, we can see, turns on the contrast between her 'childish' efforts to break free and the masculine world of the soldier who can batter down prisons. There is, however, a self-knowledge in the poem which makes us re-examine the image of the prison bars, as if they are not just physical constraints but the whole fabric of life which keeps women closed in.

This idea of the limits set on women's lives is one that runs through a great deal of women's poetry. Sometimes it is expressed through anger, sometimes through irony, as in Adrienne Rich's poem 'Aunt Jennifer's Tigers'. The tigers in question are on a woven screen that Aunt Jennifer makes by hand: they seem to represent the very freedom and naturalness denied her by marriage and by the domestic life she leads and which, eventually, kills her:

> When Aunt is dead, her terrified hands will lie
> Still ringed with ordeals she was mastered by.
> The tigers in the panel that she made
> Will go on prancing, proud and unafraid.

The 'ring' referred to is the marriage ring. Whereas in a great deal of literature marriage is viewed as the central embodiment of order and harmony, here the idea is reversed. The order marriage brings is one of submission that robs Aunt Jennifer of pride and movement. It is as if she has become a circus animal, trained and terrified into submission. Rich's poem clearly challenges traditional ideas and values. It speaks for women, making their case against the way men order the world and impose mastery on women. What should also be apparent, however, is the power with which Rich writes: the energy of the imagery of the tigers suggests just what values are being destroyed by the fear that accompanies patriarchy. The values of intelligence, imagination and independence are, though, evident in all the poems above, and suggest why women's poetry is now firmly on the agenda.

3

Drama

MOST plays are not only entertaining to watch but also enjoyable to read. Studying plays, however, is more demanding, for the student is obliged to work out a critical response, and this can prove difficult. The easiest way of overcoming the problem would seem to be to concentrate on the personalities of the main characters, saying that the play is about them. In Shakespeare's *Hamlet*, for example, we have a central character whose father has been murdered and who is uncertain what to do or how to react. The easiest way of tackling the play is to discuss Hamlet himself, almost as if he were a real person.

Character study, however, is not a completely satisfactory way of looking at drama, because it puts a false emphasis on one strand in a play at the expense of the text's larger significance. In thematic terms a dramatist is always dealing with a much larger question than that of character: he or she is focusing on concerns that are central in human experience. Our problem, of course, is how to grasp this wider meaning of the play. It is not something stated directly by the dramatist; it is only implicit in the action and the characterisation. In a sense we have to look through the characters as individuals and see that they are just a means for dramatising the themes of the play. This is, however, hard to do if we cannot see what those themes might be.

A further complication is that our discussion of dramatic themes should always go hand in hand with a discussion of dramatic form. If we are to do justice to plays it does seem essential to take into account their unique nature as a sequence of actions, structured in a certain way, and acted on a stage. In thinking about a play, then, we should be aware of its form as well as its content. The rest of this introduction attempts to provide some ideas about how to approach a play along these lines.

The basic point about all plays, both in formal and thematic terms, is that the characters are always caught up in some sort of crisis, dilemma, or confusion; they are always faced by some sort of problem. In Greek drama and medieval drama (that is, the miracle and morality plays), the question or problem the characters face always involves people's relationship with the gods or God. In the late sixteenth century, however, the emphasis shifts from religion to society and plays begin to focus on questions of social and political morality. This is true of Shakespeare and his contemporaries, and applies equally to all later drama right through from Restoration comedies to the most modern plays.

Our starting-point for discussing a play has to be an awareness of the particular problem or issue it is concerned with, and here it helps if we realise just how much plays have in common both in terms of theme and structure. All plays employ the same basic structure of exposition, complication and resolution. The first part of the play, its exposition stage, prepares the ground: some alteration in the established pattern of life occurs which means that the existing social order of the play is going to be thrown into confusion. In the central, and usually longest, stage of the play, we encounter the complication that ensues from this change. A sense of disorder prevails as the characters move around bereft of the secure roles that they previously enjoyed: in tragedy, a king might have given up his throne; in comedy, characters who previously disdained love might find themselves absurdly in love.

It is at this point that we start to see how similar most plays are, and also how they differ from novels or poems. In a poem we usually encounter personal feelings, the personal feelings of the poet as he or she faces up to life's problems. The novel, on the other hand, tends to explore the intricate relationship between individuals and their society. Plays, however, are public things acted on a public stage, and focus on public questions of the social and political organisation of society. The central section of a play, in which confusion reigns, begins to raise questions about the whole social order within which people live. As problems develop, as the characters begin to find themselves in unfamiliar and uncomfortable predicaments, we are forced to consider how precarious the social order is that has been established in the world, and how close we always are to disorder.

A play, then, is less concerned with the individual characters involved in it than with questions about the whole basis and nature of social organisation and social order. This is one reason why we have political plays but very few political poems or novels, for drama insists upon this public debate about society. Indeed, a play itself is a kind of public debate that often undermines our secure social convictions. We go to the theatre as members of the public; it is a social occasion where we see a well-structured play in acts and scenes; but within the play confusion develops and chaos takes over. There is thus always a tension in the whole form of a play between, on the one hand, social order, and, on the other, the idea of disorder.

In brief, we can say that any play is about the order that has been created in society and the awareness that social order is fragile – that all sorts of disruptive forces can intrude at any moment. Of course, we are not usually aware of such portentous matters when watching a play, so that, for example, an Oscar Wilde comedy might simply seem to be a piece of light entertainment, but the organising drive of the action is this threat to the established social order. If we start with this rather large, abstract idea, that plays are concerned with the order of society and the disorder that threatens it, we shall be able more readily to identify the particular aspect of this problem that a playwright is dealing with in a particular play. We might have noticed, for example, that Macbeth is evil, or that Antony is besotted by love for Cleopatra. These particular themes, love and evil, acquire a context if we can see that such passions or instincts are socially destructive. Drama becomes much easier to think about if, instead of saying that this play has this theme and that play that theme, we can see how all themes link together under a more general heading, and a general heading that acknowledges the distinctive public nature of drama.

This heading, this large context, however, does only provide us with our overall hold on a play, a general view of what it is about. What we are really interested in as critics is how the dramatist brings problems to life on the stage. One fruitful approach is to hold this social-order and chaotic-disorder structure in your mind, and then to look at two or three scenes from a play, scenes that you found interesting or memorable, and see how the details bring that structure to life. More often than not, in any scene, a conflict or tension will be in evidence between social normality or social order and passions or behaviour that threaten the social concord.

One implication of what we have been saying here is that plays do not have a message – they do not attempt to solve society's problems. In the resolution stage at the end of the play social order is, indeed, usually re-established, but the neatness of this ending is often satisfying simply because it is neat and ties up the problems. What we are likely to remember from the play, however, are the scenes of crisis and confrontation, the scenes that provoked questions about the fragile order we maintain in society.

The pattern of drama we have been describing is very clearly in evidence in the two dominant modes of drama: comedy and tragedy. In comedy, the disorder that threatens the characters' lives and social concord is overcome and most comedies end either with marriage or a dance, the traditional signs of harmony and order in society. In tragedy, on the other hand, what we witness is the falling apart of all signs of order as we are confronted by the most shocking form of disorder, death itself. Our response is perhaps as likely to be one of terror as pity at the wanton disregard for human life tragedy shows us. And yet the very fact that people can confront such chaos is itself positive. This is why tragedy, especially Shakespearean tragedy, is so impressive: it faces up to the worst, the most extreme forms of disorder – madness, murder, states collapsing, all family bonds torn apart – and yet in itself it is never disorderly but always patterned.

Both tragedy and comedy are discussed further in the entries that follow, as are the other major modes of drama. We also look at the major periods and such topics as character, acts and scenes and dramatic structure. Shakespeare has a separate entry because he dominates so much, but what should be apparent is that, although Shakespeare is the best-known dramatist, very similar patterns, areas of concern and methods of presentation are evident in all drama.

Act and scene. A play is traditionally divided into acts and scenes. Most plays have five acts, but nineteenth- and twentieth-century dramatists favour three acts.

One of the most productive ways of discussing a play is to focus on individual scenes, for any scene will tell us a lot about the play as a whole. What we need to remember is that all plays deal with disruption of, or threats to, an established order. Individual scenes will reveal the specific problems the dramatist is dealing with and also reveal how he or she makes his or her themes come to life.

For example, in Marlowe's *Edward II* (1592), a tragedy about a homosexual king who is deposed and sadistically murdered, the first scene shows the King quarrelling with the court about his love for Gaveston. A king should govern and behave responsibly and be trusted by his people, but here the King and nobility are at odds. This impression of political disorder becomes even stronger when Gaveston attacks the Bishop, the representative of religious values. Marlowe has thus quickly set up an idea of social order and the disruption of that order. He is not particularly interested in Edward's personality, but uses his character as a way of making concrete broader questions of social and political morality.

Once we have established this general view of a scene, we can then turn to some of its details, which should enable us to define more precisely the way in which the dramatist presents the issues. We might, in this scene, notice the clash of imagery between the sensuous language associated with Gaveston and the bloody imagery of battle. Such imagery reinforces the idea of how Edward's passionate, selfish desires are undermining the social order and points to the violence that is likely to occur when socially responsible behaviour is abandoned. If we looked at two or three scenes we could see how Marlowe extends and develops these themes.

Many modern plays, however, such as Pinter's *The Caretaker* (1960), are not divided into scenes. In such cases we can create our own scenes for critical discussion, selecting those moments we found dramatically interesting. Act II of Pinter's play, for example, closes with a long speech by Aston about brain operations and headaches but ends with his wish to build a shed in the garden. As he speaks, the lights dim, isolating him and adding to the sense of a dark, fragmented world Pinter creates throughout the play. Whereas Marlowe's play deals with public threats to the social order, what we see in Pinter is a clash between Aston's dream of normality and the mental disorder that prevents him from ever achieving a secure role in society.

Our focus in looking at a scene is, thus, twofold: we are getting hold of the play as a whole, identifying the thematic issues the play is concerned with, but we are also looking at the complex texture of the scene, trying to see how the dramatist makes these themes come to life.

Character. The people in a play are referred to as characters. We assess them on the basis of what they say and do, and what the other characters say about them. This is important: we must avoid loose conjecture and base everything we say on the evidence of the text. We only really understand the characters, however, when we relate them to the broader themes of the play.

The main character is called the **hero** or **protagonist**. The term 'hero' does not mean someone who is brave or noble: heroes may be good or evil, low or high born. Often opposing the hero is the **villain** or **antagonist**, although sometimes, as in Shakespeare's *Macbeth*, the hero himself can be a villain. What villains have in common is that their evil deeds disrupt the social order.

This kind of pattern is in evidence in Webster's *The Duchess of Malfi* (1614). Here we have a **heroine**, the Duchess, who remarries secretly; and villains, her brothers, who murder her as a punishment. Her speeches, such as this speech where she is proposing to her servant Antonio, reveal her temperament:

> The misery of us that are born great –
> We are forc'd to woo, because none dare woo us:
> And as a tyrant doubles with his words,
> And fearfully equivocates, so we
> Are forc'd to express our violent passions
> In riddles, and in dreams, and leave the path
> Of simple virtue, which was never made
> To seem the thing it is not. Go, go brag
> You have left me heartless – mine is in your bosom,
> I hope 'twill multiply love there.

The Duchess is saying she is forced to woo Antonio because of her social position. The last three lines in particular create an impression of her passionate nature and love. Yet her speech also provides pointers to the broader themes and action of the play. The opening lines, with their imagery of fear, tyranny, force and dreams, suggest a maze-like world where honesty and virtue are impossible ideals, and also anticipate the violent revenge of the Duchess's tyrannical brothers. Our focus in looking at a character's speech is thus twofold: we want to see how it relates to the larger action of the play, in this instance good versus evil or social order versus social disorder, but our main concern is with the details of the speech, for it is the details which really bring both the character and themes to life and make them seem substantial.

In some plays, however, particularly comedies, the characters are not presented in such a credible way. This is because comedy presents people as familiar types acting out familiar roles. In fact, in comedy the characters are very clearly just a means for the dramatist to express his or her real theme, which is the folly of people in the social world. In tragedy the dramatic function of the characters is less immediately obvious because they do appear more as individuals, but the thing we need to tell ourselves is that we can never separate the characters from the themes in any play.

Comedy. There are several types of dramatic comedy – romantic comedy, satiric comedy and comedy of manners are the main traditional ones – but we cannot really appreciate the differences between them unless we have some idea of how much all comedies have in common. Comedy consists of laughing at people caught in difficult situations which we know will usually be resolved; traditional comedy ends with marriage or a dance, the disorder that threatened the social concord having been overcome. At the heart of comedy, however, lies something more disturbing, for it is a way of looking at the world that regards the whole of social life as an elaborate charade which is constantly disrupted by people's folly. Comedy often shows us how people's irrational impulses, such as love or greed, or their absurd self-importance, undermine any claims of society to be a rational, civilised order. The aim of the comic dramatist is not to correct behaviour, for he or she is too aware of our irredeemable folly.

This could be a gloomy vision, but it emerges as funny because of the detached stance of the comic writer. People are seen as types acting out familiar roles. The action is meant to strike us not as real but as illustrative of human weakness, with everything being exaggerated. It is an alternative perspective to that of tragedy, informed not by a sense of how complex the problems are that face people, but by a sense of how ridiculously serious people are about themselves.

This is most evident in **romantic comedy**, such as Shakespeare's *A Midsummer Night's Dream* (1595). Romantic comedy usually deals with how seriously young people take love and how foolishly love makes them behave (*see* Shakespeare p. 94). It is a gentle form of comedy, but as in Shakespeare's *The Merchant of Venice* (1596) it can be disturbing. This darker version of romantic comedy, in which disaster and death threaten the characters, can be called **tragicomedy**. Tragicomedy complicates the basic pattern of comedy by making us aware of how unsympathetic society can prove when confronted by the excesses of love. The effect is more realistic than in pure romantic comedy, with the stress falling on society's rules and laws, how society legislates against folly.

Romantic comedy is most often associated with Shakespeare. His contemporary Ben Jonson, on the other hand, is most often associated with **satiric comedy**. Satiric comedy might appear to be more constructive than other forms of comedy in that it claims to laugh people out of folly through caricature. Characters are presented as either grotesquely ludicrous, as in *Volpone* (1606), where they are bestial versions of human beings, or as eccentric and unbalanced, as in *Every Man in his Humour* (1598). In his plays Jonson thus depicts a crazy world where moral values are overturned by roguery, self-deception and obsessive greed (*see also* p. 88). The intention may be moral, but we are usually left with the impression that people are too corrupt and foolish ever to reform.

There is an equally jaundiced view of human beings in Restoration comedy (*see* p. 93), which can be included under the more general heading of **comedy of manners**. The comedy of manners (later exponents are Sheridan and Goldsmith) is set in polite society, the comedy arising from the gap between the characters' attempts to preserve the standards of polite behaviour and their actual behaviour. As is so often the case in comedy, we see the absurdity of people, but here the focus is very directly on their morals and manners in society.

The tradition of the comedy of manners continues, for example in the works of Oscar Wilde, but a significant change does seem to take place in stage comedy in the late nineteenth century. Comedy always suggests the fragility of the social order, but earlier dramatists know that they are exaggerating; they are really fairly confident that society is in reasonably good health. In the late nineteenth century, however, this confidence disappears. Often the focus is on characters trying to maintain a certain role as their secure world crumbles. This is evident in a witty way in Wilde's *The Importance of Being Earnest* (1895), which is concerned with correct conduct in society, but polite society has really disintegrated and traditional values now seem redundant and foolish.

Shaw's plays often display a similar awareness that the traditional social order, with its traditional values, has collapsed, but it is Chekhov who focuses most directly on a disintegrating society.

His plays, such as *The Cherry Orchard* (1903), feature Russian families on their country estates which they no longer have the money to maintain. Chekhov is the originator of a more naturalistic form of comedy; the stress is not so much on human absurdity as on the absurdity of a world that shows so little concern for human beings. There is often an element of pathos, as in Synge's plays, for example *The Playboy of the Western World* (1907) which deals with the self-deceptions of characters in a bleak and barren part of Ireland.

This form of comedy, in which the characters are plausible rather than outrageous, continues into the twentieth century. As in Pinter's *The Caretaker* (1960), we laugh sympathetically at characters lost in a world they cannot understand or come to terms with. Many modern comic dramatists, however, are not concerned to present credible characters. Recognising that social order is an illusion, and believing that the world is absurd, they can, as in **theatre of the absurd** and **black comedy**, present bizarre characters in bizarre situations. In the works of Samuel Beckett, for example, comic laughter is replaced by a grimmer form of comedy involving violence, sick jokes and farce. **Farce** traditionally indicates a rather mechanical and meaningless form of comic play, consisting simply of an intricate plot, knockabout fun and comic confusion, but in much modern comedy the farce is that life itself is so devoid of any deeper meaning. People are seen as absurd pawns in a meaningless universe.

Dramatic structure. All plays have the same basic structure of exposition, complication and resolution. The exposition stage prepares the ground by showing us some sort of change taking place in the characters' lives or the social order. In the central stage of the play the dramatist develops the complication that arises from this change as the characters seek to come to terms with the problems that have developed so that a sense of disorder prevails. In the resolution, however, as the play reaches its *dénouement* or ending, order is re-established, or the characters at least come to terms with the new situation that has developed.

This, then, is the basic pattern of all plays. What makes a particular play interesting, though, is what the dramatist includes within this conventional pattern. It is his or her distinctive use of plot, characters and language that establishes a sense of life's complexity within the neat overall format. A good illustration is Ibsen's tragedy *Ghosts* (1881). The plot concerns Osvald's discovery that he has inherited his father's syphilis and is going mad. For Osvald, any notion of an ordered world has collapsed: it is partly this plot that provides us with an impression of life's problems, but also the responses of the characters as revealed in their actions and speeches. *Ghosts*, however, does not end with Osvald's death, as we might expect in a tragedy. Instead Ibsen leaves the play open with the audience uncertain whether Mrs Alving will kill her son. This ending is closer to the messiness of life than the neatness of art.

In talking about the complex themes that Ibsen develops within the received structure of plays we are moving beyond the play's skeletal framework and considering its **dramatic form**. Dramatic form means how the material is presented within the basic structure. We can use our awareness of how all plays are structured in order to find our way in to talking about the form of a play. If we know that plays usually start with a settled way of life being overthrown, and that the major part of the play will be devoted to the problems that develop, then this provides a starting-point from which to examine the distinctive way this is fleshed out in the particular play we are considering.

For example, Stoppard's *Rosencrantz and Guildenstern are Dead* (1967) opens with two characters playing a game of heads and tails. The scene might baffle us unless we knew that plays start with the collapse of a certain order: the game becomes symbolic of a world where chance dominates and where things cannot be predicted. We have used our awareness of the basic structure of plays to approach the scene, but by starting really to discuss it we are beginning to consider the distinctive form that Stoppard's play takes. Our sense of what plays have in common makes it easier for us to spot what is unique about a particular play.

Elizabethan and Jacobean drama. The dramatists referred to here are Kyd, Marlowe, Jonson, Webster and Middleton. Shakespeare is discussed in a separate entry (*see* p. 94). Many other dramatists could be included, for the period from 1558 to 1625 saw an extraordinary development of English drama. To understand why, we have to realise that this was a time of extraordinary social change: a medieval society, where people still believed in a Christian ordered universe, was yielding to a modern, secular society in which the court rather than the church became the centre of power and in which money and politics played an increasing part. Such a change obviously did not happen overnight, so in the drama of the period we find conflicting views of humanity: the medieval view of people as fallen creatures who will be saved or damned by God and who must therefore look to their eternal souls, and the more modern view of them as individuals caught between the rival demands of their consciences and their desires. It is this conflict of ideas and values that makes the plays of the period so rich.

We can see this in Kyd's *The Spanish Tragedy* (1587), a **revenge tragedy** about a man who avenges his son's murder. The hero Hieronimo longs for revenge, but also knows that he should await heaven's justice. Divided between conscience and passion he goes mad: in the last act he stages a play in which he runs amok, killing innocent and guilty alike. Kyd established a pattern for revenge tragedies, and many of the devices he uses – such as a ghost, a play within a play, scenes of violent murder, a mad hero, and the concluding blood bath – are found in later revenge tragedies, such as Shakespeare's *Hamlet* (1600). Revenge tragedies are concerned with a specific aspect of disorder in society, that is the problem of justice. Justice, like God, should be perfect, but earthly justice is corrupt and imperfect. Moreover, to take justice into one's own hands is to risk damnation. Drama in this period returns repeatedly to the question of how to act in the face of such contradictions.

The risk of damnation is made clear in Kyd's play by the use of a ghost from hell called Revenge who acts as a chorus to the play. This provides a formal framework which contrasts with the violent actions of the characters. There is something similar in *Dr Faustus* (1592), where Marlowe uses the framework of the medieval morality play, in which the hero is accompanied by a good and bad angel to guide or tempt him. Faustus sells his soul to the Devil and so rebels against God's order. Again, then, we return to the conflict between an ordered, traditional view of life and an awareness that men and women will not conform to such traditional values. In all of Marlowe's plays there is this same gap between an ideal order and the disorderly passions that beset people in society. In both *Tamburlaine* (1587) and *Edward II* (1592) the idea of order is embodied in the symbol of the crown, but what we see in both plays are the ways in which military power and political ambition create disorder in society.

In *The Jew of Malta* (1589), however, Marlowe satirises how society disguises its lust for money in religious terms. Ben Jonson, the great comic satirist of this period, develops this theme of money, lust and religious hypocrisy as disruptive forces in society.

The vision he offers in *Volpone* (1606) and *The Alchemist* (1610) is of a self-deceived society which worships the false god of gold at the expense of its true religious values. Potentially this is a disturbing view, but Jonson's plays are primarily comic: he is amused at the world's folly. His characters are often grotesque as Jonson exaggerates how bizarre people make themselves appear in their pursuit of false values (*see also* p. 85).

The comic grotesque is also found in Webster's tragedies *The White Devil* (1612) and *The Duchess of Malfi* (1614), but the depravity we witness in the plays – Webster is renowned for his macabre scenes of torture – is horrid rather than funny. The depravity is all the more disturbing in that it is found in the court, which should be the fountainhead of justice and order. In *Dr Faustus* a man seeks evil, but in Webster's plays evil is inherent in society. This sense of society as corrupt and disorderly is present again in Middleton's *Women Beware Women* (1612) and *The Changeling* (1622). Like Webster, Middleton writes tragedies that are concerned with sexual passion and damnation, but in Middleton the focus is very much on the position of women in a corrupt society where love is merely a commodity to be bought and sold.

The effect of both Webster's and Middleton's plays is to raise questions of both a moral and political nature. Yet, as with all plays from this period, the idea of damnation and salvation is still taken seriously, and so the plays are dealing simultaneously with a number of large, complicated issues. The best way to grasp the range of questions dealt with in a particular play is to concentrate on a few scenes, seeing how the dramatist creates an impression of characters caught up in a complicated world where all values – social, political and religious – are in doubt. In every case we are likely to be struck by the disordered nature of the world presented.

Medieval drama. The two basic types of medieval drama are the miracle plays and morality plays of the fourteenth and fifteenth centuries.

The **miracle plays** deal with the Christian history of the world from the Creation to the Last Judgement. Each play focuses on one major event from the Bible, such as the fall of Adam and Eve or the birth of Christ, and forms part of a series or cycle of plays named after the town where they were performed: York, Chester, and Wakefield or Towneley are the most important. Such plays can be seen as didactic drama intended to explain the mysteries of Christianity, yet there is always a gap in the plays between the ideal of God's divine order and the violent, often grotesquely comic actions of the characters. For example, what we remember most from the York play of *The Crucifixion* is the contrast between Christ's silent suffering and obedience to God and the noisy, bungling workmanship of the soldiers as they try to nail him to the cross.

This gap between religious ideals and worldly disorder is also present in the **morality plays**. Unlike the miracle plays, the morality plays focus on the moral dilemmas that confront man (and it is always a male character at the centre of the morality plays) as he journeys from birth to death. They are allegorical plays (for allegory, *see* p. 133), in which both plot and character are used to illustrate an abstract moral lesson. In *Everyman*, for example, the most famous of the morality plays, God instructs Death to tell the hero he must die. Everyman looks for someone to accompany him, but only Good Deeds will do so. The moral of the play is that everyone should be prepared for death and look to their good deeds, but what strikes us most is the sheer confusion and panic of Everyman, and how difficult religious ideals are to live up to.

The same is true in *The Castle of Perseverance*, where the hero Mankind is torn between his desire for salvation and his desire for wealth and pleasure. As in Marlowe's *Dr Faustus* (*see* p. 88), Mankind is accompanied by a good and bad angel to guide or mislead him, and indeed the whole of Elizabethan and Jacobean drama owes a lot to the morality-play tradition, especially in the figure of the Vice or the comic tempter who underlies the presentation of such characters as Iago in Shakespeare's *Othello*. As in the morality plays, both Shakespeare and his contemporaries deal with events on a cosmic scale as good and evil, heaven and hell battle for people's souls. The difference, however, is that in the morality plays this battle takes place in a world where God's order is still visible: in the more secular world of Elizabethan and Jacobean drama that order, like the order of society itself, is altogether more precarious and uncertain.

Nineteenth-century drama. With the exception of developments at the end of the century, nineteenth-century drama is not very impressive. The most popular form of play was **melodrama:** a sensational, romantic play full of impossible events where the good are always rewarded and the wicked always punished. The central interest is the plot, which usually hinges upon some sort of secret which is not revealed until the last act.

In the hands of the French dramatist Eugène Scribe this sort of neat, mechanical play became known as the **well-made play**, a concept which is crucial to an understanding of subsequent developments in drama, especially the plays of Ibsen and Shaw. These two dramatists, along with Wilde and Chekhov, revitalised the theatre towards the end of the century. Both Ibsen and Shaw use the formula of the well-made play with its melodramatic plot, but react against its trite moralising by shifting the emphasis onto contemporary social or moral questions. In *A Doll's House* (1879), for example, Ibsen deals with the position of married women in society; in *Mrs Warren's Profession* (1894) Shaw examines the economic relationship between prostitution and society. In both cases the neat structure of the well-made play is disrupted by a sense of life's complexity.

Both these plays are **problem plays**. All drama deals with some sort of problem, but the term 'problem play' (sometimes 'thesis play') refers to those plays concerned with a specific social problem. Such issues could be treated melodramatically, but these plays are naturalistic. **Naturalism** is a narrow form of realism that appeared at the end of the nineteenth century: it offers an almost photographic representation of life and stresses how heredity and environment shape people's lives. Such an approach continues into the twentieth century, for example in John Osborne's *Look Back in Anger* (1956), where we see characters trapped by society, unable to change or influence the world around them.

The problem play is the most important type of play that grew out of the well-made play and led on to a whole tradition of plays treating ideas comically, as in Shaw's *Arms and the Man* (1894), or tragically, as in Ibsen's *The Wild Duck* (1884). The effect in both these cases is a contrast between the neat structure of the play and the sense of life's complexity that the work reveals through its language. A close look at the texture of Ibsen's and Shaw's writing helps us appreciate why they are such great dramatists. They start with the ordered format of the well-made play, but subvert it in every possible way, raising so many ideas and aspects of the issue they are dealing with. Their early works concentrate on a particular social problem, but as they develop as dramatists they discover more subtle and more varied ways of presenting a picture of life's complexity.

Plot. If we tell the story of a play we are constructing a simple account of what happens. 'Plot', however, is a more inclusive term: it could be said to be the fully-developed version of the story. It takes account of the nature of the characters, the way in which events are related to each other and their dramatic effect. In talking about the plot we are trying to talk about the overall significance of the play. There is always the danger, though, that an account of the plot of a play can appear very thin; indeed, many students find that they are soon doing little more than retelling the story. The best way of guarding against this is – as suggested in Act and scene, p. 81 – to select just a few scenes for discussion. If we pick a scene from the beginning of a play, two from the middle, and a scene from the end we can report in detail on the significance of the play, and the plot as a whole should make sense in the light of this local analysis of how the play works.

Many plays, however, have not just one plot but two – that is, two fully developed stories running side by side. The **main plot** focuses on the central character, the **subplot** on another set of characters or events. This might seem to complicate matters, but in fact the subplot usually illuminates the main plot. This is particularly the case when the subplot has close parallels with the main plot. For example, in Shakespeare's *Henry IV* plays (1596–8) there are comic scenes involving a character called Falstaff which parody the court scenes, increasing our sense of political disorder in the plays. Because these scenes are comic, however, they also suggest how ridiculous our attempts to order society are. Comic subplots are common in tragedy: they suggest an alternative way of looking at the predicament, one that stresses the absurdity rather than the terror and pity of experience.

Not all plays, however, have plots in the way that we conventionally use the word. In Brecht's *Mother Courage* (1941) there is simply a sequence of unrelated events. Brecht is refusing to meet the audience's expectation that they will be offered a coherent story. The audience are alienated: they cannot involve themselves in the story of the play and are therefore forced to think more about the abstract political questions raised in the work. This idea of alienation is central in Brecht's epic theatre (*see* p. 102). In absurd drama, such as Beckett's *Waiting for Godot* (1955), there is often no plot, in so far as nothing at all seems to happen. Here the implication is that the characters are stuck in an endless world where there is no cause and effect and where everything is unpredictable. The absence of a plot is an effective way of indicating to us that we live in a world that is incoherent, where there is no significant meaning or pattern.

Restoration comedy. A type of witty, bawdy comedy written after the restoration of Charles II in 1660. Restoration comedy, which comes under the broader heading of **comedy of manners**, deals with the sexual relations and intrigues of men and women belonging to polite society. The theme is often marriage, with the dramatist leaning in one of two directions. As in Wycherley's *The Country Wife* (1675), the play can lean towards satiric comedy, emphasising the grotesque sexual desires of the characters and the corruption of society, or, as in Congreve's *The Way of the World* (1700), the play can lean towards romantic comedy with an emphasis on the plight of love in a world ruled by laws.

Underlying the plays is the basic pattern of all comedy, in which the fragile social order breaks down as characters are caught up in ridiculous situations. Our main impression is of people's folly or lust or their absurd self-importance, with both character and situation being exaggerated to illustrate this. In Restoration comedy, however, we are also aware of the potential absurdity of society itself with its elaborate rules and codes of behaviour. The complicated plots used by Wycherley and Congreve create not only a sense of confusion but also a sense of a highly suspect, artificial world. Indeed, much of the comedy of the plays arises from the gap between the characters' desires and their desperate attempts to preserve that artificial world of appearances. The odd thing about Restoration comedy, then, is the way in which it simultaneously regards society as orderly and chaotic, as civilised and yet corrupt.

At the start of the eighteenth century there was a reaction against the overt sexual concerns of the Restoration stage, resulting in the appearance of **sentimental comedy**. This is a simplistic form of comedy extolling the virtues of family life, with a stress on how goodness is rewarded. There is nothing particularly funny about such comedy except when it is mocked, as in parts of Sheridan's *The Rivals* (1775). As in Goldsmith's *She Stoops to Conquer* (1773), comedy in Sheridan is largely a matter of intrigue with an emphasis on how foolishly people behave. The plays of Goldsmith and Sheridan are comedies of manners, in the tradition of Restoration comedy, but the abrasive edge and rather disturbing stress on sexual corruption has gone, and we are offered affectionate, but very entertaining and stylish, plays about social folly.

Shakespeare. Shakespeare's plays have a great deal in common with other writers' plays. They follow the standard structure of exposition, complication and resolution, and, as is true of all plays written since the Middle Ages, deal with threats to, or disruption of, an established social order. What sets Shakespeare apart is not, then, that his plays are fundamentally different in kind from other plays. What makes him the greatest dramatist is, quite simply, the fact that he writes so much better than anyone else.

This is evident in his **comedies**. The kind of comedy Shakespeare writes is called romantic comedy: life is proceeding as usual but then various characters fall hopelessly in love, the central section of the play focusing on the comic mishaps of love. Romantic comedy might seem to offer little more than comic confusion for its own sake, but in a light-hearted way it shows us how people's capacity for irrational behaviour and folly can disrupt the settled order of society. The problems, however, are soon resolved: the plays end with the social harmony of marriage and a dance. This kind of pattern is found in plays such as *A Midsummer Night's Dream* (1596; all the dates for Shakespeare's plays are approximate) and *Twelfth Night* (1601), yet it is a pattern that other dramatists can also employ. So why are Shakespeare's romantic comedies so easily the best? His sheer skill in controlling the comic action has to be admired, but Shakespeare does not offer us a noticeably more ingenious or complex plot than other writers. Many would argue that it is the characters who make these plays so striking, and his characterisation is certainly impressive. The characters, however, only come to life because of the words they speak, and it is, therefore, Shakespeare's use of language that has to be recognised as of central importance.

What we mean by this is the way in which Shakespeare uses words, especially imagery, to make the themes of the plays come to life, bringing out the full implications of the plots. Watching a Shakespeare comedy we feel we are witnessing something more substantial than just a mechanical comedy about people falling in love. The plays are not particularly profound, but they do acknowledge that anarchic element in people that can disrupt the social order. Such ideas are always implicit in romantic comedy, but Shakespeare's language brings out and explores these implications. For example, in *Twelfth Night* a kill-joy character called Malvolio castigates the other characters thus:

> My masters, are you mad? Or what are you? Have you no wit, manners, nor honesty, but to gabble like tinkers at this time of night? Do ye make an ale-house of my lady's house?

The imagery of madness, drinking, noise and the whole idea of overturning social order touches upon the broader issue of the play of rational and irrational behaviour in society. What is happening here is evident everywhere in the work: every speech relates to the broader issues and implications of the plot. The speeches are not merely advancing the action but constantly acknowledging the bigger issues of the whole nature of human beings and the organisation of society that are implicit in the action.

This might prove easier to appreciate in Shakespeare's more serious comedies. *The Merchant of Venice* (1596) and *Measure for Measure* (1604) can be called **tragicomedies**. The basic pattern resembles that of romantic comedy, with young people falling in love, but, whereas the pure romantic comedies take place in a make-believe world, these darker or problem comedies take place in a more realistic world where the young lovers come in conflict with those in authority. The plays examine how a society attempts to control its subjects. There is always the threat of the lovers being punished, even put to death, for their reckless behaviour. Again the power of the plays lies in Shakespeare's ability to explore the full implications of the story; the particular focus is on the themes of justice and mercy, something which is made clear in the speeches, such as a famous speech from Portia in *The Merchant of Venice* which begins 'The quality of mercy is not strain'd'; it raises the question of to what extent the enforcement of society's laws should be tempered with mercy.

In all Shakespeare's plays there are set-piece speeches such as this in which the characters comment on the broader implications of the situations in which they find themselves. The best-known examples are Hamlet's soliloquies (*see* p. 152). The purpose of such speeches is to reflect on the wider significance of the action; they raise all the difficult questions about people and their role in society and the world. It is, however, not just the set speeches that confront the broader issues: every speech, every line of dialogue, touches on the deeper issues in some way.

This is both the impressive and difficult quality of Shakespeare's plays. He creates a very full sense of just how complicated life is, exploring the whole nature of the disordered world we live in, raising more issues and asking more questions than any other writer. Because the plays are so complex our critical response can never fully cope with them. We can, however, approach the plays in a systematic way. First, we can identify how there is a clash between a settled pattern of life and a new turn of events. Then we can look at how specific scenes bring this conflict to life, seeing how the speeches do not merely serve to advance the action but also reveal the implications of the incident presented. It is in particular the imagery in the speeches that forces us to look beyond the specific incident, as in the speech from Malvolio quoted above: the images of madness, drinking and noise broaden the issue, so that it is not just a comment on the folly of the characters he is confronting but a consideration of the whole nature of anti-social behaviour.

Shakespeare's ability to raise all kinds of fundamental questions about life is seen at its best in his **histories** and **tragedies**. The most common story in these plays is of a character, such as a king, who is no longer fulfilling his traditional role but finds himself in a dilemma, either because his own temperament is proving to be at odds with what is traditionally expected of him, or because unruly forces around him, at court or in the country, are threatening and undermining his authority. (The contemporary relevance of such ideas is discussed in Elizabethan and Jacobean drama, p. 87.) The history plays deal with questions about people and political and social order; the tragedies ask even more basic questions about the whole purpose of existence, asking what people are and whether there is any meaning in life.

Such deep implications might not strike us immediately. When we are reading one of Shakespeare's **history plays** we might feel that it is just a dramatised account of the life of a particular king. What the plays are really concerned with, however, is the gap between an ideal notion of kingship and the less tidy reality of kingship. The ideal notion is of a responsible king appointed by God governing justly a secure and ordered society, but there are always problems that prevent this ideal of order from ever becoming a reality. In *Richard II* (1595) we have a king who claims divine authority, but his personality and actions make him totally inadequate to fulfil the role he is trying to play. In the *Henry IV* plays (1596–8), however, the king is a competent figure: it is the rebels in the country, including a comic rebel Falstaff, who challenge and undermine his authority.

Our starting-point for a discussion of any Shakespeare history play has to be an awareness of their general pattern: the plays work with an ideal notion of kingship, but accept the inevitability of disorder, recognising that the failings and ambitions of individuals will always disrupt the social and political life of the country. If we then look at a few scenes we shall begin to acquire a sense of how Shakespeare fills out this pattern, how he explores the whole question of political and social order. The plays do not make a statement: Shakespeare is not saying that people should behave in a certain way but exploring the complex reality of political life. In order to appreciate this we might, in *Henry IV Part One*, look at a scene featuring Falstaff, the larger-than-life comic rebel, seeing how his speeches with their total lack of respect for authority and discipline undermine the very idea that there can be order in a state. Or we might look at the meeting between King Henry and his son Hal in Act III, scene ii, noticing how the King immediately starts discussing the whole question of kingship. Such scenes reveal the thoroughness with which Shakespeare presents and explores the problem of people's weakness or unruliness that makes an ordered state seem a mythical ideal.

The same issues are in evidence in Shakespeare's **Roman plays**, such as *Julius Caesar* (1599) and *Antony and Cleopatra* (1606). The former deals with the conspirators who murder Caesar: political order is the ideal, but the reality is disorder. In the latter it is the passionate love of Antony and Cleopatra that renders them incapable of playing the public roles that are expected of them: social and political order are disrupted by extreme passions, creating war and disorder in society.

This awareness of the inevitable disorder of experience is seen in its most developed form in Shakespeare's **tragedies**. At the beginning of a tragedy some act takes place – such as the murder of Hamlet's father or Lear's abdication as king – that disrupts society. The social concord is broken and more violent elements take over. With traditional social restraint gone, the very worst face of human beings is exposed: in the tragedies our human capacity for destruction and brutality is allowed full reign. It is the tragic hero who bears the brunt of these bestial passions: he is confronted by the worst things that life can offer, yet faces up to this, meeting the challenge. This is the pattern in *Hamlet* (1600) and *King Lear*

(1605; *see* p. 99). In the case of *Macbeth* (1606), however, it is his own evil instincts that Macbeth has to confront; the same is true of *Othello* (1604), where the hero is overtaken by blind, sexual jealousy unleashed by Iago's scheming villainy.

As the tragic hero moves towards death we feel that the plays are asking the most fundamental questions about experience: what does life amount to, are people anything more than violent animals? This larger awareness that permeates the tragedies is perhaps most evident in the set-piece speeches where the hero ponders on the whole nature and purpose of existence. For example, in the final scene of *King Lear*, the King carries on his dead daughter and protests,

> Why should a dog, a horse, a rat have life,
> And thou no breath at all?

Here we can see Shakespeare's method at its best, confronting us with the large question about whether human life is worth any more than that of beasts. As always, it is the language, here the animal references, that carries the weight of the larger meaning. If we looked at the rest of the speech we should see how much meaning Shakespeare crowds into a few lines, how many ideas he raises about our place in the world and the value of human life.

This crowded texture of his lines can help us focus our discussion of a Shakespeare tragedy. As the issues involved in his tragedies are immense and wide-ranging we need to discipline and control our approach: we need to be aware of the general pattern of the plays, their concern with the extremes of disorder and people's brutal nature, but the most productive way of extending our analysis is to look closely at particular scenes, seeing how they present and examine the larger issues. Whereas with other dramatists we might have to look at several speeches to grasp the essential details, in Shakespeare's tragedies we can grasp a lot from even a few lines. This is because no other writer invests his lines with so much meaning, no other writer can so consistently and economically turn to the wider issue of the complex nature of reality.

What we have been talking about in this entry is what lies behind the action of a Shakespeare play; the fact that he looks so searchingly at the disorder of life and the idea that life could ever be better or more ordered. In his last plays, his **romances** such as *The Winter's Tale* (1610) and *The Tempest* (1611), Shakespeare deals more directly with this problem of the desirability of order and the inevitability of disorder. They are stylised plays, set in a far-away magical world even more remote than the make-believe world of the comedies. Something of the human interest of the earlier plays is now lost; it is as if Shakespeare no longer needs the props of realistic characters and plausible stories as he now makes explicit what is implicit in his earlier works, that his true subject is, indeed, the whole question of order and disorder in life

Tragedy. The simplest definition of tragedy is that it is a play that ends with the death of the main character. There are two main types: the type written by Shakespeare and his contemporaries (and by classical dramatists, such as Sophocles) in which we witness terrible disorder in a society, and a narrower type of tragedy, established by Ibsen and Strindberg in the nineteenth century, which focuses on the breakdown of a family.

It is the most ambitious form of drama. Indeed, because a tragedy can carry such a weight of meaning, students sometimes shy away from a particular tragedy's full implications, creating a simplified version of what the play is about. The most common reductive approach is one which concentrates on the tragic hero or heroine, stressing his or her nobility in suffering; this is a way of making sense of tragedy in reassuring and coherent human terms. The fortitude of the hero or heroine is important, but far more central is the impression tragedy conveys of how chaotic life becomes when the established social order is destroyed. Tragedies begin with some alteration in the existing social order, and this change leads to a shocking destruction of human life. Comedy laughs at the folly of people, but tragedy asks fundamental questions about the nature and purpose of existence in a world where, if the conventional social bonds are broken, the most appalling violence and vicious self-interest become dominant. It is the tragic heroes and heroines who usually pose these large questions about life in the speeches they make as they experience the full horror of what the world can be like.

We can see all of this in Shakespeare's *King Lear* (1605). Lear abdicates as ruler of the country, a clear alteration in the social order. His good daughter, Cordelia, is banished, and Lear hands over his responsibilities to his evil daughters Goneril and Regan. A vicious power struggle develops and Lear is driven out of doors into a storm. He confronts a chaotic universe in which the state, the family, nature and reason have all been thrown into confusion. He asks whether there is any justice or order in the world, whether there is anything that distinguishes the behaviour of human beings from that of beasts. Lear goes mad, but in many ways is clear-sighted for the first time in his life.

There is also a subplot focusing on another old man, Glouces-ter, whose eyes are ripped out as a punishment for helping the King. The subplot increases our awareness of a world falling apart. The two old men, one mad and one blind, struggle towards Dover: in their plight we have an image of the state of humanity struggling through a terrifying world, and at the end of the journey is death.

This sense that we live in a world that is governed not by reason but by more animal-like instincts is present in both classical and Elizabethan and Jacobean tragedy. The plays raise fundamen-tal questions about the meaning of existence in such a world. The vision is pessimistic, yet not totally so: tragedy provokes terror and pity at the plight of human beings, but alongside this there is the positive fact that both the tragic hero and the dramatist have confronted the worst that the world has to offer. The challenge in studying a tragedy is to delay grasping at this positive element in the text and to appreciate first the forceful way in which tragedy creates an impression of the frightening disorder of life.

Modern tragedy, as produced by dramatists such as Ibsen, Strindberg, Eugene O'Neill and Arthur Miller, can, in comparison with earlier works, seem unambitious. Whereas Shakespeare and his contemporaries focus on the whole state of humanity, modern tragedy focuses on the family. It still has the power to disturb, though: the family is the central unit in society, and if family life is presented as diseased and corrupt it can undermine our con-fidence that there can ever be any coherent order in society. This is evident in Ibsen's *The Wild Duck* (1884): the play concerns a girl who is going blind through inherited syphilis and who kills herself to win back her father's love. The child is destroyed by the sins of her forefathers and by an adult world of deceit and illusion. Ibsen's plays might appear to be works with a social message, but they are correctly described as tragedies because of the fullness of their sense of a disordered and corrupt world. The same is true of Strindberg's plays, for example *The Father* (1887), which presents a father and mother vying for control of their child. In Strindberg, however, the emphasis is not only on something rotten in the very fabric of society and family life, but also on the disorder of the individual mind.

More recent tragedies, such as O'Neill's *A Long Day's Journey into Night* (1941) and Arthur Miller's *The Death of a Salesman* (1949) also focus on family life and continue Strindberg's psychological emphasis. What modern tragedy has in common with earlier tragedy is that it explores the painfulness of a world where fictions of a rational social order can no longer be maintained. Yet there is a difference. It has something to do with the fact that the central characters of modern tragedy are fairly insignificant figures: they are **anti-heroes**, meaning that they are just ordinary people as opposed to the great men and women who feature in earlier tragedies. This links up with the whole question of scale: earlier tragedies look outwards, asking questions about the position of human beings in the universe. Modern tragedy centres itself in the family, and then tends to look inwards: the emphasis is on the disorder of the mind as much as on the disorder of the wider world. The heroes or heroines are as likely to be confronting the worst elements in themselves as confronting the worst elements in the world.

Twentieth-century drama. The period from the end of the nineteenth century up to the present day has been a great age for drama. There is a substantial tradition of major dramatists from Ibsen, Chekhov and Shaw through to Beckett, Pinter, Stoppard and Churchill. In this entry, however, we do not attempt to mention every important dramatist from this period: what we are concerned with is the overall pattern of modern drama.

A good point at which to start is with Shaw's *Arms and the Man* (1894). The hero, Bluntschli, a mercenary fighting in a war, evades capture by hiding in the bedroom of Raina. As the plot unfolds, Bluntschli overturns all her romantic illusions about love and heroism. A light, comic play, it ends, as we might expect, with their marriage. What makes Shaw's play modern is its debunking of conventional attitudes and beliefs, here exemplified by Raina and her family. In terms of content, Shaw breaks the frame of traditional values. The same thing happens at the formal level: Shaw takes the neat format of the well-made play (*see* p. 91), but subverts its tidy structure, introducing a sense of life's confusing complexity. Something very similar happens in plays such as Synge's *The Playboy of the Western World* (1907) and O'Casey's *Juno and the Paycock* (1924) where traditional ideas and ideals are undermined by comedy. What marks such plays off as modern is, first, their undermining of conventional social myths, beliefs and convictions, and, second, the innovative form of such plays, the writers breaking up the neat pattern of the well-made play.

Such a form of drama, in which the audience come to the theatre to have their convictions questioned, continues to the present day. There is a very common sort of play where we see reasonably ordinary people caught in a social dilemma. Such plays often use a box set, so that we seem to be in a room of someone's house. The focus, almost invariably, is on the gap between the social and ethical framework the characters have been raised in and the reality of their predicament, where these values are exposed as limited. The trouble with a great many plays of this kind is that the formula becomes so predictable that the plays in the end are reassuring rather than disturbing. They really only make a great impact when the dramatist makes the sort of formal innovation that allows him or her to say something new. For example, Osborne's *Look Back in Anger* created a sensation in 1956 when the hero, Jimmy Porter, lambasted every social value and prejudice of the day. Osborne's originality lies both in his conception of a new sort of disaffected character and in the fury and energy of the monologues he creates for Porter.

There are other modern dramatists, though, who have turned their backs on this tradition. The security of the box set can seem very limited or even irrelevant in a century that has experienced two world wars, and some dramatists have accordingly sought a more radical form appropriate for such a chaotic period.

One response is the German dramatist Brecht's **epic theatre:** the very name suggests an ambitious form of drama which attempts to tackle the larger problems of modern history. Brecht's *Mother Courage* (1941) presents Mother Courage on a journey across Europe selling goods. One aspect of the play is that Brecht is drawing attention to the money-making that underlies war, so the play continues in the tradition of questioning established ideas. There is, however, more to the play than this. Brecht sets out to **alienate** the audience: he makes it clear that we are watching a play and does not allow us to become sympathetically involved. What this amounts to is a very radical, political undermining of the structures within which we live. Unlike Shaw, Brecht does not just question traditional social values but also questions the artifice of drama itself, making us see the way in which a play is another conventional structure. By doing this he draws attention very emphatically to the falseness of any scheme of order, including that of the play itself, and thereby highlights the violent and chaotic reality of modern life. Brecht thus introduces a form of political drama in which all the institutional frameworks of society, including the frame of drama itself, are subverted.

Another dramatic response to the twentieth-century experience, the **theatre of the absurd**, is even more disturbing, for it does not even bother to challenge our conventional systems of order. A dramatist such as Beckett starts from the assumption that we live in a chaotic and meaningless world. In *Waiting for Godot* (1955) two men wait near a bare tree for Godot, who never comes. While they wait they talk, but the dialogue never gets anywhere. Their existence is absurd and meaningless. Again a radical new approach has been found to convey a new sense of the reality of modern life: in Beckett's plays we encounter a world without causes, hopes, convictions or beliefs.

Brecht and Beckett are the two central, and most influential, figures in post-war drama, yet there are few writers who closely resemble them. They represent two extreme ways of responding to, and articulating a sense of, the disorder of life. In between the poles of Brecht and Beckett are dramatists such as Pinter, Stoppard and a great many other well-known contemporary figures: John Arden, Arnold Wesker, Alan Ayckbourn, Edward Bond, David Hare, Trevor Griffiths, Howard Brenton. The list could be greatly extended, for the last forty years have produced an extraordinary number of plays all focusing on the state of modern society. The reason for this is not hard to find: the crisis of post-war society finds its most appropriate voice in the theatre.

Many contemporary plays are, in fact, overtly political in intent and aimed at subverting their audience's comfortable illusions. Often they are deliberately shocking in their violence: in Bond's *Saved* (1965) a baby is stoned and punched to death; in Brenton's *The Romans in Britain* (1980) one male character rapes another. Informing such plays is the idea that we live in an irrational, anarchic world without any form of order or values, something that is reflected in the innovative form of modern drama. Unlike Brecht and Beckett, however, most contemporary dramatists employ fairly plausible characters, for their real interest is in how individuals survive in an irrational world. This is evident, for example, in Stoppard's *Rosencrantz and Guildenstern are Dead* (1967), which focuses on two ordinary men who suddenly find themselves in a bizarre situation. Shaw, at the start of the century, was asking questions about how people cope with a world of false social values; today, the balance has tilted towards asking how people can survive in a world where there are no values, in a world that is chaotic and meaningless.

In **feminist theatre**, however, there has been a different response to the dilemma of modern life, a response no less political than that of Bond or Brenton, but interrogative of other issues. Feminist theatre really begins with the American dramatist Megan Terry in the 1960s. From then on there has been a rapid increase in the number of feminist dramatists, including such central figures as Caryl Churchill, Pam Gems and Michelene Wandor, and acting and production companies such as the Women's Theatre Group. The endeavour of both writers and actors has been to show how the achievements of women have been suppressed by history and society, and also to show how women have been made subordinate to men. The plays set out to make the audience review the past and present from a different perspective, to see that social or political order is not 'natural' but constructed in favour of men by men. But the plays also set out to celebrate women, to be positive, challenging us with ideas about the need to change society.

Many of the above aspects of feminist theatre can be seen in Caryl Churchill's *Top Girls* (1982). The main figure is Marlene who runs the 'Top Girls' employment agency. The play, however, begins in a restaurant with Marlene entertaining a number of women drawn from history, including a Japanese courtesan and Chaucer's Patient Griselda, the stereotype of the patient wife. What Churchill does here is disrupt time so as to create a sense of continuity between women who have endured and struggled against men. But the play is not a simple affirmation of women's strength or victory; Churchill leaves us with a sense of how women are still caught in a society that prospers by conflict and pain: Marlene has given her daughter to her sister Joyce so that she can pursue her career. As in other twentieth-century drama, we are struck by the way in which the play reveals how the social order seems to require the destruction of people, and especially women. Like much feminist theatre, the play raises questions about class, money and violence and about how women are victimised both directly and indirectly by the values of masculine society.

There are now a large number of feminist dramatists writing for the theatre and also for television and cinema. While this book is not intended as a guide to these media, it is worth noting how both **film** and **television** now clearly provide the major vehicle for drama. Here we include not just plays but also television soaps, series, films and even situation comedies (to consider just one of these, a look at Carla Lane's comedies would prove both challenging and rewarding). The fact is there has been a massive change in cultural production since the Second World War as a result of the advances of technology. Yet what we see on television and on video is for the most part consistent with and continues the debates that we have drawn attention to in this section, and which have been around for a very long time.

There are still plenty of plays on television that make use of the box set and the well-made-play format. Narrative on television is nearly always very traditional, with a clearly defined exposition, complication and resolution (something that is reinforced by the two advertising breaks in a one-hour show on British television). Any police series raises serious questions about how to maintain order in society, but inevitably reinforces the dominant ideology of our society even as it shows detectives overstepping the mark. Television, above all, clings to the traditional values of the family and of the limiting of woman to the stereotype: this is most obvious in soap operas, where the nuclear family, organised along traditional lines, remains the ideal, and in which most of the dramatic situations (such as adultery, problems with children, problems over employment and unemployment, and issues of class) develop from challenges to, or deviations from, traditional gender and social roles; it is a form of questioning that tends to reinforce the conservative position. To this extent, it can be argued that television and film are less challenging and controversial than the radical drama of Ibsen or Brecht or Churchill. But the majority of texts at any time are going to be conventional and traditional; if even once a year there is a programme on television that seems to challenge the conventions of the medium and forces us to consider questions that we might not have realised even existed, then television is fulfilling a purpose that is consistent with the most traditional demands that we place upon art forms. **Media studies**, the logical extension of the traditional study of literature, will inevitably concentrate primarily on television, and has to consider the issue of how the medium, in holding a mirror up to society, reinforces ideology while, occasionally, questioning the values of society.

4

The novel

ALTHOUGH there are earlier novels, the history of the English novel really begins with the publication of Daniel Defoe's *Robinson Crusoe* in 1719. The late arrival of the novel on the literary scene tells us something important about the genre: it is, above all else, a form of literature which looks at people in society. Writers have, of course, always been interested in the world around them, but the development of the novel reflects a move away from an essentially religious view of life towards a new interest in the complexities of everyday experience. Most novels are concerned with ordinary people and their problems in the societies in which they find themselves. This is often the case even when the pattern appears to be broken: *Robinson Crusoe* presents a man alone on a desert island; some novels, such as Tolkien's *The Lord of the Rings,* have animals as central characters; but even these novels are dealing indirectly with people in the social world.

Novels do not, however, present a documentary picture of life. Alongside the fact that novels look at people in society, the other major characteristic of the genre is that novels tell a story. In fact, novels tend to tell the same few stories time and time again. Novelists frequently focus on the tensions between individuals and the society in which they live, presenting characters who are at odds with that society. A lot of novels have young people as the main characters, for it is often the young who feel themselves to be most at odds with conventional standards. You will have made considerable progress in understanding the particular novel you are reading if you can see how it sets certain individuals against society or their family. Novelists return to such a basic pattern repeatedly because it is really the story of everyone's life – all of us have individual impulses and desires, but all of us have to face up to the fact that we are members of a family and a society.

So, in thinking about a novel, try to see this informing structure: a society, and characters who are in some ways at odds with this society. Do not, however, make the mistake of believing that the novel is written to put across a point. It is true that some novelists are moralists – they examine the relations between individuals and society and put forward their ideas about how people should behave – but it would be too simple to say that the important thing about their novels is the message they preach, just as it is too simple to say that a writer such as Dickens is a novelist with a social purpose who writes to reform society. Such an attitude to novels exists because of the feeling that a story must have a point and a purpose.

Novels, however, are long works with a great amount of detail on every page. They thus present all the complicating facts that need to be taken into account before we can reach any sort of judgement. The effect of this detail is that we come to recognise the complex reality of a character or event in the story. The easiest way to describe this effect is to talk about the difference between the story and the discourse. 'Discourse' here means the language and texture of the writing in a novel. The story in a novel is almost a parable, a tale that makes a point, but in producing a novel the writer complicates the basic story by the addition of a great of deal of detail. This detail, the novel's discourse, serves to create an impression of just how complicated problems and people are when we look at them closely. The novelist's beliefs might be apparent – a writer generally leans in one of two directions, either suggesting that individuals should conform to society's standards or suggesting that society is in such a bad state that individuals are bound to feel alienated – but a sense of the general tendency of the work must be complemented by an awareness of the richness of texture of the novel. As readers, our real interest lies in the complications the novelist creates within the familiar pattern of characters at odds with their society that enable us to gain a vivid sense of what it is like for particular individuals to be caught in certain events. A productive critical method for achieving a sense of a novel's complexity is to look closely at scenes which you found interesting or memorable, seeing how the details create a vivid and distinctive impression of an individual and society conflict.

To a substantial extent such an approach works with all novels, but is particularly relevant to novels in the realistic tradition: that is to say, novels which seem to present an accurate impression of ordinary life. Jane Austen and George Eliot are realists. Many novelists, however, are not, and studying a novel becomes more difficult when the novelist departs from straightforward realism. As in Melville's *Moby-Dick*, for example, the novelist can tell a more adventurous story which clearly goes beyond everyday experience. Critics sometimes divide novels into those in a realistic mode and those which present a more dramatic story, the latter being referred to as prose romances. American novels are often romances. In reading a realistic novel we are most impressed by the picture of life that is presented, but in a romance we are far more aware that we are reading a story.

This is also the effect when the novelist intervenes directly in the telling of the story. Even Austen and Eliot do not just present us with a picture of life: they are both present as narrators. But the novelist can be more perversely intrusive: for example, in a comic novel events which could be treated seriously are presented as funny, while in some novels the writer deliberately draws attention to the fact that he or she is writing a story, making it perfectly clear that the events and characters are fictional. A term commonly used for such novels is reflexive, that is they examine or draw attention to their own status as novels. All these terms – 'realistic', 'comic', 'narrator', 'romance' and 'reflexive novels' – are discussed in this section. We must recognise, however, that the novel is an untidy genre and that a novel can, say, be both comic and realistic, and this is something that should be borne in mind in reading the definitions that follow of different kinds of novel. A general point we can make here, though, is that, although our first response might be to think that novelists are mainly interested in presenting an accurate picture of life, because novels also involve a made-up thing, the story, the novelist can tilt the balance away from a direct picture of life and make more of the fact that a story is being told.

We can, however, delay looking at this sort of complication. What we want to stress here is the extent to which novels are concerned with presenting a picture of how people relate to' society, for this provides a starting-point for looking at any novel. As suggested, the way to appreciate the distinctive qualities of a novel is to look for the broad pattern in the text – how some of the characters in the novel are at odds with society – and then to turn to specific incidents, for it is the page-by-page texture of the novel that makes the conflicts come to life and seem substantial.

Character. The people in a novel are referred to as characters. We assess them on the basis of what the author tells us about them and on the basis of what they do and say. This is important: we must avoid loose conjecture about a character and establish everything from the evidence of the text. Another point to remember is that the characters are part of a broader pattern: they are members of a society, and the author's distinctive view of how people relate to society will be reflected in the presentation of every character. Details are not included just for their own sake but relate to the overall pattern of the novel.

For example, in George Eliot's *The Mill on the Floss* (1860) the main character, Maggie, makes her first appearance as a child:

> Mrs Tulliver, desiring her daughter to have a curled crop, 'like other folks's children', had had it cut too short in front to be pushed behind the ears, and as it was usually straight an hour after it had been taken out of paper, Maggie was incessantly tossing her head to keep the dark, heavy locks out of her gleaming black eyes – an action which gave her very much the air of a small Shetland pony.

Such a passage suggests that Mrs Tulliver wants her daughter to conform, but that Maggie cannot – from her gleaming eyes we sense that she is spirited, yet she also seems as lovable as a Shetland pony. The details create our impression of her personality; at the same time they raise the broader themes of the novel, for here, as so often in fiction, is a rebellious character who will come into conflict with society. The novel will present this character caught in various dilemmas; at the end of the novel she will either make or fail to make an accommodation with society. Most characters in most novels are either like Maggie or social conformists like her mother. It is important to spot these broad patterns, but equally important to see how the use of detail makes the character substantial and individual.

In some novels, however, particularly comic novels, the characters are not very substantial or credible. A different approach to characterisation is involved here. Whereas George Eliot stresses the individuality of characters, comic novelists, such as Fielding and Dickens, tend to emphasise how the characters are familiar types involved in familiar dilemmas. This might seem a simpler, because less psychologically convincing, approach, but the point to remember here is that the comic novelist is writing from a different stance. It can be an unnerving approach because it mocks the idea of uniqueness and stresses how we are all acting out roles in society. Acting images are often used in comic novels, and there is an emphasis on outward appearance (such as clothes, bodily peculiarities and speech mannerisms). In looking at a comic novel, try to understand the thinking behind such character presentation: the novelist seeks to show how desperate, foolish or pathetic people can appear as they attempt to present a face in society.

Comic novels. Novels primarily intended to make us laugh. Students are sometimes grudging in their praise of comic novels, as they can appear lightweight compared to realistic novels, which present such a substantial picture of life. A common, but misguided, approach is to ascribe some social purpose to the writer, and then to argue that the comedy makes the social criticism entertaining.

Comedy is, however, at the heart of comic novels. Comedy consists of laughing at characters caught in difficult situations. Unlike the realistic novelist, who is sympathetically involved, the comic novelist writes from a detached position in which he or she surveys the whole picture in an amused way. People are seen as types acting out roles in familiar stories. The action is meant to strike us not as real, but as illustrative of human traits, exaggerating human weaknesses such as greed and lust. It is an alternative perspective to that of the realist, prompted not by a sense of human complexity but by a more jaundiced sense of what people have in common in a corrupt world. It is a potentially gloomy vision, but it emerges as funny because it sees the absurdity of human pretensions.

The comic stance can be a cruel one, merely laughing at human misfortune, but in practice the comic novelist can become more realistic when the situation demands it. Similarly, there is often comedy in realistic novels: Jane Austen and George Eliot are often funny, laughing at how seriously people take themselves and their problems. Comedy in realistic novels is often gentle and affectionate, frequently laughing at youthful naïvety. The simplest form of comic novel is satiric – for example, Thomas Love Peacock's *Nightmare Abbey* (1818) – although there is a satiric element in many novels. Satire mocks affectation, attempting to laugh people out of their folly.

However, whereas satire is essentially constructive, comedy can be more disruptive. It presents a picture of a crazy, irrational world where there is nothing we can hold on to, no social value we can trust. Fielding and Thackeray, who have much in common, both present a vast panorama of self-interest. In *Tom Jones* (1749) and *Vanity Fair* (1848), both use a narrator who castigates human folly, but the narrator also mocks himself, for his views cannot be taken any more seriously than those of anyone else in the social world. The effect is simultaneously amusing and disturbing. Dickens is the finest comic novelist: not only is his panorama of folly the most inventive and full; he is also the most disturbing of writers. Other comic novelists touch on the irrational impulses that motivate people, but Dickens takes this idea further, conveying a sense of the darker, more unfathomable lusts and desires that lurk beneath the social façade. His novels follow the usual pattern of much comic fiction of a vast array of absurd, villainous, pathetic or pretentious characters set against a small band of good characters who display more wholesome qualities, but Dickens, for example in the repeated use of murders in his novels, probes far more deeply into the disturbing nature of irrational impulses in life. Most comic novelists are content just to look at the folly of people in society, but Dickens looks beneath the surface.

Comedy, then, is not just a surface characteristic of comic novels, but a way of looking at the world which sees the whole of social life as an elaborate charade, where any sense of a civilised social order will always be disrupted by people's basic desires of greed, lust and self-interest. The emphasis, for the most part, is on the surface of things, with a simple sense of character, and plenty of illustrative examples of the sort of greed and corruption that prevails in society. The odd thing about comic novels, however, is that they are often very serious novels, presenting a disturbing view of how society conducts itself.

Eighteenth-century novels. Defoe's *Robinson Crusoe* (1719) introduces us to some central features of novels in general. Crusoe is shipwrecked on a desert island: by presenting him in isolation Defoe can convey a full impression of how human beings structure their world; then, when other people appear, he can examine them in a social context. From its start, then, the English novel looks at a person coming to terms with the world in which he or she finds himself or herself. The manner is realistic, with a detailed account of Crusoe's feelings and the ordinary business of life.

Robinson Crusoe, however, is not just a realistic novel. There is another narrative pattern in the text. There are certain archetypal stories that predate the novel, but which some novelists continue to employ. The most basic is a story of an individual on a quest. Such stories recur because they provide an effective focus for considering our journey through life: their presence in novels is always interesting because they hint at something grander than the novel's tendency to become absorbed in the complications of ordinary life. In *Crusoe* we can trace a religious story of a man sent into isolation who has to rediscover his faith. The novel holds this religious search for an ideal in tension with the distractions of daily experience. In Defoe's second novel, *Moll Flanders* (1722), there is a similar gap between the ideal – the heroine should be devout – and how things are in a fallen world, where people are preoccupied with the daily business of life.

After Defoe the next significant novelist is a more straightforward realist. This is Samuel Richardson, author of *Pamela* (1740) and *Clarissa* (1748). Both novels present women whose virtue is at risk in a socially corrupt world. In Richardson's treatment of this individual and society conflict we see a characteristic strength of novels, for the details accumulate to present a very disturbing impression of the lives of these women trapped in difficult dilemmas. The stress is on the complications of real life rather than on an ideal notion of how life might be. Richardson's novels are **epistolary:** written in letters from the main characters. It is a method that offers us a very direct insight into the characters' minds, and Richardson can be regarded as the first **psychological novelist**.

Curiously, Richardson's *Pamela* was almost immediately parodied by Henry Fielding in *Joseph Andrews* (1742). Fielding, who also wrote *Tom Jones* (1749), is the first great comic novelist in England. He reacted against how seriously Richardson took his characters and their dilemmas, preferring, like all comic novelists, a stress on human folly. The realistic novelist offers a subtle analysis of his characters, but the comic novelist takes a simpler view that people's lusts and desires disrupt life: it might be a less subtle view, but it is a disturbing one, as it emphasises the irrational impulses that motivate people. Another important aspect of Fielding's novels is his intrusive presence as narrator, where he makes it quite clear that he is making up the story. The direction in which this leads is towards mocking the whole activity of novel-writing, for, if human nature is irrational, who is the novelist to presume to order and explain life in something as contrived as a story?

Such scepticism is characteristic of the eighteenth century when writers were questioning the ability of this new form to present a convincing picture of life. The realistic novel only becomes dominant in the nineteenth century. Fielding's stress on the gap between fiction and life is carried much further by Laurence Sterne in *Tristram Shandy* (1760–7), where the hero tries to tell the story of his life but in his desperation to include everything can hardly make any progress at all. This is widely recognised as the greatest reflexive novel – that is a novel which constantly draws attention to its own existence as a novel (for more on Sterne, *see* p. 121).

Although a realistic novel and a novel such as *Tristram Shandy* are very different there is some connection, for what all novels do is disrupt a neat ordered story. In the background of a novel there is always an idea of order, indeed a story is an ordering of the events in life. The realistic novelist disrupts this neat fictional pattern by the introduction of complicating detail in the narrative. The non-realistic novelist relies more on the narrator to disrupt the neat fiction as he or she points out that people are too foolish ever to settle their differences, or that life is a lot more complicated than a story. This disruption of a story is evident in the other main strand in eighteenth-century fiction, the **picaresque** novel. Fielding's novels are picaresque tales, as are Smollett's, for example *Roderick Random* (1748). But the forerunner of all novels, Cervantes's *Don Quixote* (1605–15), provides the model of such picaresque works. It describes the events on a long journey: Don Quixote believes he is on some glorious mission, but he is repeatedly caught up in farcical situations. Picaresque takes the quest story from romance (*see* p. 122), in which somebody is in search of an ideal, and deflates it, emphasising that there is no goal to be reached and that one is simply entangled in the complications of life. Once again the impulse to disrupt a story is in evidence: order is an illusion, or, in other words, a fiction. But order – the religious ideal Defoe acknowledges, the social order that Richardson and Fielding know is uncommon in a corrupt or foolish society, and the order that Tristram Shandy would like to impose on his own life – remains a desirable, even if impossible, ideal.

Narrative structure. Narrative is the organisation of a series of events into the form of a story. This is obviously what we have in novels; what is less obvious is how similar the narrative structure is in most novels.

A novel usually begins with a description of a place or a character. The setting is likely to strike us as either an attractive one, where the characters should feel comfortable, or an unattractive one, where people are bound to feel unhappy and alienated. A character introduced at the beginning of a novel will usually come into collision with society. The opening chapters will expand the picture of the characters and the society they live in. The novel will then progress by taking the characters through a sequence of events extending over a certain time span. Some conflict will always be in evidence, as novels always deal with characters who are at odds with their family or conventional social values. The novel will bring various characters into confrontation and put characters into problematic situations.

The simple sequence of events in a novel is the **story**. **Plot** is slightly different. To quote E. M. Forster, '"The king died and the queen died", is a story. "The king died and then the queen died of grief", is a plot. The time sequence is preserved, but the sense of causality overshadows it.' To talk about the plot of a novel, then, we have to provide a fuller description of the work, taking into account the nature of the characters. An account of the plot, as opposed to a summary of the story, provides some idea of the ways in which a particular novel is distinctive. We cannot, however, really appreciate the unique qualities of a specific novel unless we are aware of how much novels have in common in terms of the basic stories they employ. For example, one of the most common patterns is that of the **education novel:** this takes a rebellious character through a sequence of testing situations. By the end of the novel the character has either matured or at least discovered something about himself or herself. If you can recognise that basic format, and it is the format of the majority of classic novels, then you are well placed to comment on how an individual novel develops this story in a new way. All novels which start with the main character as a child and then present the child's growth and development towards adulthood are essentially education novels telling a very similar story. In most instances a plot develops as the writer shows how, when we look closely at people and events, life is a lot more complicated than the simple story. Our concern as critics is with the imaginative skill with which the writer adds complications to the simple pattern. The novelist complicates the neat pattern of the story either by offering us a full and complex impression of life, or, as is discussed in the next definition, by the way in which he or she handles the narration. The received pattern of fiction is set against a more complicated sense of life's complexity.

The story, however, is not there merely as a starting-point for the novelist. A story suggests that events can be arranged into a meaningful order. The story often dominates at the end of novels, where the complications are overcome: novels often end with the marriages of the main characters, who settle down anticipating a quiet future. In addition, such an idea of an ordered and harmonious existence is often an implicit ideal in a novel. Indeed, the story itself acts as an ordering frame for the novel. This is because a novelist is interested not only in the complications and sheer untidiness of experience, but also in seeing what order can be detected or created in the confusion of life. In this way a novel often strikes a balance between story and plot, between order and the disorder of experience.

Narrator. The narrator tells the story in a novel. Novels contain simple stories which, in their telling, become complicated. There are two overlapping ways by which the novelist can complicate matters. One is by introducing complications in the content: the inclusion of a mass of details about people, places and events makes the story seem substantial and real. The other way in which the writer can complicate matters is by the way in which he or she chooses to narrate the story: a story can be told in many ways, for every narrator will see things from a different **point-of-view**.

In a **first-person narrative** the central character relates the events he or she experienced. As in Dickens's *David Copperfield* (1850), this allows us a very direct insight into the character's mind; often the experiences are viewed retrospectively, so that we are aware of the differences between the character's immature and mature personality. In all other methods of narrative the narrator or narrators are principally observers of the events. In **omniscient narration** a narrator who can see everything relates the story. The omniscient narrator can be **unintrusive:** that is to say, we are not really aware of a persona telling the story because the action is presented without many explicit comments or judgements. Such an impersonal method is common in modern realistic novels, such as the works of E. M. Forster and Graham Greene, yet we do gain a sense of a narrator from the style the author adopts. Earlier realistic novelists, such as Austen and Eliot, use an **intrusive** narrator who comments on the events and characters. Such narrators frequently point to the significance of what they are presenting, often providing a moral interpretation of events and characters.

The narrators in Austen and Eliot are thus constructive figures, but the intrusive narrator can be disruptive, particularly in comic novels. The narrator in Thackeray's *Vanity Fair* (1848) is self-mocking, as if saying that life is more complicated than his view of life. This leads us on to a standard complicating technique that can be found in novels. When the narration becomes at all self-conscious, or complicated, as when several narrators are used or when a character on the fringe of the events relates the story, the impression that comes across is that the events are more puzzling than any interpretation can do justice to. Emily Brontë in *Wuthering Heights* (1847), for example, presents an extraordinary love story which is conveyed to us by two main narrators: they are characters involved in the story but incapable of appreciating its significance. Conrad, as in *Lord Jim* (1900), sometimes uses a character called Marlow as narrator: he is an intelligent man, but his understanding of what he perceives is limited, simply because, like anyone, he interprets events according to his own beliefs and values. Such narrators are often called **unreliable narrators**.

It is, however, only in realistic novels that we really regard the narrator as reliable, as providing a true picture and, sometimes, a true interpretation of events. In non-realistic novels the narrator is usually either dramatised or self-conscious. The realistic novel attempts to offer us a true picture of life, but the non-realistic novel makes far greater use of the method of narration to hint at the complexity of experience, principally by suggesting that there is always a gap between life itself and any reading or interpretation of life. Such scepticism about the ability of the novel to get at the full truth has always been present in fiction, but becomes far more common at the end of the nineteenth century. George Eliot is confident in her grasp and understanding of life, but at the end of the nineteenth century, in the works of Hardy, James and Conrad, all sorts of experiments with methods of narration take place: a certain confidence disappears, and suddenly all the major novelists are aware of the gap between reality and interpretations of reality.

Nineteenth-century novels. The novelists referred to here are Austen, Dickens, Eliot and Hardy, but many other names could be included as this was the great age of the novel, when it became the supremely confident form for consideration of an increasingly complex world. All four of these writers look at conflicts between individuals and society, but, whereas Austen and Eliot feel that society, for all its faults, is in reasonable health and that individuals should conform, Dickens and Hardy are fiercer critics of the existing social structure, and so fully aware why characters might always feel at odds with the world.

George Eliot's novels feature egotistical heroes and heroines who come into collision with society. The experiences they undergo, however, usually have a maturing effect, so that they see the error of their ways and become more responsible members of society. Eliot is, then, a moral writer, but her novels, such as *Adam Bede* (1859), *The Mill on the Floss* (1860) and *Middlemarch* (1871–2), are effective because she presents the experiences sympathetically and with a perceptive understanding of why the characters might be at odds with society. Indeed, some, such as Maggie, the heroine of *The Mill on the Floss*, never find a secure role in society. When reading Eliot, we notice how convincing her presentation of life is and how perceptive her sympathies are. Austen (*see* Realism, p. 119) has much in common with Eliot, but she is a sterner moralist who is quick to rebuke those who flout society's rules.

Dickens is far more critical of society than either Eliot or Austen, presenting a picture of a dehumanising society motivated by greed and lust. He is not, however, merely a social novelist, for his is a comic, although disturbing, vision of a corrupt world. He can, as in *David Copperfield* (1850), come close to realism, using a story of a boy's growth to maturity, but he generally prefers a more elaborate structure. For example, in *Dombey and Son* (1848), *Bleak House* (1853), *Little Dorrit* (1857) and *Our Mutual Friend* (1865), he presents a panorama of many grasping characters caught up in a corrupt social and business world, setting against this a small group of good characters. His good characters are too good to be true, but this is how they have to be, for, if the world is as corrupt as Dickens suggests, the idea that good people can change anything is only a fiction. A fictional ideal of goodness is thus set against the terrible reality of the social world; we contrast how things might be and how they really are.

Hardy is also a social critic, but more of a realist than Dickens. He concentrates on social rebels, sympathising totally with these characters, but one of the most impressive qualities in his novels is his ability to create an impression of the awful mess these characters – such as Henchard in *The Mayor of Casterbridge* (1886), Tess in *Tess of the d'Urbervilles* (1891), and Jude and Sue in *Jude the Obscure* (1896) – get into as they reject conventional behaviour. They are not rebels by choice; it is just that their passionate nature leads them to break society's rules, and they inevitably come to grief. Hardy's novels make a great impact at this realistic level, but there are other elements in his work. For example, some of his novels follow the structure of tragic drama and he emphasised the fact that he was a story-teller. It is perhaps inevitable that the story should be more noticeable in Dickens and Hardy than in Austen and Eliot, for the latter try to make sense of life in social terms, searching for a social order that can make life coherent. Dickens and Hardy do not expect to find order in society, so have to provide an alternative form of order in their works. With Dickens, this is usually a case of setting the disorder of life against a pleasant fictional ideal of good characters winning the day. With Hardy, we could say that he reads a tragic significance into the lives of his characters, as if their lives have a meaning and value that is grander than anything merely social. Hardy at times also toys with the idea that human life might be controlled by Fate: he does not expect to find order in society, so seeks another ordering framework that might make sense of life.

Realism. Realistic is the label we apply to those novels that seek to provide a convincing illusion of life as we normally think of it. Readers who are just beginning to study novels often feel most comfortable with realistic novels because they appear relatively straightforward. The realistic novel can seem like a clear window on the world – and as readers we can become fully involved with the characters and events – while non-realistic novels seem to look at the world through a distorting mirror, with the result that we are forced to consider the relationship between the work of art itself and life.

A realistic approach allows the writer to create a very full impression of what it must be like for certain people to be caught in certain dilemmas: there is a searching presentation of the full range of psychological and social factors that are involved in every experience. In Jane Austen's novels, for example, such as *Sense and Sensibility* (1811), *Pride and Prejudice* (1813) and *Mansfield Park* (1814), the standard story concerns young women living in a society where they are expected to make a good marriage. Austen examines the very real difficulties her heroines experience, and we feel that she is acknowledging all the issues that need to be taken into account. Realistic novelists are often moralists, concerned with how correct conduct can be achieved in the complex conditions of the real world. Austen is concerned that her characters should achieve a balanced response to life, balancing emotion and common sense, but she shows how difficult this is to achieve by presenting a realistic enough picture to convince us that this is how it might really be if one of us was encountering these problems in real life.

In talking about a realistic novel, however, we should resist the temptation to discuss it as if it is real life. We are not so much concerned with discussing the characters as people as with discussing how the texture of the writing creates such a credible picture. Look at passages to see how the writer creates the realistic impression; try to be aware of how much art is involved in a realistic approach. Austen uses landscape, buildings, the weather, description, dialogue and her own witty comments to illuminate the characters and themes.

There are a great many realistic novelists, novelists such as Richardson, Trollope, Henry James, D. H. Lawrence and E. M. Forster, and all novels are realistic to a degree if they present a convincing environment and characters. The realistic mode is appealing because it is as varied as life itself, but we should usually be able to identify a basic pattern of a convincing examination of the experiences of characters caught in problematic situations. At the end of the nineteenth century a cruder form of realism, called **naturalism**, appeared. Naturalism is principally associated with the French novelist Émile Zola, but is carried on in American fiction by writers such as Theodore Dreiser and Stephen Crane. In naturalism a more documentary-like approach is in evidence, with a great stress on how environment and heredity shape people. The major influence was Darwin's biological theories of evolution. The realistic novel is far more subtle and varied as it is not committed to such a determinist view of life. Indeed, the realistic novel attempts to reproduce something of the complexity of life itself, of all the social and personal considerations that come together in a complex mix in any incident in life.

There is only one potential weakness in the realistic approach. Realistic novels sometimes end unconvincingly, because the aim of providing a full picture of life cannot really be reconciled with the order that is often established in the closing chapters of a book. At the end of Eliot's *Middlemarch* (1871–2), for example, the heroine Dorothea, who has experienced endless problems, suddenly achieves happiness and a perfect marriage with Will Ladislaw. We cannot help feeling that there is a gap between the novel's rich sense of life and the fictional order that is established at the end.

Reflexive novels. 'Reflexive', 'self-referential' or 'self-conscious' are labels that can be applied to novels where the writer draws attention to the fact that he or she is writing a novel. In Laurence Sterne's *Tristram Shandy* (1760–7), Tristram attempts to write an autobiography but hardly makes any progress at all. The novel includes black pages, blank pages, and endless play with all the formal features of a novel, such as the standard organising-device of dividing a novel into chapters. The intention is simple. Sterne draws attention to the gap between life and attempting to reproduce a life in a work of art. The novel would, however, be tedious if it were only concerned with discussing the problems of fictional discourse. It works so well because Sterne has a complex vision of life: central themes in the novel are the vulnerability of the human body, anxieties about sex, and death. It is a comic novel, but the humour is nervous, making jokes about the most worrying things in life. The method of narration is justified because the novel deals with subjects such as death and sex which are beyond rational analysis. The novel, therefore, points to the absurdity of trying to write about such matters in a coherent work of fiction. Yet there is also a desperate desire, revealed in the manic energy of Tristram's narrative, to try to confront, understand and get the measure of such problems.

The basic pattern of *Tristram Shandy* is found in a less radical form in other novels. Fielding, in *Joseph Andrews* (1742) and *Tom Jones* (1749), is a reflexive novelist, and there has been a great deal of reflexive fiction recently, such as the novels of Vladimir Nabokov and John Fowles's *The French Lieutenant's Woman* (1969). The good reflexive novelist must offer us a sense that life is complex, so that we feel that it cannot be processed within a novel, yet we must also feel the author's urge to confront and try to understand experience. Many reflexive novels use an intrusive narrator, but not all: the elaborate artifice of many modern novels, such as Joyce's *Ulysses*

(1922), poses the same questions about the relationship between art and life. The explanation for the often peculiar nature of Joyce's prose is that this manner of writing raises questions about what is an appropriate style for conveying a sense of reality. It is eighteenth- and twentieth-century novels that most frequently advertise their own fictionality in this way. Nineteenth-century novelists tend to be more realistic, but even George Eliot does frequently stop to discuss her own novels and their relationship to life, and Dickens, particularly in *Bleak House* (1853), can make great play with the difference between the order of fiction and the disorder of life.

Romance. We use the term 'romance' to describe those novels where the story is more adventurous or more fanciful than in realistic novels. Something grander than the novel's familiar concern with social issues is involved, for 'romance' suggests a search for some truth beyond that which we might encounter in ordinary experience. Both characters and events are removed from the everyday, so that there is always an air of the extraordinary about romance.

The American novel has always been more romantic than realistic: the very idea of the New World suggests a search for something new, and there is a repeated pattern in American novels of characters setting out on a journey of discovery. This is a reworking of the traditional romance story of a knight on a quest as the hero seeks a life that is more heroic, exciting and purposeful than ordinary existence. Sometimes, as in Edgar Allan Poe's *The Narrative of Arthur Gordon Pym* (1838) or Herman Melville's *Moby-Dick* (1851), this is also a symbolic journey exploring buried desires. There is something similar in English fiction in Joseph Conrad's *Heart of Darkness* (1902), which describes a river journey up the Congo, but this is also a journey into the disorder of the mind. The romantic journey suggests an escape from the mundane routine of ordinary life, but this departure from social routine always involves travelling into dangerous and violent places, including the dark world of the mind.

Novelists who use the romance idea, however, can use it in a sceptical way: Mark Twain's *Huckleberry Finn* (1884) takes two friends on a trip down the Mississippi, but there is a gap between the adventurous ideal and the reality of what they encounter on their journey. Similarly, the central character in Scott Fitzgerald's *The*

Great Gatsby (1925) seems to have escaped from everyday concerns into a world of fabulous wealth, but it is clear that Gatsby's ideal existence is not secure, for all the ordinary pressures of existence threaten and undermine the life he has created for himself.

Even here, however, we are still aware of that romantic aspiration which characterises American fiction, that search for some ideal dream or better life that might be reached at the end of the journey. This is evident in Henry James's novels, such as *The Portrait of a Lady* (1881), which often feature young American heroines arriving in Europe. Their romantic ideals are crushed by the realities of European life, yet the initial aspirations remain attractive. Such a commitment to a romantic ideal is less common in English fiction. An exception is Emily Brontë's *Wuthering Heights* (1847), where we encounter the extraordinary love of Cathy and Heathcliff; it is a love that proves impossible in the real world, but Brontë goes much further than most English novelists in actually dramatising an alternative to ordinary experience. Walter Scott is another English novelist who writes romances, but he writes from the perspective of society. In *Waverley* (1814) he contrasts the romantic, if violent, life of the Highland rebels and the more moderate manners of the English. There is a reverence for the heroism and idealism of the Scots, but such values are seen as belonging to the past. Scott's sense of reality undercuts his sense of romance.

This tension between romance and reality is present in many novels. Cervantes's *Don Quixote* (1605–15) presents Quixote on what he thinks is an important quest, but shows how he is repeatedly caught up in the farce of everyday life. Romance suggests that it is possible to escape to a more purposeful life, but Cervantes mocks this ideal of a better, more heroic life. Yet the romantic ideal is always attractive to writers, even if they only use it as a make-believe alternative to reality, because it does convey the idea of the possibility of a life that is exciting and meaningful. European novelists tend to undercut the romantic ideal; American novelists, however, tend to take the romantic dream seriously, often presenting characters who have turned their backs on society to embark on a search for a different sort of life.

This desire for an ideal world and a better way of living is seen in its most extreme form in the **utopian novel**, such as William Morris's *News from Nowhere* (1891). Utopian novels present a perfectly ordered society where all the problems of the real world have been eliminated. This is, however, more than simple day-dreaming:

often the intention is that this should reflect back on the imperfections of the existing world. In **fantasy** literature and **science fiction** we again have the creation of make-believe worlds. The informing impulse can be to present a world where the problems of ordinary life are transcended and where the characters can live a more heroic or more ordered life. Some fantasy novels, though, especially tales of the supernatural – as in the **Gothic** novels which flourished in the late eighteenth century – concentrate on the more sensational side of romance; they depart from the social world, not to seek an ideal goal, but to explore the irrational passions of the mind.

Stream of consciousness. A technique which seeks to record the random flow of impressions through a character's mind.

Some writers, whom we can refer to as **psychological novelists**, offer a very full impression of the mental life of their characters. One way of achieving this is to allow the character to speak in the first person, either through letters, as in Richardson's *Clarissa* (1748) and Alice Walker's *The Color Purple* (1982), or directly, as in Charlotte Brontë's novels *Jane Eyre* (1847) and *Villette* (1853). But the novelist can present a third-person analysis of a character's thoughts, as is the case in George Eliot's novels. Towards the end of the nineteenth century, however, there developed an increasing awareness of the complexity of the human mind; this new awareness of inner feelings led to the eclipse of the intrusive omniscient narrator, for if one acknowledges the unique character of every mind then it becomes impossible for any one person to provide an authoritative view of experience. A move away from omniscience is evident in the novels of Henry James, who, as in *The Portrait of a Lady* (1881), offers long passages of introspection and self-analysis by the main character.

In James's novels, though, the thoughts are ordered and logical. There is an immense leap from James's practice to

> My missus has just got an. Reedy freckled soprano. Cheeseparing nose. Nice enough in its way: for a little ballad.

These are some of the phrases flowing through the mind of Leopold Bloom in Joyce's *Ulysses* (1922). When students first come across writing like this they naturally find it baffling. It seems as if anything can be included, as if the untidy abundance of the phrases is all that matters. Indeed, in theory this is how a stream-of-consciousness novel should be, presenting nothing except a chaos of jumbled phrases.

In practice, however, most stream-of-consciousness novels do not operate like this. The almost forgotten novelist Dorothy Richardson offers the purest form of stream of consciousness, consisting of just the random impressions of a mind. In her novel *Pointed Roofs* (1915) we really do seem to encounter the disorder of the mind rather than the order of art. In the novels of Joyce, Virginia Woolf and William Faulkner, though, the flow of ideas does have some pattern, and there are larger elements of structuring, for stream of consciousness is only one aspect of their novels. The overall organising principle of Woolf's *To the Lighthouse* (1927), for example, is the idea of a trip to the lighthouse. There is a tension in the work between the way everything disintegrates into the characters' isolated consciousness and the possibility that they might visit the lighthouse together. Similarly, Joyce's *Ulysses* presents all the complexity of a Dublin day and all the untidiness of the characters' minds, but this is set against the organising frame of the Ulysses story. In the course of the novel Stephen could be said to meet his spiritual father in Bloom, just as the original Ulysses story deals with a reunion between father and son. In both novels characters come together and are united in a significant way. Both novels thus hold the diffuseness of life in tension with the possibility of some overall order, and therefore significance, in life.

The principal point about stream of consciousness, then, is that it is a method that acknowledges how complex and chaotic the human mind is, but it is used in novels where the writer is still engaged in the novelist's traditional activity of trying to find or create an order and meaning in the confusion of experience. *Ulysses* might well exhaust us with the complexity of its method as we try to follow a character's thoughts, but an ideal of order and a significant story are present as a pattern in the background.

Style. Style means the writer's characteristic manner of expression. What in the end distinguishes one writer from another – so that the experienced reader could identify a passage as coming from, say, a Lawrence novel – is the style. Styles change from age to age, but every novelist has his or her own 'voice'. A critical approach that looks closely at style is a productive one, for the style of a novel reveals the author's attitudes, and from a small section of the text we can infer a great deal about the work as a whole.

Here are several short passages describing characters. The first is from D. H. Lawrence:

> In feeling he was developed, sensitive to the atmosphere around him, brutal perhaps, but at the same time delicate, very delicate. So he had a low opinion of himself. (*The Rainbow*, 1915)

The sentences add one impression after another, rather than presenting a detached analysis. The emphasis is on feelings and emotional characteristics, on the internal psychology of the man. The colloquial, repetitive style aids this impression of getting at the heart of the person. We begin to see the way in which Lawrence concentrates on the emotional side of life, how people are composed of contradictory impulses and desires, and how Lawrence is sympathetic to such a character.

George Eliot, in contrast, seems to speak in the voice of society:

> The face was large and roughly hewn, and when in repose had no other beauty than such as belongs to an expression of good-humoured honest intelligence. (*Adam Bede*, 1859)

The style is detached and educated. Eliot judges by external characteristics rather than plunging into the character's soul. She offers standard social judgements, and this begins to indicate her general stance as a novelist – that is, as a confident, reasonable, educated observer of human affairs.

Thomas Hardy's style can resemble Lawrence's:

> Eustacia sighed: it was no fragile maiden sigh, but a sigh which shook her like a shiver. (*The Return of the Native*, 1878)

The emphasis is on emotional characteristics, making us feel that Hardy is a novelist who probably sympathises with the discontented individual. Yet at other times his style is a sort of awkward parody of Eliot's, as if he cannot shake off a social perspective. In fact, Hardy's style presents problems, because it is inconsistent, but generally the division between an emotional and a social style is one of the easiest ways of categorising novelists. If novelists write in a polite, literary manner they are, on the whole, speaking from the point of view of society. If, however, they are more sympathetic to the social rebel they will probably write in a less polite style.

One aspect of this is that novelists such as Lawrence and Hardy will employ far more imagery and metaphor in their writing than, say, Eliot, as they are often trying to express a feeling that cannot be expressed in rational language. They can only hint at such ideas through metaphor. For example, in Charlotte Brontë's *Jane Eyre* (1847) the heroine describes her feelings when happiness suddenly turns into misery:

> A Christmas frost had come at midsummer; a white December storm had whirled over June; ice glazed the ripe apples.

To say she is unhappy would not be enough; figurative imagery is required to suggest a state of mind which cannot be expressed in straightforward terms.

In discussing style, then, the starting-point can be whether it seems like polite, social discourse or whether it is more emotional. We might, however, encounter a comic voice, but this also gives us a clue to the direction the novel will take. Or the style might be convoluted and intricate, as in Henry James's later novels, such as *The Wings of the Dove* (1902). The explanation for such a style is that the writer is aware of the complexity of experience and therefore indicates in his or her writing how difficult it is to describe and present reality. Once we have got an initial idea of the manner of the writer, the various stylistic choices within a passage will fall into place in relation to this governing idea. (*See also* Language and style, p. 150).

Twentieth-century novels. Modern novelists can be divided into those who continue within a broad tradition of realism and those who experiment far more with the form of the novel. Writers such as John Galsworthy, Arnold Bennett, Graham Greene, Iris Murdoch, Doris Lessing, Ernest Hemingway, John Updike and Saul Bellow are essentially realists. They are less intrusive than nineteenth-century realists, presenting a credible picture in which we are not particularly aware of the narrator's presence. They deal with social, personal and ethical problems, and offer us an entertaining yet at the same time instructive look at how people cope with life in the twentieth century. The outstanding novelist within this tradition is D. H. Lawrence, whose novels conform to the usual pattern of presenting characters at odds with society, but Lawrence goes much further than other writers in a romantic quest for an alternative way of life. He feels that there must be a new way in which people can relate to each other. However, in his best novels, *The Rainbow* (1915) and *Women in Love* (1921), as committed as Lawrence is to exploring fresh areas of experience, writing in an emotional style that suits his subject matter, he never forgets that his characters are bound by all the demands of ordinary existence.

The other major novelists of the century all employ the same basic pattern of individuals in conflict with society or their families, but the most noticeable feature of many great twentieth-century novels is the extraordinary degree of formal experiment and innovation. This begins with the works of Joseph Conrad and Henry James. Conrad often uses a dramatised narrator, Marlow, and sometimes disrupts the time sequence of events. James's late novels, such as *The Wings of the Dove* (1902), repeat the story he had been writing for years of innocent young women coming in contact with a corrupt society, but become more and more elaborate, with extremely long sentences where it is often impossible to trace the line of thought.

The reason for such innovations was the disappearance of shared values and shared beliefs. George Eliot writes confidently, as if she and her readers can share a view of the world, but at the end of the nineteenth century this confidence disappeared. A new awareness of individual psychology came into existence at this time. It began to be realised that everyone has a unique perception of the world. Conrad, therefore, employs a fallible narrator, who presents his own limited view of the experiences he describes, and in James's novels the sentences become confusingly long as he acknowledges that it is impossible to provide a definitive analysis of experience.

Such changes in thinking have two overlapping consequences for the novel. There is far more emphasis on the mind of the individual, something that is most apparent in the technique of stream of consciousness: a new way of writing that reflects a new view of the human mind (*see* p. 124). The other consequence is that many of the great novels of this century advertise their own fictionality. Joyce's *Ulysses* (1922), for example, is written in a sequence of different styles: there is the world and various styles that try to make sense of the world, but each style is inadequate and incomplete. In the works of such writers as Joyce, Viriginia Woolf and William Faulkner there is thus a mixture of the exploration of characters' minds and a way of writing that draws attention to itself.

Whereas the realistic novelist presumes to read the world, the experiments in fiction this century instead draw attention to the ways in which fiction tries to structure experience, for reality is always beyond the grasp of the text. This can become an arid approach if the writer is simply concerned with discussing the nature of fiction, but in Joyce, Woolf and Faulkner such an approach is effective because the technical experiments are prompted by a genuine awareness of life's complexity. Their oblique method of writing draws attention to itself, but in doing so does indirectly offer us a new view of the world.

This awareness of the problematic relationship between art and life continues to be a major characteristic of much of the best contemporary writing. It perhaps reaches its most extreme form in the French *nouveau roman*, where, as in some novels by Robbe-Grillet, we can even be deprived of a plot and characters to hold on to, so that we have none of the conventional fictional devices for making sense of life. Rather more accessible is the work of Vladimir Nabokov, who constantly draws attention to the fictionality of his novels. Many other contemporary novelists play with art and life in this way, but possibly the most original English-language novelist since Joyce is the American writer Thomas Pynchon. *Gravity's Rainbow* (1973) is a novel about the Second World War: the novel endlessly tries to structure and understand the chaos of war, but every time it holds out a promise of coherence or a thread of order it destroys it. A novel such as *Gravity's Rainbow* might not be easy to read, but this is because it is suggesting that the world cannot be read. Yet the novel also acknowledges the human refusal to concede to chaos, and how we are constantly engaged in trying to order and understand life. We might be aware of the disorder of life, yet we none the less strive to arrange life into a coherent story.

A similar sense of the complexity of the world and the neatness of narrative is encountered in **magical realism**, the generally accepted name for a kind of novel originating in South America: writers who have been referred to as magical realists include Gabriel Garcia Márquez (Colombia), Mario Vargas Llosa (Peru), and Alejo Carpentier (Cuba). Perhaps the single most celebrated magical realist novel is Márquez's *One Hundred Years of Solitude* (1967). The novels of Salman Rushdie, for example *Midnight's Children* (1981), can also be described as magical realism. Like most modern literature, magical realism reflects the ontological uncertainty of our times (ontology is a branch of philosophy concerned with the nature of being). Magical realists no longer share traditional realist fiction's confident assumption of our ability to understand and describe the world. In a variety of ways, their novels challenge the traditional perception of an ordered and coherent world which underpins realist fiction's pretensions to reproduce reality in literature. A conventional linear plot might be abandoned, the stance of the traditional, omniscient narrator might be shunned, or, at the opposite extreme, the narrator might flaunt his or her presence, the novel might reflect at length on the nature of fiction, or a novel might accord the same status to the world of the mind as that of the physical and social world. But what is most likely to strike the reader in magical realism is the bizarre nature of the events and stories that are included in the plots, many of them calling upon and exploiting myth. Implicit in such inventiveness is a questioning of the rational cultural tradition of the West: the narratives mimic, subvert, exaggerate and parody the ways in which Western European culture has used the novel to make sense of experience. But it amounts to more than a critique of the West: magical realism challenges Eurocentrism by expressing a Third World experience and drawing on local cultural traditions. At the heart of many of the works is resistance to the dominant culture imposed by Western imperialism; and at that point we realise the political force and engagement of such texts, that they are attempting to make sense of the experiences of Third World countries in terms which are not dictated from outside. (The best analysis of Eurocentrism is Edward Said's, in *Orientalism* (1978), where he illustrates how, over the course of two centuries, Islamic culture has been distorted and misrepresented by Western commentators, who have presented prejudice and the ideological agendas of imperialism in the guise of objective analysis.) The label magical realist can also be applied with some justice to the work of an East European novelist such as Milan Kundera, who plays with narrative in ways not unlike those of South American novelists and whose works also constitute a political challenge to an imposed order, in his case the former Communist regime of Czechoslovakia.

The sense of a political challenge leads us on naturally to the work of **feminist novelists** such as Angela Carter, Alice Walker, Toni Morrison, Jeanette Winterson and Margaret Atwood. But in various ways the central, and most radical, writer in women's fiction in the twentieth century remains Viriginia Woolf. Both in her novels, such as *Mrs Dalloway* (1925) and *To the Lighthouse* (1927), and especially in her essay *A Room of One's Own* (1931) and her later novels, such as *The Years* (1937), Woolf sees the need for women and fiction to challenge boundaries and a social system that limits and defines women and men into feminine/masculine, emotional/rational roles. Woolf's vision of a new sort of writing by women has its critics, but it opened up the possibility of a whole series of changes which would not only see women writing a diversity of fiction but also the possibility of re-reading women novelists from earlier centuries from a feminist perspective. It should make us realise that more is involved in feminist writing than the production of fiction. Many feminist writers are also literary critics or are engaged in the writing of feminist criticism. Their writings as novelists and as critics are intended to be complementary. Their project is nothing less than a sea-change in the position of women in society and literature. In order to grasp this point fully it is necessary to think about the way in which women have largely been excluded from the literary canon, from the traditional list of 'great authors'. It is only really with the advent of feminism and feminist writing that we have come to see how limited that canon was and how it has been built around white male writers. Feminism has opened the door onto a vast new range of literary experience from all sorts of groups of people previously excluded from the syllabus. What the feminist novel does is make us realise again how the world is structured, but, as with magical realist fiction, it also has the great strength of not just despairing at the state of the world but also offering us something positive by carrying within it a sense of challenge and renewal, the possibility, however utopian, of restructuring the world.

5

Critical concepts

THE previous sections of this book have dealt with traditional terms, such as 'tragedy' and 'sonnet', which are used in relation to one of the three major genres of literature: poetry, drama and the novel. In studying English, however, you will come across a number of terms and ideas which refer to a broader aspect or quality of literature. This section lists some of the most commonly used terms and also deals with terms which are used in relation to more than one genre. Most of the definitions are very short, but we have devoted more space to such important concepts as allegory, form and content, irony, language and style, metaphor, satire and structure.

In addition to such terms, we have also included in this section a number of terms associated with modern theories of criticism and recent ideas about the place and function of literature. Modern criticism has introduced a great many new terms: we have sought to include those, such as contradiction, desire, ideology, patriarchy, subject and text, which are central to recent critical thinking and which link up with the discussion of critical theory in the next section of the guide. You may well find it useful, therefore, to read some of the entries in this section in conjunction with section 6.

Affective fallacy. In *The Verbal Icon* (1954) Wimsatt and Beardsley drew attention to what they saw as a common error in poetry criticism. Critics, they suggested, confused the poem with its results or emotional effect upon themselves, paying too much attention to the personal feelings and memories it conjured up. They called this 'the affective fallacy'; as an alternative they advocated a more objective form of criticism which would attempt to describe and analyse the text in a detached way. Their view is open to objections – a poem cannot be totally separated from the reader's response –

but for practical purposes it is wise to follow their advice. Their position is the standard one in academic critical practice: you will be marked down if you become too subjective or personal in your response. It is better to concentrate on the text itself, trying to analyse how the poem works, rather than describing your own feelings as you read a poem.

Allegory. An allegory is a work which has a meaning behind the surface meaning. For example, Bunyan's *Pilgrim's Progress* (1678) is more than just an account of the hero's adventures; because of his name, Christian, and because of the nature of his experiences, we recognise the text as having a more general significance as an allegory of the Christian's journey through life.

A great deal of medieval literature is allegorical, the underlying meaning always being religious. This is because the allegorical way of thinking is one in which the everyday world is seen as an imperfect reflection of the divine world. Things on earth are only an imperfect shadow of the true pattern, so any account of worldly experience is informed by this awareness of a more fundamental significance behind the surface of things. The kind of story employed in allegory, be it in prose narrative, poetry or medieval morality plays, is often a quest narrative of someone's journey through life. Such a mythic story is well-suited to a mode that attempts to deal with universal facts and forces. In reading an allegory we are aware of the ideal religious order behind the text, but our attention is usually held by the disorderly trials and tribulations the hero or heroine experiences that indicate the gap between the ideal pattern and the nature of life in this imperfect world.

The last two great religious allegories are Spenser's *The Faerie Queene* (1596; *see* p. 31) and *The Pilgrim's Progress*. An allegorical manner of thinking died out in the course of the seventeenth century as Western Europe moved from an essentially religious to a secular view of experience. From that point on allegory ceased to be a way of perceiving life and became merely a mode that writers could employ. This is evident in such works as Swift's *Gulliver's Travels* (1726) and George Orwell's *Animal Farm* (1945). Both writers use allegory not to point to some greater truth but for the purpose of political and social comment. They tell bizarre stories, involving absurd and corrupt characters, but we can see that there are disturbing parallels with the real events of their day. Allegory of this kind is a favourite mode of present-day writers in countries where free speech is restricted and where any political comment has to be veiled and indirect. Such political allegory is, however, quite unlike that of earlier works which are informed by a belief in God's divine order.

Allegory differs from symbolism (*see* p. 68) in that in allegory there is a fixed meaning behind the surface meaning. In symbolism the meaning behind the surface meaning is elusive and cannot be translated into other terms. In allegory we can state confidently what the precise meaning is that lies behind the surface, because we are meant to see through the text to its underlying significance.

Allusion. An allusion is a passing reference to a person, place or event beyond the obvious subject matter of a text, or a reference within a text to another literary work. Allusion enhances or complicates a text: an instructive or interesting parallel is drawn with another area of life or literature. When the writer looks out to life, history or literature, our sense of the immediate events being described is modified by this reference. A love poem, for example, might incorporate a phrase from Shakespeare's tragedy *Othello*: by including this allusion to a work which deals with love and jealousy, the writer might be adding a tragic dimension to the view of love being offered in his or her own poem. Of course we might not always spot the allusions, but when we do they add to the complexity of the meaning of the work we are reading.

Ambiguity. Ambiguity refers to the fact that words can often have several meanings, thus making us uncertain what is meant. It became established as a widely used critical term with the publication of William Empson's *Seven Types of Ambiguity* (1930). Empson pointed out that different views can often be taken of what the words mean in a line of poetry. He extended the concept to cover any verbal nuance which gives room for alternative readings.

Ambiguity is central in poetry because poetry deals with the complexity of experience: the writer tries to confront and understand an experience, but ambiguity acts as a counterforce to this organising impulse. As one word suggests various or opposed meanings we come to feel how life burgeons beyond the absolute control of the writer. The words have an indeterminacy which can help incorporate within a poem a sense of the indeterminacy and complexity of life.

The instinctive critical reaction, particularly if one is just beginning to study poetry, is to search for a single meaning in a
poem, a clear statement of what it is saying. Criticism is not, however, really concerned with searching for a simple, reductive interpretation of a poem, but instead acknowledges the complicating
effect of imagery and the levels of ambiguity that can exist in a text.
This is a matter of seeing how the poet uses language to indicate
the complexity of the experience he or she is trying to understand.
We should attempt to reverse our instinctive attitude of looking for
one meaning in a poem in favour of seeing that the language of
poetry is full of conflicting, ambiguous meanings. The danger in
such an approach is that everything can be represented as ambiguous and the plain sense of the poem can disappear unless one
remembers that ambiguity is concerned with complexity of meaning in the words, not with improbable meanings of the poem as a
whole.

Aporia. Aporia is a term taken from Greek rhetoric and was traditionally used to describe a figure of speech in which a speaker or
character deliberates on an irresolvable question. The term has, in
recent years, been taken up by deconstructive critics.

Hamlet's famous 'To be or not to be' soliloquy is an example
which we might well see as an extended series of doubts and
questions all arising out of the opening aporia: 'To be or not to be,
that is the question.' In the soliloquy, Hamlet is struggling to arrive
at a conclusion about how he should act, but the opening statement sets up an impasse of meanings that prevent him from reaching any resolution or conclusion. Hamlet's situation is that he has
been ordered by a ghost that resembles his father to avenge his
murder by killing his stepfather Claudius but by not killing his
mother Gertrude. The Ghost's contradictory commands place
Hamlet in a double-bind, a situation where he has both to act and
not act. Discussed in these terms, aporia moves beyond its original
sense and starts to approach the sense in which it is used by
deconstructive critics, where it indicates a point where we are faced
not by a simple choice of readings but by a plurality of 'undecidable'
meanings or where a 'gap' or lacuna opens up between what a text
wishes to say and what it is constrained to say. The deconstructive
critic is centrally concerned with looking for the aporias, blindspots
or moments of self-contradiction where the text begins to undermine its own presuppositions. In the example from Shakespeare,
we are describing a deliberate effect in the text associated with a

particular moment or speech, but in the examples sought by deconstructive critics the effects are not so much deliberate as an indeterminacy in the text. It is this indeterminacy of meaning which the deconstructive critic focuses on, showing how language always moves beyond and eludes fixity. (*See also* Binary opposition and Contradiction, pp. 136, 138.)

Archetype. An archetype is a basic model from which copies are made. It can be argued that at the heart of all works of literature are certain simple patterns which embody fundamental human concerns, the primary concern being the place of people in the natural world. The most basic archetype, a story of death and rebirth, expresses the fond hope of human beings that they can find a pattern in human life that resembles the pattern of nature. Other basic archetypes are the story of a journey through life and the story that deals with a search for a father. The most interesting work on archetypes has been produced by a Canadian critic, Northrop Frye. An awareness of archetypal patterns has two benefits for the student of literature: it can help us see the informing concerns of literature, how similar problems are returned to again and again; second, if we can see the underlying pattern of a text it helps us appreciate what writers add to the basic pattern in order to make their work distinctive.

Binary opposition. The phrase binary opposition refers to two mutually exclusive terms such as left/right, man/woman, nature/culture. The concept is one of the underlying tenets of structuralism: structuralism argues that such oppositions are basic to all cultural phenomena, to everything from language to cooking. More narrowly, structuralism argues that meaning itself is relational in this way: that is to say, we only know the meaning of the word 'left' by virtue of its contrast with the word 'right'. In effect this means that language, like culture, is built on a self-contained system of interrelationships.

What structuralism initially sought to achieve, in the 1960s, was an almost scientific analysis of the codes and conventions operating in literature. Its very premises, however, have been challenged by deconstructionist critics who argue that meaning is not oppositional in the way structuralists assume. Structuralism maintains, for example, that the terms nature and culture are external to each other; deconstruction argues that such terms are never isolated or single or pure: there is always a trace of the other term in them. In other words, deconstruction seeks to undo the binary oppositions set up by structuralism, emphasising the plurality of differences rather than difference fixed as opposition. An example should clarify the point. In Shakespeare's play *Titus Andronicus*, there is a struggle between the Romans and the Goths: a structuralist reading might analyse the play in terms of an opposition between Roman nobility and Gothic barbarity; a deconstructionist reading might point to the way these terms invade each other and how each shows traces of the other, so that, in the end, we cannot decide the difference between nobility and barbarity. There is a further aspect of the structuralist position: it sets up its oppositions in a hierarchical way. This means that in the man/woman opposition, for example, the first term, 'man', is seen as positive (or privileged), the second, 'woman', as negative (or subservient). Feminist critics have used this opposition to show the way in which patriarchy has constructed women as negative and marginal; the feminist critic can then go on to deconstruct the opposition to reveal its instability.

Carnival. The idea of carnival in literature has become important through the work of the Russian critic Mikhail Bakhtin. By carnival, Bakhtin means the way in which popular humour subverts official authority in classical, medieval and renaissance texts and culture: for example, the feast of the ass in the medieval church when an ass was taken into church and the clergy brayed out their responses, or the ceremony of the boy bishop when a choir boy replaced the bishop in the service. Carnival overturns the established hierarchy and sets up a popular, democratic counter-culture. In the place of repressive seriousness comes laughter. A single voice is challenged by a plurality of voices. Familiar examples are Bottom and his fellow actors in *A Midsummer Night's Dream*, and Falstaff and his cronies in *Henry IV, Part One*.

The question of voice, however, goes beyond carnival. Bakhtin argued that all utterances are **dialogic:** they all imply a situation of dialogue or are directed at a listener. In addition, they are all **polyphonic**, that is made up of several voices. Whenever we speak we use words and phrases that have circulated through other conversations, those words and phrases carrying with them traces of the meanings of those conversations. The importance of these points lies in their implications for the novel and for language itself. The novel for Bakhtin is the dialogic form, the genre of literature which is open, and in which, as in carnival, the voice of authority is disrupted by other voices in the text. More broadly, language itself is open to constant redefinition as different classes struggle for control over it: for example, the meaning of the word 'liberty' is something that changes depending upon who is doing the defining. Bakhtin's work clearly has implications for novel criticism, and also for political criticism in general in its ideas about the text as a **site of struggle** between authority and popular culture. The notion of the text as a site of struggle is widespread in contemporary criticism: it shifts authority away from the author to those forces acting on, and within, the text from society and politics.

Contradiction. Contradiction occurs where we are faced with two or more meanings that cannot be reconciled or resolved. To this extent it overlaps with ambiguity (*see* p. 134), but there are important differences. Critics such as Empson tended to use ambiguity to demonstrate the richness of the texts being discussed. Contradiction, however, which has become a central term in poststructuralist criticism, points to incoherences or divisions in a text that undermine its apparent stability.

The idea of contradiction is often used by critics when exploring the politics or ideology of a text. For example, in her reading of *Jane Eyre* as a contradictory text, Mary Poovey demonstrates how the novel both challenges and supports contemporary social ideas about gender and class. The aim of such criticism is to reveal how the text is built on and reproduces divisions in the values, ideas and beliefs of the society that has produced it. Both feminist and Marxist critics are interested in such divisions in literary texts because they expose the ways in which the seeming order of texts is deeply troubled by irreconcilable impulses. The idea of contradiction is also used, however, in a narrower and more specialised way by deconstructionist critics. Deconstruction starts from the premise that language itself is an endless chain of meanings that cannot come to any fixed, final position: it is an endless chain in which final meaning is always deferred and differential. For this reason, texts can never be coherent or stable. The task of the deconstructive critic is to pursue within the text the **aporia**, or contradiction (*see* p. 135), that undermines its seeming unity, and to show how the text's meanings are, in fact, 'undecidable'. This does not represent a negative view of the text; on the contrary, deconstructionist critics are interested in the intricate play of language in and between texts. J. Hillis Miller, for example, one of the leading exponents of deconstruction, suggests how Shelley's poem 'The Triumph of Life' is full of echoes and allusions of other texts so that it can never be reduced to a single, univocal meaning or reading.

There is one further complication: the French philosopher, Jacques Derrida, the main proponent of deconstruction, uses the ideas of contradiction and the deferral of meaning in language to attack what he calls **logocentrism**. Logos means word and also concept, so what Derrida is criticising is the way in which Western philosophy has tried to make meaning seem full, unified and immediate, centring upon an ultimate principle or **presence**. He attacks the desire for what he calls the **transcendental signified**, for a stability of meaning which derives from outside language. For Derrida there is only language and *différance* – that is, meanings which are always differential and deferred.

Différance is a central concept in deconstructive thinking and involves a number of ideas simultaneously: it includes difference, divergence, delay and deferral of meaning and of reference. Derrida coins the term in order to get away from the idea of there being fixed differences in language as proposed by Saussure and structuralists; where they argue for a system of binary oppositions, Derrida sees a constant sliding between meanings and a plurality of differences in which opposites always bear traces of each other. (*See also* Binary opposition, p. 136)

Conventions. A literary convention is a feature of a text which is in evidence in a large number of texts. For example, there are many poems written in fourteen lines and rhymed according to an established pattern. We call all such poems sonnets. The term 'sonnet', like all literary terms, identifies a particular convention, in this case a conventional form of poetry: the length is conventional, there are conventions about where a change of direction occurs in a sonnet (either after eight lines or after twelve), and the rhyme scheme of sonnets follows one of two conventional patterns. In addition, the subject matter is often conventional: sonnets are most commonly love poems.

Such conventions, both of form and subject matter, are found in all works of literature. All writers accept a traditional framework and operate within its broad rules or conventions. What we are interested in as critics is how the writer makes his or her work distinctive within this received pattern. This is the theme of the previous three sections of this book, which discuss the literary terms we use to describe the major conventions of poetry, drama and the novel, and indicate some of the ways in which a writer can create something new within an established format.

Desire. A term used in psychoanalytic criticism, primarily associated with the French psychoanalyst and theorist Jacques Lacan, whose work has had a considerable influence on feminist criticism and post-structuralism generally.

In order to grasp something of what Lacan says (much of his writing is extremely opaque), we need to know about Freud and the Oedipus complex. Oedipus, in classical literature, killed his father and married his mother. Freud used this story as a model to explain human desires as the child passes from infancy to adulthood. The child, Freud argued, to pass successfully into society, must abandon the desire for an incestuous relationship with its mother, submit to the law imposed by the father and transfer the affections felt for the mother onto another. In the case of the male child, the threat that hangs over it is castration if it continues to desire the mother. The child must move out of the triangular family into a world where it is no longer the centre.

Lacan takes Freud's theory about the child and desire and rereads it in the light of contemporary ideas of language. According to Lacan, the child of 6–18 months enters the **Imaginary**, pre-Oedipal period. This is a period of illusory unity and mastery of its world. Subsequently the child acquires language and enters into what Lacan calls the **Symbolic Order**, that is the order of social and cultural life and language. This entry into language is the equivalent of the Oedipus crisis in Freud's theory: in Freud, the child begins to fear castration; in Lacan, the child becomes aware of its own difference and also of meaning through difference. Submitting to the symbolic order of language, the child now comes under what is called the **Law of the Father**. In the Symbolic Order the child becomes a subject, that is a figure who calls itself 'I' but who is not the originator of meaning since meaning resides in the language the child has learned. The child, now excluded from 'imaginary' unity and mastery, experiences as a result of its construction in language the loss of existence as pure organism, and it is this lack which begets desire in the subject. This desire (a sort of symbolic castration) creates the unconscious in the subject.

Central to Lacan's analysis are the ideas of the split human subject with its desire for unity, and the idea of the unconscious being structured like a language. It is these ideas which critics have exploited and also modified in various ways. Thus, for example, Julia Kristeva argues that the pre-Oedipal period is characterised by the **semiotic**, a kind of language of babble which does not disappear when the child enters the Symbolic Order: indeed, it becomes evident whenever the order of language is disrupted. As is the case in all post-structuralist thinking, both language and identity are thus characterised as unstable. If we consider a novel such as Thackeray's *Henry Esmond*, in which the hero eventually marries a woman who has acted more or less as a mother to him throughout the text, the framework of recent criticism enables us to look beyond the mere oddness of this (and beyond the kind of biographical approach that would attempt to psychoanalyse Thackeray's mind), and relate it to a broad argument about history, politics, gender, the construction of the self in language and the ways in which the Victorians thought about ideas of the subject.

Part of the difficulty of explaining Lacan's ideas lies in the plurality of some of the terminology. For example, in discussing lack and desire Lacan writes of '*manque-à-être*' which can be translated both as 'lack in being' and 'want-to-be'. A similar complication occurs with the term 'other': with a lower case 'o' 'other' here means other people or things or places (*see also* p. 143). However, 'Other' with a capital 'O' is the imagined source of meaning and truth (language): it is, variously, the unconscious, the analyst, God. In Lacan the subject constantly seeks for unity with the imagined source of truth, with the 'Other'. But because this 'Other' is not available, the result in the subject is unassuaged desire, a desire occasioned by its own lack.

Didactic. In everyday usage didactic means 'teaching a lesson'. As applied to a literary text, however, didactic means a work dealing with a moral or religious or philosophical theme. Thus a great deal of medieval literature can be described as didactic because it is concerned to explain the mysteries of Christianity.

It is often argued that the aim of literature is 'to teach and delight'. This should not be taken too literally: students sometimes wrongly assume that what they are supposed to look for are the

GOT IT !!!

moral messages in a text. The commonest complaint of all examiners is that students have failed to see the implications of the questions set. This is because they have failed to see the implications of the texts. The examiner wants you to demonstrate how an author creates a complex impression of the issues raised by his work, not to say it has a simple moral message. A poet such as Chaucer, for example, is often underestimated as a writer because it is assumed that his main purpose in *The Canterbury Tales* (about 1400) is to offer simple moral judgements about the pilgrims who tell the tales rather than to create a rich comic world of confused moral values.

Discourse. The term discourse is used in a number of different ways. On page 108 of this guide we use it in the sense of the language and texture of the writing in a novel. This is the usual meaning of the word when applied to discussions of narrative: it describes 'how' a text is written, not the content (some critics reserve the French spelling *discours* for this meaning). To some extent this first usage overlaps with the second, more specific use of the term by the French philosopher and historian, Michel Foucault, whose work has been very influential on post-structuralist criticism.

The first thing to be said about Foucault's use of the term discourse is that it is always related to concrete examples of language being used in specific areas of knowledge. For example, Foucault argues that madness, sexuality and criminality are all discursively constructed: each of them is an example of the way in which in different historical periods human behaviour is shaped by a specific vocabulary and knowledge. But there is more to his argument than this. Foucault maintains that specific discourses such as medicine, law and psychiatry serve specific interests, and that power and control of the human subject are exercised in discourse. More particularly, discourse is a way of classifying and ordering. We can see this more clearly if we look, as Foucault does, at the history of madness and how knowledge is used as a power to control and define those who are then labelled as mad. The point here is that language operates in the interests of the institutions of society to construct people in certain ways. It is not only power, however, but also resistance to power that is embedded in each discourse. It is not possible, in other words, to have a discourse which simply maintains the status quo. The power which is inscribed in discourse is shadowed by resistance to that power which is also inscribed in the discourse.

For example, in Shakespeare's *The Tempest*, Prospero has been deposed as duke and now rules an island where he has taught a figure called Caliban how to speak. But Caliban resists Prospero's white colonial rule and uses his knowledge of language to curse him. The play shows the way in which Prospero's colonial rhetoric contains the seeds of its own failure as well as its fear of that which is 'other'. The term **other** is used in a number of ways in post-structuralism: here it is used to describe the way in which groups of people characterise outsiders who threaten them as 'other', in this case as non-human. Racism is a practice, for example, that operates by categorizing ethnic groups as 'other', as outsiders, as threatening, as alien. At work here is the way we use discourse to divide reality up into binary opposites – black/white, man/woman. As Foucault reminds us, however, it is discourse that masters and divides us and only seems to put us in control of the world. It is we who are the sites of discourse and constructed by it.

Empathy and sympathy. Empathy means 'feeling into', becoming totally absorbed in and physically participating in an object. For example, in 'Ode to a Nightingale' (1820) Keats shares in the ecstasy of the bird's flight away from mundane reality and for a moment is totally caught up in its existence.

Sympathy means 'feeling with' the emotions and state of mind of, for example, a character in a play. The most obvious device for creating this effect is the soliloquy where the hero addresses us alone on stage. Drama, however, traditionally engages our sympathy at one moment, then distances us the next. As a result we find ourselves both involved in the issues of the play but also able to see them in a wider setting. Thus, for example, while we may sympathise with Hamlet in his soliloquies, we may also feel horror or antipathy at his killing of Polonius. When reading a novel or play we shall often find ourselves sympathetically involved with the characters, yet at the same time we should try to maintain a degree of critical detachment.

Fancy and imagination. Coleridge, in his literary autobiography *Biographia Literia* (1817), argues that fancy and imagination are two distinct mental processes producing two distinct types of poetry. Fancy he associates with light verse, but all serious, passionate poetry comes from the imagination. He values the imagination so highly because he sees it as a faculty which can unite separate elements: 'It dissolves, diffuses, dissipates, in order to re-create: or where this process is rendered impossible, yet still at all events it struggles to idealise and unify.' The idea that is really being stressed here is finding an order in the disorder of experience. Seventeenth-century writers, and all earlier writers, know that the only true source of order is God. Eighteenth-century writers such as Pope, on the other hand, seek an order in society as well as in religion. Romantic writers such as Coleridge, Wordsworth and Keats seek their source of order in the mind with the imagination serving to create order and unity in experience. Yet, as the quotation from Coleridge makes clear, this often proves impossible, so that in romantic poetry there is frequently a tension between an ideal of order and the failure of the imagination to cope with the disorder of life.

Form and content. Content is *what* is said in a literary work, form is the *way* in which it is said. Strictly speaking, form and content are inseparable: there is no paraphrasable content in a text which we can separate from the way in which it is presented. We can, however, summarise the subject matter or theme of a text. In fact, producing a short summary is a useful starting-point in criticism, for we then have a base from which to consider the two sorts of formal choices a writer makes when developing his or her subject matter.

First, there is the overall form adopted within the genres of poetry, the novel and drama. The writer might, for example, decide to present his or her material in the form of a sonnet, or, if writing a play, he or she might decide to write a tragedy. Such a choice involves certain limits: a sonnet has fourteen lines, a tragedy usually ends with the death of the hero. By deciding what kind of poem, novel or play he or she is writing, the author has opted for a certain type of pattern in the work. The writer still, though, has considerable freedom within this structure. He or she might modify the overall pattern that is being used, but far more important is the second kind of formal choice made: the line-by-line decisions about what words to use.

To take a simple example: a poet might be declaring his or her love. Once we have seen that this is the theme we can then move on to describing how the poet actually writes about the emotion. We need to look at the overall structure employed: if it is a sonnet, we need to say something about how the brevity of the form is exploited. We then need to look at the other formal choices made; here we have to look at the individual lines, trying to decide why certain words were chosen, why the poet decided to write in a particular way. We also need to look at the imagery employed, attempting to describe the effect it creates within the poem. Our formal analysis does not have to be exhaustive: if we note the overall structure and the imagery employed it means that we have identified the central formal characteristics of the work. The all-important point, however, is to make a connection between these formal features and the content of the work. It is never enough, for example, to say that 'this poem contains various images connected with the sea'. We must go on to say how such images contribute to the overall effect of the poem: we must justify their presence. At the end of this process we should have a clearer idea of what the poem is saying, but only because we have attempted to describe how it says it.

This kind of analysis in which we discuss the relationship between what is said and the way it is said is variously called formal analysis, practical criticism, and critical appreciation. Most often it involves looking at a poem or a piece of prose or an extract from a play which the student has not read before. The purpose behind such exercises is to get you into the habit of reading closely. Such an approach, however, is also the main critical method you are expected to employ in writing essays and doing examinations. Indeed, the question that is asked most frequently in examinations, however it is phrased, is 'What is this author writing about and how does his or her way of writing relate to what is being said?' In other words you are asked to discuss the relationship between the content of the book and its form.

Hermeneutics and interpretation. When we look at a text we are trying to interpret what it means. Interpretation is concerned with clarifying the meaning of the work by analysing its language and commenting on it. This is what we normally do both when we write an essay and when we do such exercises as practical criticism.

Hermeneutics, by contrast, refers to the general theory of interpretation, the procedures and principles involved in getting at the meaning of texts. What we say about a text depends to a large extent upon our ideas about what we are looking for. Traditionally most critics have assumed that the correct meaning of a text is the one the author intended. Recent critical thinking, however, has emphasised both the extent to which the reader possibly creates the meaning of the text and also the inadequacy of all interpretations. These issues are discussed more fully in the section 'Critical positions and perspectives' (*see* p. 165).

Ideology. In a general sense, ideology means the beliefs, concepts, ways of thinking, ideas and values that shape our thoughts and which we use to explain or understand the world. More precisely, we can define ideology as the system of beliefs or ideas of an economic or political system. This second definition takes us towards Marxist criticism where the term ideology is central. Marxists argue that in any period human understanding is constructed by ideology. For example, in the middle ages the standard view was that humanity was fallen as a result of the sin of Adam and Eve. In our own time the dominant ideology is that of the property-owning class, the bourgeoisie. Marxists argue that ideology is the expression, or the 'superstructure', of the economic system, or 'base', and that our beliefs and values reflect, in a complicated way, the economic/class system we live under. The function of ideology, they suggest, is not to reveal these conditions but to disguise the real relations between the classes, to disguise the real power relations in society. What this means, in effect, is that ideology serves the needs of the dominant class. It does this by ensuring that subordinate classes believe they share the same interests as the ruling classes. Ideology thus seeks (invisibly) to make social relations appear natural and, by gaining the consent of the subordinate classes, to bring about political control or **hegemony**.

Marxist criticism is as much about history and politics as it is about literature, and so, inevitably, it is also interested in how change occurs if ideology works in the way described above to keep the ruling classes in power. The point is that ideology may set out to disguise the power relations by presenting them as natural or normal or desirable or safe, but it cannot finally disguise the problems or contradictions that exist within it. It cannot, for example in Shakespeare's *Coriolanus*, convince the citizens that everything in the state is well-ordered when they have nothing to eat and the nobles have stores of grain. At this point, gaps appear in the dominant ideology of Rome, the belief that the citizens enjoy the efforts of the nobility on their behalf. We can see in this example how texts not only reproduce the dominant ideology of a period but also how they often foreground the gaps and problems in that ideology.

The question of ideology in contemporary literary criticism has been much influenced by the ideas of the French Marxist philosopher Louis Althusser. He argues that ideology is not just a set of ideas that shape our thinking, but the common sense we learn when we learn language, so that it makes us the subjects we are. In other words, it is ideology that constructs us and which allows us to recognise our identity as individuals. We are never in a position to choose ideology: in a sense it chooses us. Althusser also argues that ideology is not just an abstract set of ideas but actually has a material existence in what he calls the state apparatuses or the social institutions: the family, the church, schools, the law. All institutions play a part in the ideological formation of the human subject. Althusser's ideas clearly have far-reaching implications both for the study of institutions in literary texts – for example, how marriage is presented in the novel – and for cultural studies in general.

Intentional fallacy. In *The Verbal Icon* (1954) Wimsatt and Beardsley drew attention to a number of misleading ways of interpreting literature which they called fallacies. The most important fallacy they identified was the intentional fallacy: this is where the critic seeks to interpret the text in the light of what he or she believes was the author's aim. They saw this as misleading because it diverted attention away from the text itself to external matters such as the author's life or state of mind when writing the work. They argued that the meaning of the work lay solely within the words on the page and that the author's intention is irrelevant in criticism. While not everyone accepts all their ideas, the general approach they recommended – of concentrating on the work itself, discussing the effect rather than trying to identify the author's intention – is the standard and accepted approach in academic criticism.

Irony. Irony is a way of writing in which what is meant is contrary to what the words appear to say. Pope, for example, might praise someone extravagantly in his poetry, but the terms used can be so extravagant that they signal to the reader that the person referred to does not deserve such praise.

One effect of such verbal irony with its contrast between fine phrases and sordid reality is that the writer can suggest the gap between how things might be and how they really are. The author seems to write from a position of detachment, sharing with the reader a private joke at the expense of the person ridiculed. In this way irony is superior to the follies of society, and it is therefore not surprising that irony is common in satiric writing: Dryden, Swift, Pope and Johnson are the satiric writers who most consistently adopt an ironic stance, and Swift is often praised as the finest ironist in English. As in *Gulliver's Travels* (1726) and *A Modest Proposal* (1729), which might seem to advocate the eating of babies as a method of population control in Ireland, Swift often uses an **ironic persona**, an invented narrator who is smug, self-confident or foolish. The irony is at the expense of the narrator, who is used to express all manner of foolish social ideas and prejudices. The touch of excess in the narrator's manner signals to us that his views are suspect: the detached author and reader both look down on his folly and that of the society he speaks for. Yet satiric writers such as Pope and Swift are not really detached, for they are disturbed by the fact that people can be so foolish.

In satire we encounter irony as a specific method that the writer can employ, but the 'New Critics' (*see* p. 180) expanded the meaning of the word, identifying irony as an informing attitude in good poetry. Their idea is best understood if we imagine a totally non-ironic poem in which the poet expresses his or her views honestly: the author has something to say and says it. It can be argued, however, that a good writer is aware that there are a great many sides to any issue, and so good poetry is always ironic as the author always undercuts any straightforward statement of his or her views: the tone is ambivalent, as in the poetry of John Donne, where we are never quite sure whether he is being comic or serious.

This view of poetry can be criticised in that it seems to favour witty, detached art that refuses to commit itself to any position. Yet the New Critics do draw attention to an important characteristic of irony, which is that the ironist does not necessarily write from a confident position but can be baffled by life's complexity, and this can explain the refusal to adopt a straightforward stance. In satire, irony might appear to serve a didactic purpose – a confident writer instructing us how to behave – but irony can reflect the writer's awareness that there is a discrepancy between how one person might view things and how they might be viewed from other angles or in a different context.

Irony of this kind is common in novels. Novels often feature people who take themselves terribly seriously, but the narrator, adopting an ironic manner in which he or she seems to take them seriously too, will often be laughing at the characters. This does not mean, however, that they are simply to be dismissed for their foolishness. The point is that for these characters their predicaments are serious, but viewed from another angle their lives are absurd. The author is not committing himself or herself to a single view: on the contrary, the author relies upon irony to imply that there is no simple way of summing up an experience, that there is no single correct perspective. Irony, then, can be a method of conveying a sense of the complexity of life because it undercuts any statement that appears to sum things up too glibly.

This applies equally to good satiric writing. The emphasis so far has been on how Pope and Swift as satirists use irony to mock folly, but it is often difficult to pinpoint an authorial position in their work as their irony is extremely devious. In Pope's poetry we can never be really sure what he is seriously saying; this is how it should be, for it would be yet another version of social folly if Pope were to believe that he is in possession of the one view of reality which is the correct one. Swift lashes projectors of schemes and proposals; it is unlikely that he would be naïve enough to believe that he has a superior view of what needs to be done to reform society.

Distinct but related forms of irony are **situational irony** and **dramatic irony**. Situational irony depends upon a discrepancy between how characters see a situation and the true nature of the situation. In Conrad's *The Secret Agent* (1907) the central character believes that his wife loves him, but in reality she only married him to provide for her retarded brother. Again we see the discrepancy between one way of viewing things and how the same situation might be seen from another angle: the individual perception of truth is shown as inadequate. In dramatic irony we know more than the characters on the stage or in the novel know. We see that they are going to encounter problems because their perception of the facts is inadequate. In both these forms of irony, then, as in verbal irony, the events are always more complicated than any individual can grasp or understand.

To sum up: when a writer uses irony it is a way of drawing attention to the gap between how things seem and how complicated they really are. In satire irony serves to ridicule the follies of the world, yet it can also indicate that the writer is not committing himself or herself to a single-minded interpretation of reality. In novels and plays irony is often used to reveal the inadequacy of the characters' view or grasp of events. In every case, however, the effect of irony is one of detachment, with the reader being placed in a superior position of judgement, able to see the full play of events and made aware of the complex nature of life where all views are partial or faulty.

Language and style. In talking about literature we are, directly or indirectly, talking about language and the way in which language is used. It might seem easier to concentrate on the content of a text, but we can never ignore, or at least should try not to ignore, the fact that literary texts are built out of words. I. A. Richards (in, for example, *Principles of Literary Criticism*, 1924) and others who have attempted to construct a general theory about the language of literature have drawn a distinction between 'ordinary' language and 'literary' language. 'Ordinary' language refers to such things as newspaper reports, where the emphasis is on conveying information. In literature, however, they argue, language is used in an 'emotive' way – that is, in a skilful way to arouse an emotional response in the reader.

The validity of such a distinction can be questioned. It can be argued that all writing is 'literary' and that even the journalist makes artistic choices about how to phrase and present material. In addition, the idea that the language of literature is somehow special creates enormous problems for the critic, for it suggests that we are trying to describe something rather intangible and elusive. The use of the word 'emotive' in particular tends to encourage the idea that a discussion of literary language is concerned with the emotional effect a text has upon a reader rather than with the meaning of the words.

A much more productive and precise way of talking about the language is to concentrate on style. This involves describing how a particular piece of writing functions and discussing what words are used and why. How, though, do we set about discussing style, what can we say about language? The answer is simple and straightforward: the style of a text is always appropriate to the subject. After reading one of D. H. Lawrence's novels, for example, we might feel that he is interested in the emotional life of his characters: a discussion of his style then becomes a matter of looking at how he finds a way of writing that manages to convey these emotional qualities. The method, then, is to summarise what the text is about, to say what its basic content is, and this provides us with a starting-point for discussing its style. Thus, for example, when we read Wordsworth's poems we might sense that he often celebrates the natural world: when we have seen this is what he is writing about we can then proceed to an examination of his style, the ways in which he uses language to create the appropriate sense of joy and wonder. The secret really is that we have determined in advance what we are looking for: we have seen what the author's subject is and then turned to the words used to see how they match this subject. An ability to talk about style depends mainly upon taking a conscious decision to look at a text's language, but we cannot analyse how the words create the appropriate mood, feeling or idea unless we have already arrived at some idea about what the subject matter of the work is.

Our stress so far has been on the practical question of how to discuss the language of a text, but the whole issue of language and literature can be approached at a different level. The emphasis of a great deal of twentieth-century criticism has been on the idea that language, far from being just a tool the writer uses to put forward his or her ideas, actually creates the content of a text. This is the emphasis of 'New Criticism' (*see* p. 180), but some subsequent thinking, in a structuralist and post-structuralist vein (*see* p. 190), has suggested that there is nothing outside language in a literary text, that, while literature may appear to refer to the real world, it is in fact a self-contained thing concerned only with its own artifice. This leads to a type of criticism which concentrates almost totally on the way in which the language of the text works. Because such criticism dismisses the referential dimension of language (what the text says about life) as illusory, it tends to focus on the way in which literary texts are very self-conscious, discussing their own use of language. You might find such an approach unappealing and hard to grasp, and there is obviously no reason why you should adopt this view of literature. Appreciation of a text's style, however, is something that should be fairly central in your critical approach. It is never enough just to talk about the content of a work of literature: you should always try to see how the author uses language to create a full impression of his or her subject matter.

Metaphor. A figure of speech in which one thing is described in terms of another (e.g. wafer thin). A simile is very nearly the same, but, whereas metaphor identifies one thing with another, a simile involves the notion of similarity, using the words 'like' or 'as' (e.g. as thin as a rake).

Hamlet's famous soliloquy begins,

> To be, or not to be, that is the question:
> Whether 'tis nobler in the mind to suffer
> The slings and arrows of outrageous fortune,
> Or to take arms against a sea of troubles
> And by opposing end them.

Hamlet is trying to decide which is the nobler course of action, suffering the blows of fortune or fighting them. The third and fourth lines both employ metaphors: 'outrageous fortune' is described in terms of 'slings and arrows', and 'troubles' are described in terms of 'a sea'. The subjects (or tenors) of the metaphors are 'fortune' and 'troubles', the figurative terms (or vehicles) which describe them are 'slings and arrows' and 'a sea'. Language is being used figuratively to make the ideas vivid. Rather than talking about Shakespeare's use of metaphor we could just as validly describe this as his use of figurative imagery; it is just that metaphor identifies a particular figure of speech, while imagery is a more comprehensive term.

The obvious attraction of metaphor is that it makes an idea vivid: it can prove difficult to grasp the thread of an abstract thought, but when the idea is described in concrete terms it comes to life. This is the basic appeal of metaphor, but there is far more that can be said about the device. Indeed, some critics have suggested that metaphor is the most important device in poetry. This is because of the way in which metaphor adds to and enriches the meaning and weight of poems or indeed plays written in verse, such as Shakespeare's. Thus Hamlet's 'troubles' are only his personal feelings of unhappiness, but, by associating his feelings with such large and chaotic subjects as warfare and the sea, the individual experience is linked with vast and important aspects of life. Within the space of a few lines a writer, through metaphor, can thus seem to incorporate within a text concerns that go beyond the stated subject matter, with the result that a poem or passage in a play that might essentially be an expression of personal emotion can appear to be a huge statement about human experience.

Another aspect of metaphor is that it demonstrates how a writer can respond to the complexity of experience, for metaphor is an ordering or reconciling device that enables a writer to establish connections between different areas of experience. This can be seen at its most extreme in the use of **conceits** in metaphysical poetry (*see* pp. 24 and 45). A conceit is a far-fetched metaphor, making very unexpected and unlikely connections: for example, in one of his poems Donne compares himself to a besieged town. Such conceits demonstrate clearly the way metaphor works: its logic rests upon finding similarity in dissimilarity, so that disparate and hitherto unconnected things are brought together.

Metaphor is in fact central to any notion of poetry that sees it as an art form concerned to confront a disordered and baffling world, for metaphor allows the artist to connect dissimilar areas of life. In writing about 'outrageous fortune' Shakespeare is dealing with a chaotic aspect of life, but he manages to confront the idea by connecting it with another chaotic facet of life, warfare. We are struck by the way in which the writer can, even in a baffling world, perceive and establish connections.

It can also be argued, however, that, rather than establishing some pattern of connectedness in a baffling world, metaphor can work in the opposite direction, breaking up the conventional ways in which we think about the world. Metaphor can be said to create an effect of **defamiliarisation:** that is, it can be said to challenge our normal way of thinking about things, restructuring our perceptions. This and the idea put forward in the previous paragraph might seem incompatible, but the common thread is that metaphor is a device for making connections, for ordering the world, even if it sometimes does it in an unexpected way that jolts us out of our usual patterns of thinking and perceiving. Indeed, metaphor is such a central device in poetry because it acknowledges the diffuseness of experience and yet reveals the human desire to organise and make connections.

As it is so central, many critics have attempted to work out a more precise and technical theory about the role of metaphor in literature. The most important contribution in this area has come from the linguist Roman Jakobson. Jakobson builds upon the difference between metaphor and a related rhetorical figure, **metonymy.** Metonymy is a figure of speech in which the name of an attribute of a thing is substituted for the thing itself (e.g. 'the crown' for the monarchy). Metaphor works on the basis of connecting different areas of experience, while in metonymy there is already a connection between the words. In his expansion of the contrast between the two, Jakobson suggests that, while some texts, such as realistic novels, tend to favour metonymy, poetic texts, which can include certain novels, rely more on metaphor. In the metonymic text there is an attempt to create an illusion of life, while in the metaphoric text we are more aware of the play of language and how baffling experience is. One of the benefits of Jakobson's work is that it moves beyond just talking about the role of metaphor in poetry and begins to suggest a way of talking about both poetry and prose. A book which illustrates how Jakobson's theories can be put to use is David Lodge's *The Modes of Modern Writing* (1977).

Motif and theme. The theme of a work is the large idea or concept it is dealing with. In order to grasp the theme of a work we have to stand back from the text and see what sort of general experience or subject links all its details together. The easiest way of doing this is to sum up the work in as few words as possible. For example, we can say that the theme of Shakespeare's *Macbeth* is evil. We might feel that this is the theme of several of Shakespeare's plays, and we should be right. Many texts do have the same basic theme, and all texts deal with common or familiar themes. What we are interested in as critics is the particular way in which the theme is handled in a particular text: we move from the general to the distinctive.

A motif is much smaller: it is a type of incident or image that occurs frequently in texts. For example, a common motif in poetry is the idea of making love while there is still time and before death comes (the *carpe diem* motif, meaning 'seize the day'), which Marvell uses in his poem 'To his Coy Mistress' (1681).

Paradox. A paradox is a self-contradictory statement. For example, in his sonnet 'Death be not proud' (written about 1600, published 1633) Donne writes, 'Death, thou shalt die.' The statement is paradoxical because we cannot reconcile the idea of death with the idea of Death dying in any logical way. A paradox is used because this is the only way in which Donne can come to terms with the difficult Christian idea of life after death. Paradox gives us a sense of the writer getting on top of complicated ideas, but only just. (Conceit, *see* p. 23, functions in a similar way.)

Paradox became established as a widely used critical term with the publication of Cleanth Brooks's *The Well Wrought Urn* (1947). Brooks argued that it was not only metaphysical poetry such as

Donne's that used paradox but that the language of poetry is itself the language of paradox. By this he meant that poetry, far from offering us simple statements about life, always acknowledges the complexity of experience which the writer seeks to reconcile through his or her language. Like many 'New Critics' (*see* p. 180), Brooke believed that the main way in which the writer managed to bring opposites together and so create a unified whole was through paradox. Paradox in a work always suggests an attempt to confront and come to terms with the contradictions of experience. At the same time, because it is such a self-conscious device, paradox also always suggests a sense of strain, a sense that things cannot be ordered in a logical, rational way but only by a deliberate effort.

Pathetic fallacy. A term invented by the nineteenth-century writer John Ruskin, who objected to the way in which poets attributed human feelings and actions to natural objects. For example, Ruskin disliked Coleridge's description of a leaf 'That dances as often as dance it can' ('Christabel', 1816), because it is false or fallacious: leaves cannot dance. What Ruskin could not see was the effect of the description: the landscape is made to reflect the mood of the poem by this metaphor. The poet is not primarily interested in the leaves as such, but in creating an image.

The same is true of personification. Here, as in Keats's 'To Autumn' (1820), an abstract concept is given a human shape and actions: autumn in Keats's poem is seen as a woman reaping and gathering the harvest. Personification makes the idea seem solid so that we can grasp and understand it, but it also serves to relate the season to human life so that the theme becomes relevant to us.

Patriarchy. A central concept in modern critical thinking, especially in feminist criticism. A patriarch is the male head of a family, and a simple definition of patriarchy is that it means rule or government by a man, with authority passing through the male line from father to son. This definition, however, excludes the political implication of patriarchy, which is that it is a social system of rule that ensures the dominance of men and the subservience of women. Two related ideas follow from this: patriarchy means that the relations between the sexes are not just personal but also political, and it also means that the relations between the sexes are built on inequality. A way of summing-up these ideas is to use the American feminist Kate Millett's phrase 'sexual politics'.

Central to most feminist criticism is the view that Western culture and society are male-centred, and that women are made subordinate in every area of life: the family, the state, in law and in religion. In all these areas, women are usually defined only by reference to men, and usually in a negative way: negative because women are implicitly defined as lacking male authority, male power, and, most of all, lacking male sexual organs. Patriarchy, feminists argue, privileges masculine sexuality, especially the male phallus as the symbol of power. What is meant by this is that patriarchy regards being masculine and possessing a penis as the norm, and builds the social order around masculine sexuality: the term used to describe this is **phallocentricism:** that is, centring on the idea of the superiority of the phallus.

Patriarchy, however, goes even further than this. Not only does patriarchy involve the subordination of women but it is also a social process or conditioning whereby women come to accept in their thinking the idea of male superiority. In addition to this, feminists have pointed out that the concepts of **gender** (that is, the features thought of as making up masculinity and femininity), largely reflect the thinking and bias of patriarchy. Sex is a matter of biology, of anatomy, of being male or female; gender, on the other hand – what is feminine or masculine – is a matter of culture, and in Western society this has always meant patriarchal culture. Patriarchy defines the masculine as active, rational and brave, and the feminine as passive, quiet and emotional. In other words, it constructs stereotypes. One branch of feminist criticism, referred to as **gender studies**, explores the different meanings attached to masculinity and femininity in literature, history and culture.

Feminists also argue that patriarchy constructs the literary canon, the so-called great authors and great books. They point out that literary criticism has not only been dominated by male assumptions and ideas but also chosen to study and praise texts that reflect male interests. It has chosen texts where women are **marginal** or **oppositional** and men are central and heroic. This feminist analysis has a number of consequences. As well as 're-reading' many of these patriarchal texts – Shakespeare is often referred to as the patriarchal bard – feminists have shown how literature written by men often presents women in simple antithetic terms: as idealised virgin figures and pure, innocent angels, or as demonic temptresses, witches, and Eve figures who deceive men. Secondly, feminists have not just re-read the canon but also turned towards

gynocriticism, that is towards criticism that focuses on women as writers, as distinct from the feminist critique of male authors. Gynocriticism is also concerned with rediscovering women writers who have been devalued by the male literary canon, and with developing critical theories and practices for women. Elaine Showalter, who invented the term, describes gynocritics as 'the history, styles, themes, genres, and structures of writing by women; the psychodynamics of female creativity; the trajectory of the individual or collective female career; and the evolution and laws of a female literary tradition.'

A third consequence is that feminist critics have also been concerned with the question of a specifically female/feminine mode of writing, what the French feminist Hélène Cixous calls *écriture féminine*. This involves the idea of a woman's language, a language opposed to patriarchal language by its diversity and multiplicity, a language where fluidity opposes the order and logic of standard writing where women are assigned to the margins. It is from the margins that feminists have not only contested patriarchy but also permanently changed the critical and literary landscape. This is evident in the range and diversity of courses and books on feminist issues, in the study of women writers, in a general and widespread reconsideration of many 'classic' texts, and also, and just as significantly, in the study of black authors, of gay and lesbian literature, and in the ever-increasing flow of new writings from people previously excluded by patriarchy.

Readerly/writerly. In his book *S/Z* (1970) the French structuralist critic Roland Barthes drew a distinction between two basic types of text: the readerly (*lisible*) and the writerly (*scriptible*). The readerly work is one that we passively consume because it seems to offer us a real world of characters and events. We do so because its language seems transparent, acting as a sort of window through which we can see the world. The writerly text, however, forces us to produce its meaning rather than consume it. Because the text (as in the case of Joyce's *Ulysses*, 1922) constantly draws attention to its own status and procedures as a verbal artifact, we are made conscious of language's role as a mediator between us and reality. Thus, whereas the readerly text seems eminently readable, the writerly text seems to focus attention on how it is written.

Barthes's distinction has been taken up and widely applied by structuralist and post-structuralist critics (*see* p. 190) since it provides a useful framework for talking about the differences between realistic novels and more self-conscious works of fiction. Yet, as Barthes himself demonstrates by his analysis in *S/Z* of an essentially readerly story by Balzac which he discusses as a writerly text, the distinction is not an absolute one. The critic, in fact, is free to regard any text as extremely self-conscious and read it either as a readerly text or as a writerly one. Indeed, a great deal of recent novel criticism has concentrated on the ways in which a realistic novelist such as George Eliot is as much interested in the problematic relationship between art and life as a writerly novelist such as Joyce.

Satire. Satire is a mode of writing in which social affectation and vice are ridiculed. The satirist mocks errant individuals and the folly of society, the purpose being to correct conduct. The golden age of satire in English was the late seventeenth century and the first half of the eighteenth. Great satirical works have been produced at other times, but satire flourishes best when there is a consensus of opinion on how people should behave. The common feature of all satirical works is that they present a picture of people in society, and by exaggerating or distorting the picture draw attention to how people often act in an outrageous or absurd manner. Human beings are presented as motivated by lust: lust for sex or money or power, or all three. The satirist, who can express his or her views in a poem, play, novel or essay, writes from a stance of moderation, aiming to correct vice and folly.

In considering a satiric work we need, first, to be aware of its targets: who or what is being attacked. It will always be some form of social folly that is in evidence. By the same token, the satirist will always be in favour of moderation and responsible behaviour. The focus of our analysis should be upon the method of the text: how the writer creates a vivid and disturbing impression of a society that has lost its sense of responsible values. There are, however, times when we might also feel that the satirist is half in love with what is being ridiculed: the writer might criticise outrageous behaviour, but is also fascinated by the spectacle of human folly.

Satire is obviously a form of comic writing, but the distinction between satire and comedy is that, whereas the satirist wishes to correct conduct, comedy takes the view that all human conduct is absurd and self-interested. In practice the dividing-line between the two is often uncertain. Dickens is a comic writer, but his works include a great deal of incidental satire, and great satirists, such as Pope and Swift, can seem to move beyond satire when they become self-mocking, recognising the limitations of their own moral convictions. (*See also* Irony, p. 147; on individual satirists – Jonson, Dryden, Pope, Swift and Peacock – consult the Author index.)

Semiotics. Semiotics means the study of signs. Morse code is a simple sign language in which the dashes and dots represent letters. It is possible to say that everything in life sends out a coded message in a similar way: that clothes, body gestures, our social rituals all convey shared meanings to other people within our culture. Semiotics is concerned with looking at this conveying of meanings. Some of the most persuasive semiotic analysis has been concerned with popular culture: for example, Roland Barthes's essay on professional wrestling in his collection of essays *Mythologies* (1957). In literary criticism semiotics is concerned with the entire signifying-system of the text and the codes we need to be masters of in order to read it. The general characteristics of such an approach to literature are more fully defined in the entry on structuralism (p. 190), to which semiotics is closely related.

Structure. The structure of a text is its overall shape and pattern. This is sometimes referred to as its form, though strictly speaking form is a more inclusive term which embraces every aspect of the work's technique.

There are two basic types of pattern found in poetry, generally referred to as **imposed form** and **organic form**. Imposed form is a pre-existing format: most poetry before about 1800 is written within received patterns, such as the sonnet form, because it was recognised that the particular forms were suitable for certain subjects and certain ideas, and the writer worked within these limits. The good writer, though, always manages to say something new even within the conventional structure. This respect for traditional models was at its height in the eighteenth century, a writer such as Pope despising originality and preferring to imitate or even rewrite classical poems, yet in the line-by-line texture of his work there are always plenty of ways in which he reveals his individuality.

Around 1800 there was a move away from using traditional structures in poetry: in imposed form the ideas are fitted into the structure, but with the romantics, such as Wordsworth, Coleridge and Keats, we see the introduction of organic form where the structure of the poem follows the ideas. The exploratory, irregular shape of the romantic ode as opposed to the symmetrical pattern of a seventeenth-century ode is a good example of what is meant by organic form. The distinction between the two approaches is, however, not absolute: artists can modify the imposed form they are using, while organic forms are not as free as they seem, for the shape of traditional structures is always evident behind them.

The terms 'organic' and 'imposed form' really only apply to poetry, but there are also traditional patterns to be found in drama. Both comedy and tragedy have their conventional structures – comedy ending in marriage, tragedy with the death of the hero or heroine – and all plays follow a standard format of exposition, complication and resolution. The novel, on the other hand, is a freer form, but even here certain structural patterns, particularly the pattern that follows the central character's progress towards maturity, are repeated.

All these patterns are discussed in detail under the definitions of literary terms in the previous three sections of this book, where we have attempted to describe the structure of every major literary type. It is useful to be aware of such patterns because so much of our response to literature depends upon recognising what the writer adds to the basic pattern he or she takes over from earlier writers. If we can identify a text as belonging to a certain class or mode of writing, or if we can see that its structure is more innovative, as in the case of the romantic ode, then we are well placed to make a number of initial, confident statements about the general character of the work we are studying. In turn this provides a base from which we can move forward saying how the work is distinctive. In other words, we can move from looking at the overall structure of the text, its general pattern, to looking at the line-by-line texture of the writing, examining the particular details of the work. Every text shares a number of larger features with other texts, but it is in the individual lines and sentences that the writer says and does something new. Our job as critics involves both recognising the general characteristics of the work and seeing how the writer adds something to the traditional pattern that is being used.

Subject. Most post-structuralist critics reject the idea of the individual and prefer to talk about the subject. The individual (woman, child, man) is a concept that comes from traditional humanist thinking. Such thinking sees the individual as autonomous, as consciously and fully in control of language and meaning, indeed as the author of meaning. This view has been questioned by post-structuralist critics who see the human subject not as the author of meaning but as the product of it. This leads to the idea of the human subject not as the centre of meaning but as interpellated (i.e. created by language or ideology).

The choice of the term subject is not accidental. It carries both grammatical and political meaning. In the political context, the subject is literally in the subject position, that is obeying and subject to the power structures of society. In grammatical terms, the subject is author of the verb: literally, the subject is the speaker who says 'I'. Post-structuralists argue, however, that there is a split between the actual speaker who says 'I' and the 'I' that is spoken in the sentence. The point of this is that the stress falls on how the subject is unstable and constantly being reshaped (and, as such, open to change: contemporary criticism disputes fixed terms such as 'human nature' because they presuppose things will always be the same). At the same time, post-structuralists often draw attention to how the subject thinks it is in charge of meaning and at the centre of control. This, it is argued, is one of the illusions of Western culture and our political tradition, to make the subject believe it is the author of meaning.

The concept of the subject is of interest both to Marxist critics and to psychoanalytic critics, though from different perspectives. Whereas Marxists see the subject in a political manner, as constructed by ideology or the political ideas and values of society ('I am made what I am by the values I have been given by society'), psychoanalytic critics see the subject split by the entry of the child by means of language into the **Symbolic Order**, that is into the order of social life and culture (*see* p. 140). We can apply both approaches to Dickens's *Great Expectations*, in respect of which we can argue either that Pip reflects the values of a society built on the manipulation of people and money, or that, as Pip looks back over his life, he seems to be divided from the innocent child who could barely read the names of his dead family on their tombstones in the novel's opening scene. Behind the political notion of the subject lies the work of the French Marxist Louis Althusser (*see* the entry on Ideology, p. 146). The major influence on the psychoanalytic approach to the subject has been the French psychoanalyst Jacques Lacan (*see* the entry on Desire, p. 140).

Syntax. Syntax is sometimes used loosely to mean grammar. 'Grammar', however, is a much wider term than syntax, involving the study of every aspect of the system of language. Syntax, on the other hand, is concerned with the placing and relationship of the units of language within sentences. More simply, syntax refers to the way in which word order affects meaning.

Most sentences follow a pattern of subject, verb, object. This is the normal syntactic structure of English, which we all recognise just as we all recognise when a sentence departs from this pattern. Indeed, almost the first thing we notice about poetry is the way in which the sentences are written, how the words are arranged differently from ordinary, everyday usage. Such departures from the usual syntactic pattern often involve the inversion of natural word order either for the purpose of emphasis or to draw our attention to the contrived nature of the utterance. For example, a poet such as Pope consciously manipulates his syntax when he arranges his sentences in neat antitheses: we are struck by the witty way in which he writes. Such deviations from ordinary language should not, however, be regarded as abnormal, for they are an important part of the conventional nature of poetry and one of the ways in which it manages to compress meaning and achieve its effects. In *Paradise Lost* (1667), for example, Milton makes extensive use of inversion in order to create an elevated feel in the language matching his elevated subject. Everything is invested with an extraordinary degree of grandeur; the language deals with large concepts of heroic dimensions, but the syntax, too, plays its part in this, for it is never ordinary or mundane.

There are, as we might expect, many technical terms for describing syntax. One feature which it is useful to be aware of is the difference between **hypotactic** and **paratactic sentences**. A hypotactic sentence is one using subordinating conjunctions (such as 'when', 'how', 'which', 'though'), which serve to create an involved, complex structure where we have to follow the sense through a series of subordinate clauses. A paratactic sentence, on the other hand, is one where the clauses are joined together by such words as 'and', 'or', 'but', with the result that the sense is altogether much simpler to follow. Both types of sentence can be found in Milton's sonnet on his blindness, 'When I consider how my light is spent' (1652), where the structure of the first eight lines is hypotactic, while the rest of the poem is paratactic. The result is a striking contrast between the poet's struggle to make sense of life and the idea of God's order.

We could, however, spot this contrast in the poem without knowing the correct terms for describing it. Knowing the technical terms is less important than trying to be aware of the way in which writers arrange words and phrases in a sentence so as to create certain effects in their work. Two complementary points help here. First, sentences which are simple in construction suggest that things are straightforward, while convoluted sentences suggest that the poet's mind is in turmoil. Second, contorted or complex sentences in a poem will often disrupt or break down the patterns of the poem. Thus, for example, the Shakespearean sonnet usually divides into three quatrains and a final couplet, but these divisions may be breached by the syntactic patterns of the poem, resulting in a much more complicated effect. Syntax, then, can either help reinforce our impression of order in a work or emphasise the sense of the poet struggling with the disorder of life.

Text. In contemporary criticism the word text has by and large replaced the term 'literary work' for a number of specific reasons. First, 'work' implies the ideas of an author, authorial control, and the idea of aesthetic completeness. Modern theory, however, sets itself against assumptions which give authority over the meaning of the text to the author rather than the reader. This is what is meant by Roland Barthes and other theorists when they speak of **the death of the author**, that the idea of authority and meaning resting with the author is no longer tenable. Secondly, the term 'work' privileges literature at the expense of other writing and suggests it has some special power or truths to deliver. By contrast, in recent theory the term 'text' covers all forms of writing, as well as photographs, records, adverts; indeed, anything that can be read as a text, including the world itself. We can, that is, insist on the textuality of almost everything.

The issue, however, goes one step further if we bring in the notion of **intertextuality:** this refers to the way in which one text echoes or is linked to other texts either by direct quotation and allusion or simply by being a text. To this idea we can add the concept, associated with the American deconstructionist Harold Bloom, of the **anxiety of influence:** the suggestion is that writers have to wrestle with the writers that come before them in a sort of Oedipal mixture of love and rivalry. Bloom argues that writers always 'misread' their forebears, whom they then try to correct by their own writing. Bloom then extends this idea to the whole process of making a reading, so that all readings of all texts become misreadings or **misprisions**. As with contradiction (*see* above), we must recognise how such a critical position is the exact opposite of traditional criticism: whereas traditional criticism sees the critic's job as one of interpretation and evaluation (with some traditional critics trying to define the author's intention), post-structuralist approaches deny the possibility of 'accurate' reading and emphasise instead the critic's role as one of creative misreading.

6

Critical positions and perspectives

THE preceding sections in this book have concentrated on literary modes and the critical vocabulary conventionally employed to help us discuss them. This section, however, takes a broader view, looking at the whole activity of criticism and some of the ways in which critics, particularly twentieth-century critics, discuss literature. It should become clear that what a critic says about a book depends to a large extent upon the critical approach he or she adopts. As a student of literature you are likely, consciously or unconsciously, to be influenced by some of these critical approaches. Before dealing with such complicated matters, however, it seems logical to look at some basic questions.

(i) *What is literary criticism?* Literary criticism has traditionally been regarded as the analysis, interpretation and evaluation of literary works: it does not mean 'finding fault with'. Criticism as an academic activity expresses the reader's sense of what is happening in a text.

(ii) *What are the basic guidelines?* As criticism starts with the reader's response it would be possible to produce impressionistic criticism in which you wrote about your feelings, perhaps saying how moving you found a poem or how it reminded you of something in your own experience. Academic criticism, however, must be more analytic than this, commenting on the subject matter and method of the text. Criticism thus involves spotting the central themes of the work and then seeing how the text presents and develops these themes. In order to begin you have to decide, in the broadest terms, what the text is about, what kind of experience, feeling or problem is being examined; you then have to look at how the text brings its subject matter to life, and this should in turn lead you to a fuller sense of what the text is about. In starting to build your closer analysis of the text you have to show how the various choices the author has made – for example, the details included or the words chosen – serve to develop what you perceive to be the central issue. Your critical account becomes something more substantial than a mere summary or description the moment you begin to highlight some of the distinctive ways in which a text develops and presents a theme.

(iii) *Is there a correct view of what a text is about?* No, there is not, and it is this fact that makes the study of literature both difficult and fascinating; the text is a source of endless speculation, argument and debate. When students start to study literature it is very often the case that a teacher or lecturer provides them with a very clear guide to the meaning and method of a text. A moment's thought, however, will lead you to realise that this is just one person's analysis. Another reader might take a different view of what is the central theme of the text; or, while agreeing about the central theme, choose to emphasise other aspects in different sections, and this could lead to a very different overall impression and analysis of the text. To this extent it might appear that all criticism is purely subjective, as if every reader will see a text in his or her own way, but a critical response is also conditioned by the social and cultural context within which the book is read. For example, up to and including the eighteenth century the main view of literature was as 'pleasurable teaching', and criticism was concerned with how the text achieved its moral effect upon the reader. In the romantic period the emphasis changed. The romantics stressed the importance of the individual, and, consequently, much of the focus of romantic criticism was on the unique value of what the individual author had to say. This can be called an expressive theory of literature – it concentrates on what the author says or expresses – and is still a widely held view. Indeed, many readers could see little point in studying literature if they did not believe that the author has something profound to communicate to us.

As the following pages seek to make clear, however, it is precisely this view of literature that contemporary criticism has turned its back on. Recent years have seen a rejection of the idea of the author as the source of meaning in literature (some critics refer to this as 'the death of the author', *see* p. 163), and the development of broader critical objectives. One way of summing up these changes is through a consideration of the term 'critique'. A critique is not just an analysis of what a text means, but is concerned with the cultural or political or psychological conditions that helped produce or 'write' the text. It is also concerned with why certain texts are singled out for criticism, and how 'criticism' itself constructs the meaning it finds. These are complicated matters and, before going on to them, it may be helpful if we look at the question of modern criticism in a broader way under two further headings.

(iv) *What are the main features of twentieth-century criticism?* Twentieth-century criticism as a whole can be characterised as displaying a shift from an emphasis on the author to an emphasis on the text, and then a shift from the text to the reader. It is the second of these – the shift from the text to the reader, showing how the reader might collude with the assumptions of the text, or impose meanings on it, or find what he or she wants to find in it – that much modern criticism, starting with structuralism, concentrates upon. In a lot of modern criticism there is a questioning of all the strategies by which meaning itself is produced, a questioning of all the conditions that surround the production of literature. This might seem to make for a rarefied and abstract criticism, but as the entries below, starting with feminist criticism, should show, such criticism can lead to an important discussion about how society is structured, about our place in society, and, in more general terms, about how, as human beings, we organise and make sense of the world.

In order to grasp such matters, however, we do need to have a picture of how criticism developed in the first half of this century. One thing to bear in mind is that it is only in this century that literature has become a widely-taught subject in schools, colleges and universities. As English became established as an academic discipline, there developed an increasing attention to the text rather than the author's life; essays had to be rigorous, and had to be based upon the student's careful reading of the text. The focus became the exploration of the meaning and significance of the text through a close and sustained analysis of the words on the page. This is seen in England in the work of a critic such as F. R. Leavis and in America in the work of the 'New Critics'. Such critics did not reject expressive criticism, indeed they were very concerned with the value of what an author has to say, but they also looked at the text as an aesthetic form, appreciating it first and foremost as literature rather than as a philosophical or social statement by the author.

It is this blend of attention to the text and the importance of what it says that is often the most common approach to literature at school and university today. Indeed, it might seem such a natural response – looking at the text in order to appreciate both its intellectual and aesthetic qualities, at what it says and how it says it – that it might be hard to conceive how any other approach could be valid. Contemporary criticism, however, has drawn attention to the way in which critics such as Leavis and the 'New Critics' did, in fact, approach literature with a number of assumptions: they appeared to be focusing on the text itself, but they also had preconceptions about what mattered in a text. They admired complexity, but they also expected to find a coherent moral view in a text, as if the author was managing to impose some kind of pattern on life and as if the text made some kind of positive overall statement. Such a view of literature has not disappeared; indeed, many readers could not see the point of reading novels, poems or plays unless they felt they conveyed some sort of universal message (you might, yourself, have written sentences starting with phrases such as 'Wordsworth believes . . .' or 'Lawrence is stating that . . .'). We are not saying such an approach is wrong, but the fact is that more recent criticism has tended to take a step back and detach itself from the way in which traditional critics have found a scheme of values and a coherent statement in texts. Contemporary criticism has tended to emphasise the contradictions and uncertainties in texts, and the way in which criticism itself can, productively, be equally uncertain and undecided. The simplest way of putting this is to say that whereas criticism from the first half of the century tended, in the end, to praise the overall coherence of a work, recent criticism, influenced by the ideas of critical theory, has been much more struck by the idea of incoherence in texts.

(v) *What is critical theory?* Critical theory is concerned with establishing general principles about how literature works and how criticism works. In recent years there has been a great surge of such thinking, much of which challenges established ideas about literature and rejects the assumptions inherent in traditional criticism. The effect of this has been the development of a number of new types of criticism. The entries that follow cover the main strands in twentieth-century criticism but with a particular emphasis on these new approaches. Because the approaches are arranged alphabetically, however, it may be helpful if we first give a brief outline of their historical positions.

Chronologically, the main steps in critical theory are as follows:

1. Modern theory started with the work of the Russian Formalists, which emerged in Russia around 1915. Slightly earlier, the Swiss linguist Ferdinand de Saussure explained his concept of the sign in a series of lectures given in Geneva between 1906 and 1911. The Prague School, around 1929, then reformulated Formalist theory within the framework of a linguistics derived from Saussure. This was labelled structuralism, but it differs in various respects from modern structuralism which came into existence in France in the 1950s: the leading figures of French structuralism were Claude Lévi-Strauss and Roland Barthes.

2. Marxist criticism starts with Marx himself, but the most important Marxist literary critic before the advent of structuralism was Georg Lukács, who was writing mainly in the 1930s. Since the 1960s, Marxist criticism has had to take account of structuralism: significant names are Louis Althusser, Lucien Goldmann and Pierre Macherey.

3. Feminist criticism can also be traced back throughout the twentieth century, but as a socio-political movement it began its resurgence in Western Europe and the United States in the late 1960s.

4. By the 1970s it became more common to talk about post-structuralism than structuralism, although sometimes, and rather confusingly, the term deconstruction was used interchangeably with post-structuralism. Deconstruction, originating in the writings of the French philosopher, Jacques Derrida, took further structuralism's insights into the nature of language. Post-structuralism is more of an umbrella term, covering the whole ferment and interchange of new ideas between critical movements in the seventies and eighties; principally here, mention should be made of the psychoanalytic criticism of the French psychoanalyst Jacques Lacan.

5. Since about 1980, however, there has been a fresh twist and a change of direction with the advent of New Historicism. This is not, though, an entirely new movement, as it owes much to Marxist criticism and in particular to the work of Raymond Williams. It made an impact partly because it seemed to run counter to the direction taken

by deconstruction: deconstruction seemed to head off in the direction of the allusiveness of all texts and to their endless play with meaning; New Historicism, owing a great debt to the French philosopher and historian of ideas Michel Foucault, reinserts texts in a historical and political context, but a much more open and subversive context than that ever offered in traditional versions of literary history.

As this brief account indicates, modern criticism can seem a confusing mass of names, ideas and movements. In the entries below we do not attempt to expound all the details of these theoretical positions (supplementary information about some of the terms used can be found in section 5, Critical concepts), but we do attempt to show where and how new ideas might affect your practice as a critic. The intention is to provide some indication of the approaches you can adopt and the directions in which you might, or might not, wish to move in your study of literature.

Feminist criticism. Feminist criticism is concerned both with the representation of women in literature and with changing women's position in society by freeing them from oppressive restraints. Central to those restraints are essentialist definitions of what it is to be a woman: definitions that assume human nature is universal and which refuse to see how culture plays a significant part in constructing and fixing identity. Feminist criticism is, of course, part of the larger movement in the contemporary world for women's equality. That movement itself grows out of previous centuries of struggle by women to win equal rights, and out of previous writings, in texts such as Mary Wollstonecraft's *A Vindication of the Rights of Woman* (1792), which articulate the case for women. We need, however, to gain a sense of how contemporary feminist criticism has new things to say and to see how it fits into the overall pattern of modern criticism.

Feminist criticism includes a great variety of practices and is itself constantly developing and changing, so it probably makes more sense to speak of feminist criticisms in the plural rather than the singular. Nevertheless, nearly all feminist criticism starts from one fundamental perception: that is, a recognition of the patriarchal structure of society, that the world is organised on terms dictated by men, and to the advantage of men. This perception is central to two of the seminal works of feminism: Virginia Woolf's *A Room of One's Own* (1928) and Simone de Beauvoir's *The Second Sex* (1949). While these works have influenced a lot of later critics, it is only in the late sixties and early seventies that feminism really began to make a substantial impact on literary criticism. Initially, as in the works of Kate Millett, the emphasis fell on the misogynist nature of much great literature. At the same time, feminist criticism began to praise certain works, such as Charlotte Brontë's *Villette*, which offered a strong valuation of woman's experience. Perhaps the obvious point that needs to be made here is that such feminist criticism, and the same is true of all feminist criticism, is political criticism, always aware of the oppression of women. One consequence of this has been the rediscovery, and republication, of a whole tradition of books by women 'silenced' by the traditional male canon; and criticism itself, as in Gilbert and Gubar's *The Madwoman in the Attic* (1979), often concentrates on the figure of the suppressed female. Gilbert and Gubar's book is perhaps the most accessible of all the major texts of feminism, offering a celebration of the realisation of female identity in a way that has parallels with the emphasis on distinctive female experience (such as motherhood) that emerged at around the same time in other feminist works.

By the eighties, books like *The Madwoman in the Attic* had helped to place woman's experience at the centre of attention. Once there, some feminists wanted to focus the debate exclusively on the political issues, and indeed this remains a powerful line in feminist thinking today. But other writers began to raise questions about the nature of woman, and, indeed, questions about the nature of men as well as women: the three most influential figures in this area were the French theorists, Julia Kristeva, Hélène Cixous and Luce Irigaray. Their work not only introduced further challenges to the old order but also raised complex questions about our understanding of human subjectivity and its relationship to language.

The writings of Kristeva, Cixous and Irigaray were in part influenced by, yet also a reaction against, the deconstructionist criticism of Jacques Derrida and the psychoanalytic theories of Jacques Lacan. To simplify far too much, both Derrida and Lacan draw attention to the fragility and spuriousness of the rational order that exists in society. Lacan talks instead of the Symbolic Order of language and culture, with its rules centred around the phallus and the father (*see also* p. 140). In a sense, he takes the central feminist perception of the patriarchal structure of society, but shows how it permeates even such fundamental things as the structure of language and the mind. In exposing the reach of patriarchy, however, Lacan, like Derrida, also exposes its fictionality, how it is constructed in language. Against this male order, Irigaray and Cixous posit a feminine writing, an *écriture féminine*, which can operate outside the patriarchal structures. Kristeva also challenges the rigidity of the symbolic order, suggesting that women can work in a different, more fluid, open space. These French theorists, therefore, challenge an inherited world view; they see women as learning to speak outside the phallocentric order of society (*see also* p. 156).

Such a line of reasoning both found favour and attracted fierce criticism. Critics such as Alice Jardine, Mary Jacobus and Jacqueline Rose all produced feminist criticism within this deconstructive, psychoanalytic frame; but others criticised the French perspective as remote from practical and political ends. In the context of the entries within this section, however, perhaps the main thing to grasp is how the thinking in French feminism is in line with the whole instinct of modern criticism and theory to question the traditional categorisations and definitions our society has inherited. In the case of feminism, this becomes nothing less than an attempt to rethink and re-examine the whole issue of gender.

A second theoretical injection of energy into feminist criticism came along in the 1980s when the ideas of Michel Foucault and New Historicism were seen to fuse effectively with work being done by feminists. New Historicism questions the received view of the past: it discusses how power is concentrated, and who is excluded and marginalised. In the work of such critics as Catharine Gallagher, Nancy Armstrong, Gillian Beer and Mary Poovey there is a consideration of gender and class relations within nineteenth-century society. Deconstruction, Lacanian psychoanalysis and New Historicism also look questioningly at the notion of self as it has been constructed in Western culture, and this, too, fused well with feminism's questioning of the construction of identity and gender. The kind of development and movement that took place during the 1970s and 1980s is, therefore, from an energetic discovery of how neglected women's experience had been, to a much more wide-ranging analysis, and re-reading, of the whole structure of society, of male and female roles, indeed of the whole notion of gender: gender came to be seen as a construct of society, designed to facilitate the smooth-running of society to the advantage of men.

An extension of this awareness of how central to patriarchy is the establishing of firm gender roles has been the rise of **gay and lesbian criticism**, which, amongst other things, draws attention to the homophobic nature of the recent history of Western society. **Black studies**, too, can of course also work out from similar perceptions and a similar set of ideas. But the perception in black studies that the feminist debate has been primarily about white experience, and that race makes a radical difference to any analysis, has led not only to black feminist criticism but also to the sort of critique by Gayatri Spivak of the way in which even feminism, albeit unwittingly, sometimes co-operates with imperialism.

When we look at the early writers of feminist criticism we see the energy of discovery of, and celebration of, women's experience, but the position reached now is no longer as straightforward as that: there are no general rules or principles that enable us to define and discuss women's experience in a simple way. As with other movements in current criticism and theory, the move has been away from a coherent view of the past (and, indeed, the present) to a sense of the complexity of the range of issues involved. Feminist criticism will not stop still – nor, for that matter, will Marxist criticism or New Historicism or any modern critical movement – for it is a critical movement that starts from an acknowledgement that fixity and generalisations were part of the old order for making sense of and controlling society. Feminist criticism works with a shifting agenda, of endlessly acknowledging both the complexity of the past, and the limits of any schemes of interpretation we place on the past. It questions the patriarchal order of society, but is ready to accept and work with the provisionality that is the consequence of questioning or abandoning that old, containing fiction.

F. R. Leavis and twentieth-century British criticism. A lecturer at Cambridge University from 1937 to 1962, F. R. Leavis was a leading figure in the critical revolt against the outmoded approaches to literature that still prevailed in universities in the earlier years of the twentieth century. Instead of concentrating on literary history and biography, Leavis advocated close reading of the text itself, arguing that the critic should analyse the words on the page rather than work from extrinsic evidence. Others, such as I. A. Richards, the pioneer of **Practical Criticism** – an approach in which a poem is discussed without the aid of any supporting evidence about when it was written or who wrote it – had moved, and were moving, in a similar direction, but it was Leavis who became the most influential British critic of this century.

The blend in Leavis's criticism is in many respects that which we subsequently encounter in much modern criticism. The critic looks at the text, often examining representative passages, and discusses the artistry and effect of the work. The purpose of such close attention to the texture of the writing is to reveal the complexity and subtlety of what is being said. The critic does not look for a simple 'message' but attempts to see how the text makes a complex statement about human experience. Earlier critics had tended to talk in rather bland and woolly terms about the aesthetic qualities of literature, but Leavis's approach enables the critic to use the text in order to show the connection between how it is written and what it says.

There was, however, more to Leavis's approach than this. Above all, there was a stress on 'moral seriousness' as a central quality in literature. Leavis felt that a great book illuminated the complex moral nature of experience: 'moral' here does not mean a set of injunctions about how to behave but a sense of the complex web of feelings and responsibilities that exist between people in society. The novel was in many ways the best place to find such a moral sense, and Leavis's best-known book, *The Great Tradition* (1948), is about the English novel: the novelists he regarded most highly – Austen, George Eliot, James, Conrad and Lawrence – were praised for their quality of 'felt life' and for the seriousness with which they confront experience.

Part of the attraction of Leavis's approach and general stance was that it managed to combine an appreciation of the text as an aesthetic construct with a firm sense of its value and importance: the text, for Leavis, always has something substantial to say about life. Many critics followed this approach. Indeed, one might go so far as to say that Leavis established the dominant pattern of modern British criticism until the seventies. Critics might have distanced themselves from his rhetoric (for Leavis was often a pugnacious critic), and an emphasis on the moral substance of literature is less explicit in most criticism, but the general approach resembles that of Leavis. The critic focuses on the text, but, unlike the

American New Critics (*see* p. 180) who are exhaustive in their examination of the words on the page, British critics tend to move fairly swiftly from a discussion of the text to an impression of the view of life it expresses. The main interest is in what the text says and how it says it, and this dual focus, on the form and content of literature, is something that is likely to remain central in English studies. Such an approach can, in fact, be combined with biographical or historical approaches, for the critic can combine these lines of investigation with close discussion of the text in order to move towards an appreciation of what sort of complex statement it is making.

This kind of traditional British criticism is sometimes described as **pluralist**; in other words, it is an approach that seems to look at the text with an open mind and without any apparent commitment to any particular ideological position. In the seventies, however, this approach began to be referred to rather dismissively by structuralist and Marxist critics as 'liberal humanist', a vague term but one which suggests a broad tradition of respect for the individual and a belief that problems, however complex, are capable of being rationally understood. This connects with the desire of many critics, including Leavis and his followers, to trace a coherent response to life in a literary text. Structuralist critics pointed out that a text might not make a coherent statement in this way, that all works contain all kinds of confusing and contradictory elements. It is but a short step from this to suggesting that critics who seek a coherent understanding of experience in literature might well be imposing such coherence on the text, ordering the work to fit their own orderly notions of how life and literature should be. Political critics – and Leavis was very much against Marxist criticism – could point out that, by and large, Leavis did not look at a text in context, but tended to stress what he regarded as universal moral qualities that the text could be said to illustrate and endorse. This, it could be argued, is in essence a political agenda: that by being overtly non-political, Leavis wants to play down differences and divisions within history, and interpret the whole of experience in terms of liberal humanist values. Similarly, liberal humanists in general might be said to cling too committedly to the notion of the individual as a source of order and meaning in society; in endorsing the individual, critics might seem to be echoing the values promoted by a great many classic texts, but it could also be said that such a critical approach plays down or even ignores the anxieties such texts might voice about the whole construction of the self.

From all kinds of positions, therefore, the assumptions inherent in the Leavis school of criticism, and, more generally, in the whole liberal humanist tradition, are open to question and attack. This does not mean, however, that traditional criticism has been overturned or defeated, or that the notion of a 'canon' of literature (the notion that there are only certain great works of literature worth discussing) has disappeared. There are a great many contemporary critics who, like Leavis, believe that literature does have something worthwhile to say and whose critical methods reflect this belief. But anyone these days who sets out to defend a traditional position has to write with an awareness of the arguments against old values and assumptions. A traditional critic needs to have as subtle a view of literature and language, and how we relate to, and impose patterns on, literature, as the most progressive theoretical critic.

Marxist criticism. What a critic says about a book depends to a large extent upon the ideas he or she brings to the text. Sometimes these premises are undeclared or vague, but the Marxist critic is very clear about the stance from which he or she writes: the text has to be read in the light of an all-informing philosophy. It has to be seen in relation to a Marxist view of history, in which the idea of class struggle is central; the connections between literature and the economic structure of society in which it was written must be made evident.

This does not, however, produce a uniform critical response: Marxist criticism is lively and varied, and, despite the collapse of communism throughout Eastern Europe, still evolving. A crude Marxist might simply dismiss all literature as a bourgeois luxury in which middle-class authors write about their middle-class problems. Such a response, however, has not been widely expressed since the 1930s. Indeed, Marxist critics have often revealed a reverence for art, feeling that, through literature, the writer can stand apart and see the faults of society. The method of much traditional Marxist criticism has been to reconstruct a view of the past from historical evidence, and then to demonstrate how accurate a particular text is in its representation and understanding of this social reality. Not surprisingly, Marxists, such as the best-known Marxist critic, George Lukács, have always been most interested in the realistic novel, which presents a suitably full picture of society. There is, in fact, nothing particularly contentious about much Marxist criticism. F. R. Leavis and the American New Critics focused more on the text than anything else, but there has always been a form of criticism in which the text is seen in context. Traditional Marxist criticism is simply one way of relating the text to a view of the social reality of the time in which it was written. A very accessible, and influential, example of such criticism is Raymond Williams's *The English Novel from Dickens to Lawrence* (1970).

At the same time, we should recognise that, although the essence of Marxist criticism is a concern with material living conditions, the Marxist critic must consider more theoretical questions about the ideology of texts and the function of art in society. Such concerns have been sharpened with the advent of structuralism. Whereas traditional criticism – even traditional Marxist criticism – has always stressed the fullness and coherence of literary texts, structuralism draws attention to the constructed nature of the literary text; structuralism prompts questions about the nature and function of a text, and more recent Marxist criticism has inevitably taken account of structuralism. The two critics who have been most influential in developing theoretical Marxist thinking about literature have been Louis Althusser and Pierre Macherey. Macherey stresses the gaps in a text, arguing that the reader can see what the text is hiding from itself. Althusser sees texts as incomplete and contradictory as their **ideology** (the ideas, values and political beliefs inherent in a text; *see* p. 146) runs into difficulties. Both critics are essentially saying that the issues raised in a text are too complex for the author – or the ideological code of the period in which the text was written – to control and contain. A critical approach this can lead to is one in which the Marxist critic looks searchingly at the contradictions and problems inherent in bourgeois culture, exploring the text to see the way in which ideological values prove inadequate or incomplete or disruptive. This might appear a dismissive approach to literature, and handled crudely it might well be, but it can also prove a rewarding way of exploring both literature and history, making a connection between the text and the world.

One of the obvious strengths of such criticism is that it gets away from the idea that literary texts convey timeless and universal truths about life and human nature. Marxist criticism sees how a text belongs to a certain period, and expresses how people at that time organised and made sense of their world. In the hands of the committed and sophisticated Marxist (in England, critics such as Raymond Williams and Terry Eagleton, and in America, Frederic Jameson) this is, of course, tied to a radical political agenda, in which the critic hopes to bring about changes in the way society currently conducts itself, but many non-Marxists practise a Marxist-influenced approach to literature in that they are committed to a questioning re-examination of literary texts and their function in society. It is a re-reading of the past that has much in common with feminism, and is often combined with feminism (and New Historicism) as in Nancy Armstrong's book, *Desire and Domestic Fiction: A Political History of the Novel* (1987), or Mary Poovey's *Uneven Developments: The Ideological Work of Gender in Mid-Victorian England* (1989). In all such approaches, the critic attempts to write from a position outside the received views of society, as, indeed, do structuralist and deconstructionist critics (*see* p. 190). The structuralist critic, however, and the same is true of the deconstructionist critic, refuses to become involved in social and political questions. Marxism, feminism and New Historicism, on the other hand, all raise political questions about the sense of order conveyed in a literary text and how men and women stand in relation to society.

Narratology. Narratology means the analysis of narratives. It is a by-product of structuralism, which encouraged an interest in the structures that underlie literary texts. Essentially, narratology is concerned with the sequence and pattern of events in a story, and, as such, it must be admitted that much work on narratology is highly technical and not all that interesting (this is particularly the case when technical terms are coined for minor effects in a text, for example 'anisochrony', which means a variation in narrative speed). The most accessible technical book on narratology is probably Gérard Genette's *Narrative Discourse* (1980).

Narratology could be said to begin with the work of the Russian Formalist Vladimir Propp, who, in *The Morphology of the Folk Tale* (1928), drew attention to seven basic patterns in stories. All narratology shows a similar concern with establishing such general rules about how narratives function. Where it becomes useful and relevant to the literary critic, however, is when the narratologist moves beyond technical description to speculate more broadly about the consequences of perceived devices. An outstanding example is Mikhail Bakhtin, a Russian critic from the 1920s whose work has had a tremendous influence on novel criticism since its translation into English in the 1970s (*see also* Carnival, p. 137). Bakhtin describes the '**polyphonic**' effect of a novel: rather than there being one narrator who controls the entire view of the world offered in the novel, there are a host of voices jostling for attention in the text. This does not mean just the direct speech of the characters; a variety of discourses enter into the narrative discourse. The appeal of this idea is that it ties in with a great deal of recent criticism in suggesting the instability and incoherence of literary texts: rather than a text offering a unified and coherent world view, the literary text can be seen as the clash of voices and positions within a historical period. It ties in, too, with the idea in much recent Marxist criticism (and Bakhtin could be described as a Marxist critic) of how a text, rather than just expressing a straightforward ideological stance, also challenges and undermines what might seem to be its central assumptions.

Another very influential narratological critic is D. A. Miller, particularly in his book *Narrative and its Discontents* (1981). Miller is especially interested in the tension between suspense and closure in fiction: how there is a 'narratable disequilibrium' and how set against this is a state of 'non-narratable quiescence'. The openness of the text enables the novelist to create uncertainty and ask disturbing questions, but there is also an impulse to pull everything together into a pattern: in a curious way novels both subvert and reconfirm. This again relates to a good deal of current critical practice: if traditional criticism tended to view texts as coherent statements from the past, the effect of deconstruction was to refocus attention on the uncertainty and uneasiness of literary texts. But Miller (whose book is in part a riposte to the deconstructive criticism of J. Hillis Miller) reminds us that a text is not endlessly open and uncertain, that formal coherence (in the way that a novel pulls all the strands together) reflects ideological coherence.

As is so often the case in current criticism, various approaches inter-relate. D. A. Miller's work on narratology can, for example, be related to changing approaches to Charlotte Brontë's *Jane Eyre* over the past few years. Traditional criticism took a rather patronising view of Charlotte Brontë's novel, with some critics dismissing it as a self-indulgent fantasy. Charlotte was often compared, to her disadvantage, with her sister Emily, author of *Wuthering Heights*. Feminist criticism, however, alerted us to a much more radical, subversive and angry *Jane Eyre*; focusing on the language of the text, critics drew attention to how Jane speaks out in her own voice within a dominant patriarchal discourse. But recent feminist criticism has moved beyond looking at the subversiveness of *Jane Eyre* and begun to focus on the more conservative elements in the text, how the views on race and empire in the novel collude with the dominant ideology of the day (see, for example, the essay by Gayatri Spivak, in *Race, Writing and Difference* (1985), ed. Henry Louis Gates, Jr).

The openness of this debate, the way in which there is no settled view of even the most widely-discussed novels, should indicate how there are no final answers to questions about the nature of a text and how it relates to its period; and how it is open to every student of literature to make his or her own contribution to such a debate. The main point in relation to narratology is to appreciate that you should avoid getting bogged down in technical details; as quickly as possible, try to see how the theory can affect your critical practice. In what ways might it enable you to look for different things in a text? Traditional critics tended to say, 'This is an important text and this is what it says . . .'; recent approaches privilege the idea that what the text is saying is far from clear-cut. Narratology is one route into an understanding of the fact that there are competing instincts within a text, that it can simultaneously be subversive and conservative, open and closed. At the same time, narratology, by being so concerned with repeated patterns, reminds us that the critic is always imposing a shape or pattern on the text, but this is not incompatible with a desire to acknowledge the complexity of the text and the complexity of its social and cultural impact.

New Criticism. An American critical movement characterised by its very close discussion of texts. New Criticism was at its height from 1940 to 1960. Some central figures were Cleanth Brooks, R. P. Blackmur, Allen Tate and John Crowe Ransom. The movement was greatly influenced by T. S. Eliot's ideas about literature and I. A. Richards's ideas about how to discuss a text. Every time you look closely at a poem or passage of prose, discussing it as a more or less self-sufficient entity, you are carrying on an approach initiated by Richards and developed by the New Critics.

New Criticism, however, had several distinct features. The New Critics tended to concentrate on short lyric poems, particularly intellectually complex works such as the poems of Donne. The poem was looked at in isolation. No assumptions were to be made about the author's intention; the meaning was to be found exclusively in the words on the page. Poetry was seen as a special kind of language, saying things that could not be paraphrased, and therefore a poem was said to possess organic unity, with form and content being inseparable. The role of the critic was to analyse the complex verbal texture of the poem, the meaning revealing itself through such close analysis.

This seems an objective approach, concerned to respond to the evidence of the text itself. The problem is, however, that the New Critics were not objective. They favoured those works that were most likely to reveal the qualities they sought in literature, preferring, for example, the intellectual complexity of the metaphysicals to the emotional complexity of the romantics. Qualities they praised in literature included irony, paradox, ambivalence and tension, yet their criticism also included the idea that a poem reconciled these opposites of experience. In a sense they were saying that a good poem both confronts the complexity of life and manages to reconcile discordant elements. A great deal of New Criticism is, in fact, informed by religious convictions: there is both a belief that experience is complex, puzzling and paradoxical and also that there is some ultimate source of order and meaning in life. Such informing convictions were, however, unclear when New Criticism was at its height: much more apparent was the skill and ingenuity with which a New Critic discussed a poem.

An increased emphasis on the text was also a feature of British criticism at this time, but British critics were seldom as detailed in their technical analysis of the text. In addition, whereas a British critic such as Leavis (*see* p. 173) tended to be concerned with the moral and social convictions evident in a work, the New Critics were more concerned with the spiritual convictions informing a text. This distinctive quality of New Criticism is perhaps best illustrated by a comparison with the work of William Empson, who, in the ingenuity and thoroughness of his close analysis, seems the British critic closest to the practice of the New Critics. Empson, however, was more of an open-minded liberal, responding to the various levels of meaning a text can contain, and not concerned to stress the reconciliation of opposites that takes place in a poem.

Much subsequent American criticism has been written in conscious reaction against the ideas of the New Critics, especially against the idea that an author can finally order life (*see* Structuralism and post-structuralism, p. 190). New Criticism is regarded as having made moves in an interesting direction in indicating the extreme complexity of any piece of writing, but the objection raised against it is that the New Critics ultimately interpreted everything in the light of their own coherent religious view of life. Yet an approach that rejects all notions of order in a text, which is a characteristic of some deconstructive criticism, is likely to prove unappealing to many readers. For this reason, a much modified form of New Criticism, not making all that much of paradox and less transcendental in its approach, but looking at how a poem confronts and attempts to order a complex world, is bound to remain influential in the criticism of literature.

New Historicism. One impulse in traditional twentieth-century criticism (as exemplified in the work of F. R. Leavis or the 'New Critics') has been to consider the text in isolation, but there has always been an equally strong impulse to look at texts in their historical context. Thirty or forty years ago, for example, most students working on the period of Shakespeare, Spenser and Donne would almost inevitably have read E. M. W. Tillyard's *The Elizabethan World Picture* (1943) where he attempted 'to extract and expound the most ordinary beliefs about the constitution of the world as pictured in the Elizabethan age. . . .'. In a very persuasive manner, Tillyard presented a picture of a cosmic world order which governed both human institutions and natural phenomena. The literary texts of the period were seen as an expression of that sense of order.

New Historicists have also turned to the Renaissance period, but where Tillyard found order, they have found disorder, difference and division. They point out that Tillyard's world-view makes no mention of the experiences of women or of the poor and disenfranchised. In so far as there was a sense of order, New Historicists have found anxiety surrounding this order, with contention and subversion both very evident in the period. New Historicism, then, re-reads both the literature and history of a period and displaces an essentially coherent view with a sense of incoherence and argument.

But, more precisely, what is New Historicism? The term was coined by the American critic Stephen Greenblatt and refers to a revived interest, initially amongst American critics in the early 1980s, in looking at literary works in their historical and political context. In part, the new movement was a reaction against deconstruction, which took an ahistorical approach, but at the same time it built upon the new kinds of approaches, particularly to language, associated with structuralism and deconstruction. New Historicism also overlaps with feminism and Marxist criticism in taking a questioning view of the past, looking at the production, consumption and status of literary texts. A major influence was the British critic Raymond Williams, and the British equivalent of New Historicism is sometimes said to be **cultural materialism**, which is a Marxist approach looking, to put it as concisely as possible, at how the discourses of a text embody or challenge an ideological position. A fuller description of cultural materialism is that it combines studying the implications of literary texts in history, theoretical method and political commitment; and how texts relate to the particular institutions of cultural production: in the case of Shakespeare such things as the court, the theatre and the church. Central to New Historicism is an admission that the investigation being conducted is not objective, that the nature of our interest in the past is dictated by our involvement in the present.

New Historicism seemed to arrive as a welcome relief to those who felt that deconstruction led, ultimately, in the direction of philosophical abstraction, as if nothing could ever be said with any certainty or ever be pinned down. What New Historicism has offered is a reintroduction of the substantiality of the past in which to set and discuss texts. If Derrida was the name most associated with deconstruction, the major force behind New Historicism, and a general redirection of literary studies back towards history, has been the radical French historian Michel Foucault. Foucault's work is characterised by a re-examination of the idea of the 'self' as it has evolved in Western society: liberal humanists have always clung on to the idea of the 'self' as a kind of dependable and coherent concrete reality, but Foucault, in his books on the histories of madness, punishment and sexuality, has shown how the self is the victim of specialized areas of knowledge or discourses (*see also* Discourse, p. 142). His project, then, is an alternative reading of the past, refusing to cling on to old verities, and creating a much more uncertain sense of self and a disturbing view of the power relations of society.

New Historicism is equally attracted to such re-readings of the past, getting away from a comforting, progressive, coherent view of history. A case in point is Greenblatt's striking essay 'Invisible bullets: Renaissance authority and its subversion, *Henry IV* and *Henry V*' (in *Political Shakespeare: New Essays in Cultural Materialism*, ed. Jonathan Dollimore and Alan Sinfield, 1985). The essay starts by looking at the charge of atheism levelled at Christopher Marlowe and Thomas Heriot in 1593: Marlowe was an Elizabethan dramatist, Heriot the 'most profound Elizabethan mathematician' and 'the author of the first original book about the first English colony in America'. Already the moves in a New Historicist approach should be apparent: there is a combining of the political with the literary, and with figures drawn from the wider history of the Renaissance. Unexpectedly, the essay pursues not Marlowe but Heriot and his book which tells of the colonization and conversion of the American Indian. Greenblatt, however, re-reads Heriot's book not simply as a text about authority but as a text which reveals how power both produces the subversion which opposes authority and at the same time relies on subversion for the establishment of order. It is this complex idea that Greenblatt subsequently applies to Shakespeare's history plays, showing, for example, that in *Henry V* the 'subversive doubts the play continually awakens serve paradoxically to intensify the power of the king and his war, even while they cast shadows upon this power'. What Greenblatt is interested in is not just Shakespeare, however, but the whole broader issue of the way in which the same conditions of power operate both in the theatre and in the state.

History for the New Historicists, it should be plain, is not a matter of dates and great events but of politics, ideology, power, authority and subversion. There is, however, something of a difference between British and American work in this vein: American critics tend to see texts as embodying and expressing conservative ideological positions, whereas British critics tend to see texts as offering resistance to authority. The difference can be illustrated in responses to *Henry V*: in Greenblatt's reading, power harnesses subversion, but from another angle it could be argued that, when Henry is disguised and invisible to his subjects, the text offers the audience a position from which to resist kingly power. Such differences in general stance between American and British critics may themselves be both cultural and historically specific: British criticism, calling upon a long tradition of parliamentary government and political dissent, often leans towards the idea of resistance to power; American critics, calling upon a tradition of belief in romantic individualism that combines rather uneasily with aggressive capitalism, inevitably stand in a different position in thinking about the power of the state and the possibilities of political action.

Phenomenological criticism. An approach to literature which looks at the personality behind the work has always been popular, especially with the general reader. Academic criticism, however, is somewhat out of sympathy with such an approach, as it looks at the author rather than at the text. Phenomenological criticism seeks to bridge the gap between biography and criticism by approaching the author through the text. It starts with the work and, through it, attempts to trace the pattern of the author's mind.

The originator of phenomenology was the German philosopher Husserl. He regarded it as an attempt to describe human consciousness rather than the unique consciousness of an individual author, the latter being the aim of phenomenological criticism. Phenomenology as an approach to literature is usually associated with the theory and practice of the Geneva School of critics, most notably Georges Poulet. The central idea is that the critic should empty his or her mind of all presuppositions and then, responding directly to the text, discover the unique mode of consciousness of the author. In emptying the mind of preconceptions the critic becomes particularly receptive, even coming to share the mode of consciousness of the author. This has been referred to as 'consciousness of the consciousness of another'.

Phenomenology is clearly a form of romantic criticism, intent on getting at the unique personality behind the work. Most criticism this century has been concerned to trace a view of the world in the text rather than being interested in the author in this kind of way; the stress in phenomenology is on something elusive and hidden in the mind of the writer. Any claims that phenomenology might make about detecting this, however, are extremely suspect. The critic cannot empty the mind of preconceptions and so inevitably imposes ideas on the text; therefore, we might be seeing the consciousness of the critic rather than the consciousness of the author. Phenomenological criticism thus seems a very odd blend of theoretical sophistication and a certain naïvety about what happens when we read a book. As phenomenology has been more influential in Europe than in Britain or America, the only phenomenological critic most of us are likely to encounter is J. Hillis Miller, who subsequently rejected such an approach, opting instead for structuralism and deconstruction. Yet, as Miller's early work on Dickens and Hardy indicates, in the hands of a good critic phenomenology can prove a productive approach. As is so often the case, it is not the theory that matters but the skill of the critic, and in the hands of a good critic any theory can produce good criticism.

Psychoanalytic criticism. A tradition of psychoanalytic criticism begins with various essays by Sigmund Freud, but it is only in recent years that psychoanalytic criticism has really started to make an impact. The reasons for this have a lot to do with the general re-examination of the patterns of Western thinking prompted in the wake of structuralism.

All psychoanalytic theory begins with the sense of loss the subject experiences upon its separation from its mother's body. This necessarily affects the sexuality that is the constitutive factor in the construction of the subject, and, consequently, in all psycho-analytic criticism there must be an accounting of the presence of sexuality in the text. This is seen at its simplest in **classical Freud-ian criticism** where the work is read as a symptom of the author who produced it, or as analogous to the relationship between the dreamer and his or her dream, as if the work is a symptomatic reproduction of the author's infantile and forbidden wishes. The kind of criticism produced – an outstanding example is Marie Bonaparte's *The Life and Works of Edgar Allen Poe* (1949) – is conven-tionally referred to as 'psychobiography'. In **Jungian criticism** there is a stress on the 'collective unconscious' common to all cultures; therefore, rather than looking at the text for neurotic symptoms of its author's repressed desire, the Jungian critic explores the text for its revelation of the images, myths and symbols of past cultures: texts are found to contain recurrent figures, which are produced to compensate for psychic impoverishment in human beings and society. The Jungian critic does not, therefore, explore the per-sonal unconscious of the writer, but, characteristically, sees a com-mon quest motif in works of literature: in the standard story the hero encounters the Great Mother, who threatens to devour him, but the hero manages to break free from the mother. A sustained illustration of how Jung's ideas can be applied to literature is provided in Maud Bodkin's *Archetypal Patterns in Poetry* (1934).

There are other psychoanalysts whose ideas could be exam-ined here (for example, Melanie Klein, who sees the creative act as gratifying the need to expiate and make whole again), but the principal development in psychoanalytic thinking about literature has been **Lacanian criticism**. Jacques Lacan was a French psychoanalyst who died in 1981: he reinterpreted Freud in the light of modern linguistic theories and argued that Freud and his followers had laid too much stress on the controlling 'ego', the conscious or 'thinking' self, as separate from the 'id', the repressed impulses of the unconscious. Lacan saw the ego as a carrier of neurosis: there could be no such thing as a coherent, autonomous self. The 'I' can never separate itself from the 'other', its image seen in the mirror, through which it comes to know itself and which, by enabling its identification and alienation in language, creates a condition of desire in the split subject. Such thinking struck a chord in the seventies and eighties because it was consistent with the efforts of structuralism, deconstruction, Marxism and feminism in its stress on the extent to which the various verities of Western thinking, such as a coherent or unified sense of the self, were simply historical, linguistic and fictional constructs.

It is also possible to see why, starting with Lacan, psychoanalytic criticism begins to make a significant impact, for rather than dealing, as seems to be the case in Freudian criticism, with the sick mind, Lacanian psychoanalysis offers a much more direct engagement with the whole idea of the structure of the self and its relation to the social. With Lacanian thought, psychoanalytic criticism can move from the fringes to the centre ground in considering the whole notion of the construction of the subject. This is most obvious in the effect Lacan has had on feminist criticism, for there is much that the feminist critic can do with ideas of the fictionality of the traditional male notion of the self. Part of this is Lacan's stress on the phallocentric, patriarchal structure of society, and, indeed, the phallocentric nature of his own thought. Some feminists, working simultaneously with and against Lacan, argue that his stress on the frailty of psychic identity and the mobility of desire indicates the fictionality of gender definitions. As happens so often in criticism and theory these days, there is, therefore, not just a stress on how texts construct meanings, but on how theoretical thinking itself constructs meanings: feminist criticism has not been slow to point out that in the psychoanalytic tradition it is always male experience that is central.

The very fact of Lacan's stress on the fragility of the subject, however, makes possible further re-examinations of the notion of the subject. As in a whole range of current critical approaches, what is returned to again and again is the nature and construction of the self, and how the subject relates to or is positioned within the social. The old safe compartmentalisations of a stable society and a stable self are no longer tenable, but current theory, as in Lacanian thinking, does not shift one on to new stable ground but into an area where all categories are up for re-examination and requestioning. This can be seen, for example, in the work of Gilles Deleuze and Félix Guattari, who start with Lacan's ideas, but reject the notion of the unconscious as characterised by want. They see the Freudian unconscious as a capitalist construction, the result of repression produced by capitalism in the family: desire is an attempt to break the system. In the work of Deleuze and Guattari, therefore, Lacanian thinking is given a further twist and new direction by being overtly politicised; it represents yet another re-reading of how Western society constructs and sustains itself.

Reader-response criticism. Although the text is always central in criticism, modern critical theory has also stressed the role of the reader. Indeed, some critics are primarily interested in the way in which a reader receives, perceives and understands literature. Their central assumption is that the reader actively contributes something to the text. Where disagreements emerge, however, is on the question of how much the reader finds in the text and how much the reader contributes.

It is in Germany that most attention has been paid to the subject of the reader's response. Wolfgang Iser, for example in *The Act of Reading: A Theory of Aesthetic Response* (1978), holds that the text largely determines the response, but suggests that the text is full of gaps which the reader fills in. Hans Robert Jauss is more concerned with the general response to literature over a period of time than with the individual response: this is an approach known as **reception theory**. Again, however, the stress is on the text providing a certain stimulus and the reader completing the process. It is a form of give and take, a dialogue between the text and the reader. Such views are uncontroversial: they probably match common assumptions about how much a text offers and how much the reader contributes. A possible criticism, however, is that these critics assume there is such a figure as an average reader who accepts conventional beliefs and who therefore can be expected to complete the text in a certain way. The same objection holds good for the structuralist approach to the reader, where the reader is presented as responding to the codes of the text, making connections with the system of literary discourse. The position taken in post-structuralist criticism, however, is different, for here the emphasis often falls on the role of the reader in imposing a meaning on the words in the text. Such issues are explored fully in the work of Stanley Fish, probably the most sophisticated of the reader-response critics: in *Is There A Text in this Class?* (1980) he sees the reader as the text's true producer.

Russian Formalism. The Formalists were a group of critics in Russia at the time of the 1917 Revolution. Their thinking about literature planted the seeds that eventually led to structuralism. Formalism started as an activity closely linked to linguistics with an interest in the scientific examination of style. Much of the work was detailed, technical research into metre, rhyme and such topics as sound in poetry, but most readers are more likely to respond to the general view of art the Formalists offered. Literary language was seen as a special kind of language. It was suggested that, rather than presenting a picture of the world, art **defamiliarises** or 'makes strange' (an idea coined by Victor Shklovsky): literary writing disrupts ordinary language, looking at the world in a 'strange' way. What the reader notices is not the picture of reality but the peculiarity of the writing itself. Literature is thus seen as a self-conscious medium. Shklovsky, for example, referred to Sterne's *Tristram Shandy* as the world's most typical novel, as if the whole business of art is to foreground its own nature as art, drawing attention to itself as an indirect way of drawing attention to reality.

The central concept that Formalism introduces is this idea that the language in a literary text is very unusual, that the text cannot simply be looked through in order to appreciate a picture of life. Structuralism and deconstruction (*see* next entry) also start from this idea of the oddness of writing: both of these modern movements are characterised by a refusal to look beyond or outside language, the text being regarded as a linguistic construct that does not offer a clear window on the world. But the tradition that the Russian Formalists initiate has much wider consequences, consequences that go beyond a philosophical concern with the nature of language. Understanding these consequences helps us understand the whole thrust of modern criticism.

The Russian Formalists were reacting against an inherited social order and received ideas about society and the self, although their lack of interest in the content of literary works invited strong disapproval from Marxist critics and from Stalin. At first sight, Czech Formalism, structuralism and deconstruction can all seem equally apolitical and inward looking. But the political consequences of stepping outside the body of received ideas, as the Russian Formalists did, and questioning the status of the texts in which the apparent 'truths' and 'values' of Western civilisation are displayed, could not in the end be avoided. To step aside and draw attention to the artifice of literary texts will, in the end, inevitably lead to a re-examination of the ideology contained within those texts. We see this in the way that structuralism not only spawned deconstruction, but also a re-energised Marxist criticism, a more radical feminism and, in the eighties, and in reaction against the introverted nature of deconstruction, New Historicism.

Something similar happened in Russia: the work of Mikhail Bakhtin (a Russian critic from the 1920s who has had a major influence on contemporary theory) is distinct from that of the Russian Formalists, even though, in his idea of the 'polyphonic' novel, he seems to share the Formalists' interest in the methods of narrative and the instability of texts. But Bakhtin's interest in re-examining the nature of narrative leads into his concern with the social dimension of the language of a text, how language is involved in social relationships which are part of broader political, economic and ideological systems. In essence, Bakhtin is interested in the kinds of debate that are going on in a novel, the way it articulates and presents the unresolved tensions of its ideology. Such concerns are at the heart of recent New Historicist criticism. The line of continuity from the Russian Formalists to New Historicism is, then, a direct one: they might seem to initiate an ahistorical, apolitical, philosophically sceptical mode of criticism, but the eventual consequences of their intervention were bound to be political. It is in this sense that we can also describe the whole movement of contemporary criticism as political: its profound questioning, and indeed rejection of a common-sense view of the relation of language to the world, has led to what can only be described as a major revolution in modern thinking.

Structuralism and post-structuralism.

STRUCTURALISM

    (i) *Introduction.* In the first decade of this century the Swiss linguist Ferdinand de Saussure introduced a new approach to language. Whereas earlier linguists had been concerned with the history and characteristics of particular languages, Saussure was interested in the structures that underlie all languages. He coined the terms *parole* and *langue*: *parole* or speech is language in performance, and this is what earlier linguists had concentrated on, but Saussure was interested in the theoretical system that shapes all language or *langue*, the rules or principles that enable language to exist and function.

It is in the work of Saussure that the movement known as structuralism has its origins. Structuralism can be defined as an analytic approach which is less concerned with the unique qualities of any individual example than with the structures that underlie the individual examples. Saussure's work, however, had been confined to linguistics. In the 1950s such an approach began to be applied in other disciplines, when Saussure's ideas were taken up by the anthropologist Claude Lévi-Strauss. Anthropology is the study of human beings, especially in relation to social groups and culture; traditionally anthropologists have looked at particular tribes or groups, but Lévi-Strauss was more concerned with the structures that underlie all societies. Subsequently, first in France, where most of the new ideas in this field have originated, and then internationally, a structuralist approach has been adopted in the social sciences and in the study of literature, as, for example, in the work of the French critic Roland Barthes.

Described in these broad terms structuralism might appear relatively uncomplicated. The difficulty arises when we consider the problem of how to identify underlying structures. It depends upon more than intuition. Saussure elaborates complex theories about language, and it is this theoretical work that provides the basis of the method of all subsequent structuralist thought.

(ii) *Theory*. We use language to talk about life. Saussure, however, was not interested in this referential significance of language. He placed his emphasis elsewhere, suggesting that language is a self-sufficient system operating by its own internal rules. It is not the existence of things in the world that determines the nature of language; on the contrary, a word is a purely arbitrary sign, defined by its difference from other words. Language is a system of relations between the constituent units; it is a form, not a substance. This point might become clearer if we introduce Saussure's distinction between the 'signifier' and the 'signified': a word itself is the signifier, the concept it points to is the signified. The two cannot

Relationship = Arbitrary.

really be separated, but structuralism is concerned with the operations of and relations between the signifiers, rather than with looking outside the system of language at the signified. The primary concern of Saussure is with the internal order of language.

There is more to Saussure's thinking than this, but it is this pattern of thinking that has been adopted by structuralist literary critics. They apply Saussure's ideas about language to literary texts, the central idea being that the text is a self-sufficient system. Traditionally critics have made sense of texts by relating them to life, but the structuralist does not wish to move outside the text in this sort of way. Instead he or she moves in the opposite direction, trying to work out general theories about how texts function.

At first this seemed a way of describing literature which could lay claim to almost scientific precision. The 'pure' structuralist hopes to establish a grammar of texts, a set of general rules about how they work. There is something of a parallel in the work of Northrop Frye, an archetypal critic who emphasised the underlying mythical patterns in literature, but structuralism aimed to be more scientific and all-inclusive, explaining the entire signifying system of the text, not just the grand structure but the operations of every word and sentence.

(iii) *Implications.* As described so far, structuralism might seem a valid, but rather dull, technical approach to literature. Yet structuralism provoked bitter rows. This is because of the implications of such an approach: rejecting a conventional interest in life beyond the text, preferring to see every book as a construct working by certain rules, structuralism adopts a position of not seeing things from within the cultural context of society. For example, whereas most critics reading Wordsworth tend to identify and sympathise with his problems and ideas, the structuralist would look at the concerns of his texts in a detached way. As a result, structuralist critics found themselves in a position of criticising the way in which traditional critics create a context for the work by relating it to their own view of life. This leads on to a sceptical view of the values and beliefs accepted by most critics. So, the whole tradition of criticism, in which a complicated and meaningful text is read sympathetically by a reader who wants to determine its relevance to life, is dismissed as a standard, although complicated, literary structure being met by a standard critical response. This is a simplification of the structuralist position, but structuralism is characterised by a desire to stand back in this sort of detached way.

This is well illustrated in structuralist criticism's use of new technical terms and unfamiliar language: this is an important way of indicating that one is not a participant in a conventional, humane discourse but writing from outside it. When structuralism has travelled this far, however, it has lost all vestiges of detachment: it has become actively involved in society, if only in a subversive role. What began as a new way of looking at literature becomes a movement intent on questioning and undermining prevailing values. What began as a look at the structures of literature becomes an examination and rejection of the structures of belief and value that have been central in our culture.

(iv) *Structuralist criticism*. In practice, structuralist criticism, as it developed in universities in the English-speaking world, was often far more moderate than this. Many critics found that structuralism – perhaps in a very loose sense in which the critic works with some general ideas about the patterns underlying certain kinds of texts before turning to a specific example – provided an illuminating way of talking about literature. The most characteristic effect of structuralism, however, has been to alter the balance of the way in which many books are regarded. A critic who looks closely at the structure and language of a text will often play down the traditional idea of what the text can tell us about life and, in a sense, make the book's own form its subject. Structuralist criticism is, by and large, reflexive, pointing out how the text might be discussing the gap between the word and the world, the gap between the structure of art and the structure of reality. Structuralist criticism, therefore, achieves an accommodation with conventional criticism by relocating the centre of interest, claiming that writing is often concerned with the problems of writing about reality. Yet this is still distinct from the prevailing tradition of criticism: whereas most traditional critics find a complex statement about life in a text, the emphasis of much structuralist criticism is on the limits of literature, how the world is more complex than the self-contained system of the text. Structuralist criticism often draws attention to the way in which a literary text fails to order the world and fails to make sense of experience.

(v) *The limits of structuralism*. Most modern critics concentrate on the text, yet their interpretation is affected by their own sense of reality and their own values. This is even the case when critics look at a text in its historical context, for the way in which we make sense of the past is inevitably determined by our twentieth-century frame of mind. Structuralist criticism attempts to focus on the text alone, rejecting interpretation in favour of a description of the text's operations. Yet this can never be an accurate description, for the work is being read in the light of ideas, of theories which are external to the text.

These theories draw attention to the fact that all writing is concerned with ordering the world through language and with the inadequacy of language to do this, including the language of structuralism. Regarding everything as a construct and order system, structuralism thus eventually turns on itself as yet another artificial ordering-system. This is the point at which structuralism becomes post-structuralism, a line probably first crossed in 1970 by Roland Barthes in his book *S/Z*. With post-structuralism we move into an area where we might appear to be in total chaos, unable to describe or make sense of anything. Yet the very fact that critics have worked out a post-structuralist position underlines how criticism is perpetually engaged in trying to respond to and order the problems and disorder it perceives in the world and the text.

POST-STRUCTURALISM

(i) *Introduction.* Post-structuralism begins at the point where structuralists start to doubt the adequacy of the comprehensive theory that they are imposing on literature. Post-structuralism is concerned less with establishing a firm hold on the text than with acknowledging the text's elusive nature and the fallibility of all readings. If this idea seems difficult to grasp it is because it is difficult to envisage a form of criticism that is concerned to stress the indeterminacy of all texts and the inadequacy of all readings.

(ii) *Theory.* Yet such criticism does exist, taking its lead from the work of the French philosopher Jacques Derrida, who has pursued to their conclusion some of structuralism's insights about a language. A central idea is that language is an infinite chain of words which has no extralingual origin or end. To describe this chain Derrida introduced the concept of *différance*: words are defined by their difference from other words, and any meaning is endlessly deferred as each word leads us on to another word in the signifying system. Language only makes sense if the reader imposes a fixed meaning on the words. Readers search for such a meaning because they are committed to the notion of presence, to the idea that there should be some referent and that words should make sense in relation to some presence outside the text. According to Derrida, however, the text should be seen as an endless stream of signifiers, with words only pointing to other words, without any final meaning.

Such a view rejects concepts such as common sense and reason as merely ordering-strategies that the reader imposes on literature: the reader wants to pull the text into his or her own frame of reference. Writers also attempt to impose ordering strategies on language, but these always prove inadequate. The form of criticism that emerges from such thinking is referred to as **deconstruction**. The terms deconstruction and post-structuralism are sometimes used interchangeably; strictly speaking, post-structuralism covers all the approaches that have developed in the wake of, and which take account of, the new insights into language that stemmed from structuralism. In the broadest terms, such approaches take a step back and look at how we conventionally organise the world. Deconstruction, which originates with Derrida, and which was taken up primarily by American critics such as J. Hillis Miller, is a rather less broadly-based outgrowth of structuralism. It is, at the same time, more overtly sceptical, tending to expose all the tactics any writer employs to marshal experience, and working with an idea of the impossibility of language achieving any kind of coherent engagement with the world.

A deconstructive reading is a sort of double reading: it acknowledges the way in which the writer attempts to order things, but then points to the contradictions and problems in the text, the complications that the writer cannot pull into her or his system. The critic's own response, however, can also be deconstructed, for the critic, too, is involved in trying to create coherence where none exists. Derrida's method is to look closely at individual texts, searching for the contradictions and, particularly in his studies of philosophical writing, the gaps in what appears to be a logical argument. He is fully aware, however, that his own readings can be deconstructed, for all readings are misreadings in that they impose ordering-strategies. The standard ordering strategy of Western culture is the organisation of our thoughts in binary pairs (for example, good and evil, black and white, man and woman). Derrida draws attention to the presence of, and inadequacy of, such an ordering strategy in texts but, as already suggested, is aware that his own text is likely to betray a similar dependency upon binary pairs in order to create a coherent case.

(iii) *Implications.* Like structuralism, deconstruction appears to stand outside the values and beliefs of society, but is even more all-questioning. The deconstructive reader appears to believe that nothing can be finally understood. In contrast, structuralism contains a strong element of reason in believing that it is possible to explain how literature works.

One criticism of deconstruction is that it fails to acknowledge the possibility that a text can confront experience in a way that communicates itself to the reader. The deconstructionist would argue that such a direct engagement with a text is an illusion, that what we are doing is imposing a determinate meaning on the words. The traditional critic could respond by saying that, although the deconstructive view has some substance, it is valid only at a theoretical level, that in practice we share a context of understanding with the writer and can quite legimately assign a meaning to what the text says. Such arguments, however, never arrive anywhere, because the two sides argue from such different premises.

Moreover, an attraction to the deconstructionist position often has more to do with the critic's attitudes than with agreement with the informing theory. The deconstructive position might appear to be one of non-involved scepticism, but implicit in it is a view of the world which finds experience chaotic and baffling. This is not particularly apparent in the work of Derrida, especially as he maintains that there is no reality outside language, but in the hands of those critics who have taken up his ideas a view of external reality becomes more explicit. Generally this view is that reality is too complex for a literary text or reader to make sense of. It is an idea that first came to the fore in structuralist criticism, but deconstruction extends it, stressing not only the limits of literature but also the limits of criticism.

(iv) *Deconstructive criticism.* Structuralist criticism often deals with those writers, such as Joyce, who are obviously concerned with discussing the nature of writing and its relation to reality. Deconstructive criticism frequently turns its attention to writers who seem more committed to expressing a view of life. J. Hillis Miller, for example, in a reading of *Middlemarch*, discusses how the principal images that appear in Eliot's novel collide with and undermine her claims for impartial vision. This is a typical deconstructive reading, emphasising the contradictions the writer cannot control. Miller was one of a group of critics at Yale University in the 1970s and early 1980s who adopted a deconstructionist position. Another was

Geoffrey Hartman, who has written about the 'vision' in Wordsworth's poetry. Whereas most critics concentrate on the substance and significance of this vision, Hartman stresses how it lies beyond the reach of language, and shows how Wordsworth's verse repeatedly becomes confused and puzzled because there is such a gap between the feeling and words.

Both these critics, then, stress the problems language experiences in trying to cope with life. Such an approach might seem negative, but deconstructive criticism is often very lively both because it recognises that the text is a complex thing and because the critic's sense that there is no determinate meaning to the text allows a degree of reckless freedom in discussing it. The method often is to take a small chunk of text and to point out just how problematic the passage is. It is sometimes suggested that in doing this deconstruction simply continues the method of close reading as practised by the New Critics, but, whereas in New Criticism the stress is on how the text finally, albeit in a complex way, holds together and makes sense, deconstruction emphasises the way in which a text becomes problematic and confused.

(v) *The limits of deconstruction.* We have written about deconstruction at length because it was the most controversial progeny of structuralism, and still attracts a great deal of attention and even anger (the majority of philosophers in British universities have very little time for Derrida, who, as a philosopher, challenges the very principles of reason on which philosophy is constructed). But there is more to post-structuralism than deconstruction; the story of criticism and theory in the last decade has been, in part, a rejection of and reaction against deconstruction, but at the same time an absorption of, and a working forwards from, deconstruction.

The old-fashioned, traditional objection to deconstruction is that it is a form of criticism which, rather than valuing what a text says, emphasises a text's difficulties in saying anything. To many this appeared a negative, destructive approach. But to anybody who had absorbed even a fraction of the message of structuralism and deconstruction, it became impossible to return to the old verities of criticism, for together they had exposed the kind of cosy complacency of much traditional criticism, in which the critic found a coherent pattern and set of values in the text which he (and in the context of traditional criticism it was a male view that was conventionally offered) could endorse. Wordsworth, for example, could be read as offering a positive vision that was relevant to, and could inspire, all of us. Structuralism, and then to an even greater extent deconstruction, stepped back from this conspiracy in which middle-class critics praised literature for its embodiment of middle-class values.

But those who had started to sense some of the political implications of structuralism and deconstruction began to question the remoteness of deconstruction, which could appear to become a kind of apolitical, endlessly sceptical game. The story, however, is more complex than a rejection of deconstruction, for what Marxist and feminist critics realised is that structuralism and deconstruction between them had offered the most radical analysis yet of the way in which Western society had constructed itself. Even something as simple as structuralism's notion of how society and thinking are constructed on the model of binary pairs, for example the pairing of man and woman, could lead on very quickly to the idea that there is something suspect in such a mode of organising life, that this particular pairing would privilege the man and marginalise the woman. What structuralism and deconstruction encouraged people to see was, in essence, that the order of the world was not something given, but something that the world had chosen to construct through language. Deconstruction, in short, provided a new angle from which to analyse the structure of Western society: for example, traditional critics had always endorsed the individual; deconstruction, taking a rather more sceptical view, could see the fragility of the construction of the notion of the individual.

The bulk of post-structuralist criticism is, therefore, more engaged, more political, than deconstruction, but although this appears to be a rejection of the non-involved stance of deconstruction, it is an engagement that is always firmly based upon a continuation of the kind of stepping outside traditional values that characterises deconstruction. This is true of Marxist and feminist criticism, and of the kind of psychoanalytic criticism which takes a step back and looks at the construction of the subject in Western society. It is also true of New Historicist criticism which, rather than just drawing a picture of a period, speculates on how and why any period constructs itself in a certain way. Traditional critics accepted that a text offered a coherent response to life and that critics could make sense of this. Post-structuralist critics, by contrast, tend to find incoherence, contradiction and anxiety in texts from the past;

they tend to stress the fragility of the ideological order of society rather than the strength or coherence of any period.

There are those who object to this aspect of post-structuralist criticism, arguing that critics are imposing the anxieties and concerns of the twentieth century on texts from the past, but post-structuralists accept that they are imposing on texts in this kind of way. Whether one likes it or not, it simply has to be accepted that Western society at the moment is endlessly engaged in a re-examination of its past, of the values it has inherited, and of the cultural and political orders, in particular the orders of black and white, male and female, Western and Eastern, that prevail in society today, and the ways in which they operate. Post-structuralist theory and criticism, which to the newcomer or outsider might seem trivial hair-splitting about books, is, in fact, the mode of writing in which a debate about all aspects of the past, present and future of society, and the place of people in society, is being conducted in the liveliest and most interesting way.

Further reading

Using a library

It is often the case that students do not really know how to make the best use of the English Literature section of a library. When it comes to finding a book on, say, Thomas Hardy there is obviously no problem: one goes to the shelves where the books are arranged by period and author. But a lot of students never realise that, as well as author and period sections, there is (usually) also a general English Literature section; nor do they realise that the most inter-esting ideas about the subject are often hidden away in these general books. Even if you do locate these books, however, there can still be a problem: it is far from clear which general books are going to be helpful and which are going to be irrelevant. It could take forever to sift through all the general books trying to find the kind of material you need. Not surprisingly, a lot of students give up looking and so miss out on much of the most rewarding criti-cism being written.

This Further Reading section is a guide to how to find the material you might want in the more general books in a library. (Remember that public libraries in Britain are obliged to obtain any book you request for a fee which is little more than the price of a stamp.) We have included the books that we have found most useful and which, for the most part, we know appeal to students. The list of books largely follows the sequence of the sections in this guide. This does, however, lead to some arbitrary decisions about where to place a book: a book by Bakhtin could, arguably, be included in the Drama section or the Novel section or the Con-cepts section. In fact, we have put one of his books in the Critical Concepts section and one in the Critical Positions section. You might, therefore, need to do some browsing before you find the reference you want. But it should be worth the effort because many of the best and most stimulating ideas about literature, indeed about history and culture generally, are to be found in the volumes listed here.

1. Histories of English literature

David Carroll and Michael Wheeler (eds), *Longman Literature in English Series* (London: Longman, 1985–92).

Martin Coyle, Peter Garside, Malcolm Kelsall and John Peck (eds), *Encyclopedia of Literature and Criticism* (London: Routledge, 1990).

A. N. Jeffares (ed.), *The Macmillan History of Literature* (9 vols) (London: Macmillan, 1982–8).

Pat Rogers (ed.), *The Oxford Illustrated History of English Literature* (London: Oxford University Press, 1987).

Anthologies of English literature

M. H. Abrams (ed.), *The Norton Anthology of English Literature* (5th edn; 2 vols) (London: Norton, 1986).

A. N. Jeffares and Michael Alexander (eds), *Macmillan Anthologies of English Literature* (5 vols) (London: Macmillan, 1989).

Anthologies of literary criticism

David Lodge (ed.), *Twentieth Century Literary Criticism: A Reader* (London: Longman, 1972).

Dennis Walder (ed.), *Literature in the Modern World: Critical Essays and Documents* (Oxford: Oxford University Press, 1990).

Period studies of literature

M. H. Abrams, *The Mirror and the Lamp: Romantic Theory and the Critical Tradition* (London: Oxford University Press, 1953).

David Aers (ed.), *Culture and History 1350–1600* (Brighton: Harvester Wheatsheaf, 1992).

Malcolm Bradbury and J. McFarlane (eds), *Modernism* (Harmondsworth: Penguin, 1976).

Marilyn Butler, *Romantics, Rebels and Reactionaries: English Literature and its Background 1760–1830* (Oxford: Oxford University Press, 1981).

Howard Erskine-Hill, *The Augustan Idea in English Literature* (London: Edward Arnold, 1983).

Donald Greene, *The Age of Exuberance: Backgrounds to Eighteenth-Century English Literature* (New York: Random House, 1970).

Stuart Hutchinson, *The American Scene: Essays on Nineteenth-Century American Literature* (London: Macmillan, 1991).

Jerome J. McGann, *The Romantic Ideology: A Critical Investigation* (Chicago: Chicago University Press, 1983).

David Norbrook, *Poetry and Politics in the English Renaissance* (London: Croom Helm, 1984).

Felicity Nussbaum and Laura Brown (eds), *The New Eighteenth Century* (New York: Methuen, 1987).

Pat Rogers, *The Augustan Vision* (London, Weidenfeld & Nicolson, 1974).

Alan Sinfield, *Society and Literature 1945–1970* (London: Methuen, 1983).

Michael Swanton, *English Literature Before Chaucer* (London: Longman, 1987).

Raymond Williams, *Culture and Society 1780–1950* (Harmondsworth: Penguin, 1961).

Post-colonial literature

Bill Ashcroft, Gareth Griffiths and Helen Tiffin, *The Empire Writes Back: Theory and Practice in Post-Colonial Literature* (London: Routledge, 1989).

Henry Louis Gates Jr (ed.), *Black Literature and Literary Theory* (London: Methuen, 1984).

Bruce King, *The New English Literatures: Cultural Nationalism in a Changing World* (London: Macmillan, 1980).

2. Poetry

John Barrell, *Poetry, Language and Politics* (Manchester: Manchester University Press, 1988).

Harold Bloom, *The Anxiety of Influence: A Theory of Poetry* (New York: Oxford University Press, 1973).

Anthony Easthope, *Poetry as Discourse* (London: Methuen, 1983).

Paul Fussell, *Poetic Meter and Poetic Form* (New York: Random House, 1965).

David Lindley, *Lyric* (London: Methuen, 1985).

Richard Machin and Christopher Norris (eds), *Post-Structuralist Readings of English Poetry* (Cambridge: Cambridge University Press, 1987).

Winifred Nowottny, *The Language Poets Use* (London: Athlone Press, 1962).

W. M. Rosenthal, *The Poet's Art* (New York: Norton, 1987).

Barbara Herrnstein Smith, *Poetic Closure: A Study of How Poems End* (Chicago: University of Chicago Press, 1968).

Period studies of poetry

David Aers, *Chaucer, Langland and the Creative Imagination* (London: Routledge, 1979).

Isobel Armstrong, *Language as Living Form in Nineteenth Century Poetry* (Brighton: Harvester Press, 1982).

Anne Margaret Doody, *The Daring Muse: Augustan Poetry Reconsidered* (Cambridge: Cambridge University Press, 1985).

Rod Edmond, *Affairs of the Hearth: Victorian Poetry and Domestic Narrative* (London: Routledge, 1988).

E. D. H. Johnson, *The Alien Vision of Victorian Poetry* (Princeton: Princeton University Press, 1952).

Hugh Kenner, *The Pound Era* (London: Faber & Faber, 1972).

John Lucas, *Modern English Poetry from Hardy to Hughes* (London: Batsford, 1986).

Lauro Martines, *Society and History in English Renaissance Verse* (Oxford: Basil Blackwell, 1985).

George Parfitt, *English Poetry of the Seventeenth Century* (London: Longman, 1985).

Derek Pearsall, *Old English and Middle English Poetry* (London: Routledge & Kegan Paul, 1977).

John Press, *A Map of Modern English Verse* (Oxford: Oxford University Press, 1969).

Anthony Thwaite, *Poetry Today* (London: Longman, 1985).

Robert Von Hallberg, *American Poetry and Culture 1945–80* (Cambridge: Harvard University Press, 1985).

John Williams, *Twentieth Century British Poetry* (London: Edward Arnold, 1987).

3. Drama

Eric Bentley, *The Life of the Drama* (London: Methuen, 1965).

Peter Brook, *The Empty Space* (Harmondsworth: Penguin, 1972).

T. W. Craik (general ed.), *The Revels History of Drama in English* (8 vols) (London: Methuen, 1975).

S. W. Dawson, *Drama and the Dramatic* (London: Methuen, 1970).

Martin Esslin, *The Field of Drama* (London: Methuen, 1987).

Francis Fergusson, *The Idea of a Theater* (New York: Doubleday, 1953).

Northrop Frye, *A Natural Perspective* (New York: Columbia University Press, 1965).

H. D. F. Kitto, *Form and Meaning in Drama* (London: Methuen, 1956).

Clifford Leech, *Tragedy* (London: Methuen, 1969).

John McGrath, *A Good Night Out: Popular Theatre: Audience Class and Form* (London: Methuen, 1981).

Richard Southern, *Seven Ages of Theatre* (London: Faber & Faber, 1962).

George Steiner, *The Death of Tragedy* (London: Faber & Faber, 1961).

Wylie Sypher (ed.), *Comedy* (New York: Doubleday Anchor, 1956).

John Willet (ed.), *Brecht on Theatre* (London: Methuen, 1964).

Raymond Williams, *Drama in Perspective* (Harmondsworth: Penguin, 1968).

Period studies of drama

Catherine Belsey, *The Subject of Tragedy: Identity and Difference in Renaissance Drama* (London: Methuen, 1985).

Eric Bentley (ed.), *The Theory of the Modern Stage* (Harmondsworth: Penguin, 1968).

Enoch Brater (ed.), *The New Women Playwrights* (New York: Oxford University Press, 1989).

John Bull, *New British Political Dramatists* (London: Macmillan, 1984).

Edward Burns, *Restoration Comedy: Crises of Desire and Identity* (London: Macmillan, 1987).

Sue-Ellen Case, *Feminism and Theatre* (New York: Methuen, 1988).

Jonathan Dollimore, *Radical Tragedy: Religion, Ideology and Power in the Drama of Shakespeare and his Contemporaries* (Brighton: Harvester, 1984).

John Drakakis (ed.), *Alternative Shakespeares* (London: Methuen, 1985).

John Drakakis (ed.), *Shakespearean Tragedy* (London: Longman, 1992).

Richard Dutton, *Modern Tragicomedy and the British Tradition* (Brighton: Harvester, 1986).

Martin Esslin, *The Theatre of the Absurd* (London: Eyre & Spottiswoode, 1962).

Michael Hattaway and A. R. Braunmuller (eds), *The Cambridge Companion to English Renaissance Drama* (Cambridge: Cambridge University Press, 1990).

Helene Keyssar, *Feminist Theatre* (London: Macmillan, 1984).

Kathleen McLuskie, *Renaissance Dramatists* (Hemel Hempstead: Harvester Wheatsheaf, 1989).

David Ian Robey, *British and Irish Political Drama in the Twentieth Century* (London: Macmillan, 1986).

William Tydeman, *English Medieval Theatre 1400–1500* (London: Routledge & Kegan Paul, 1986).

Gary Waller (ed.), *Shakespeare's Comedies* (London: Longman, 1991).

Glynne Wickham, *The Medieval Theatre* (London: Weidenfeld & Nicolson, 1974).

Raymond Williams, *Drama from Ibsen to Brecht* (London: Chatto & Windus, 1968).

James Woodfield, *English Theatre in Transition 1881–1914* (London: Croom Helm, 1984).

4.   The novel

Robert Alter, *Partial Magic: The Novel as Self-Conscious Genre* (Berkeley: University of California Press, 1975).

Nancy Armstrong, *Desire and Domestic Fiction: A Political History of the Novel* (Oxford: Oxford University Press, 1987).

Wayne C. Booth, *The Rhetoric of Fiction* (Chicago: University of Chicago Press, 1961).

George Dekker, *The American Historical Romance* (Cambridge: Cambridge University Press, 1987).

Elizabeth Deeds Ermarth, *Realism and Consensus in the English Novel* (Princeton: Princeton University Press, 1983).

Avrom Fleishman, *The English Historical Novel* (Baltimore: Johns Hopkins University Press, 1971).

George Levine, *The Realistic Imagination* (Chicago: University of Chicago Press, 1981).

Georg Lukács, *The Historical Novel* (London: Merlin, 1962).

Period studies of the novel

Gillian Beer, *Darwin's Plots: Evolutionary Narrative in Darwin, George Eliot, and Nineteenth-Century Fiction* (London: Routledge & Kegan Paul, 1983).

Malcolm Bradbury (ed.), *The Novel Today* (Glasgow: Fontana, 1977).

Hazel V. Carby, *Reconstructing Womanhood: The Emergence of the Afro-American Woman Novelist* (Oxford: Oxford University Press, 1987).

Lennard J. Davies, *Factual Fictions: The Origins of the English Novel* (New York: Columbia University Press, 1983).

Catharine Gallagher, *The Industrial Reformation of English Fiction 1832–1867* (Chicago: University of Chicago Press, 1985).

Robert Kiely, *The Romantic Novel in England* (Cambridge: Harvard University Press, 1972).

Brian McHale, *Postmodernist Fiction* (London: Methuen, 1987).

John Orr, *The Making of the Twentieth Century Novel: Lawrence, Joyce, Faulkner and Beyond* (London: Macmillan, 1987).

Andrew Sanders, *The Victorian Historical Novel 1840–1880* (London: Macmillan, 1979).

P. M. Spacks, *Imagining a Self: Autobiography and Novel in Eighteenth-Century England* (Cambridge: Harvard University Press, 1976).

Jane Spencer, *The Rise of the Woman Novelist: from Aphra Benn to Jane Austen* (Oxford: Basil Blackwell, 1986).

5.   Concepts

Roland Barthes, *Mythologies* (London: Jonathan Cape, 1972).

M. M. Bakhtin, *Rabelais and His World* (London: MIT Press, 1968).

R. L. Brett, *Fancy and Imagination* (London: Methuen, 1969).

Charles Chadwick, *Symbolism* (London: Methuen, 1971).

Terry Eagleton, *Ideology* (London: Verso, 1991).

Angus Fletcher, *Allegory: The Theory of a Symbolic Mode* (Ithaca: Cornell University Press, 1964).

Alastair Fowler, *Kinds of Literature: An Introduction to the Theory of Genres and Modes* (Oxford: Clarendon Press, 1982).

Terry Eagleton, *Criticism and Ideology* (London: Verso, 1976).

P. N. Furbank, *Reflections on the Word 'Image'* (London: Secker & Warburg, 1970).

Terence Hawkes, *Metaphor* (London: Methuen, 1972).

Linda Hutcheon, *A Poetics of Postmodernism* (London: Routledge, 1987).

Frank Kermode, *The Classic* (London: Faber & Faber, 1975).

Arthur Pollard, *Satire* (London: Methuen, 1970).

Raymond Williams, *Keywords* (Glasgow: Collins, 1976).

6.   Critical positions and perspectives
Introductions to theory

Terry Eagleton, *Literary Theory: An Introduction* (Oxford: Basil Blackwell, 1983).

Geoffrey Hartman, *Criticism in the Wilderness: The Study of Literature Today* (New Haven: Yale University Press, 1980).

Ann Jefferson and David Robey (eds), *Modern Literary Theory: A Comparative Introduction* (London: Batsford, 1982).

David Lodge (ed.), *Modern Criticism and Theory: A Reader* (London: Longman, 1988).

Rick Rylance (ed.), *Debating Texts: A Reader in Twentieth-Century Literary Theory and Method* (Milton Keynes: Open University Press, 1987).

Raman Selden, *A Reader's Guide To Contemporary Literary Theory* (Brighton: Harvester Press, 1985).

Traditional criticism

Chris Baldick, *The Social Mission of English Criticism, 1848–1932* (Oxford: Clarendon Press, 1983).

Cleanth Brooks, *The Well Wrought Urn* (New York: Harcourt Brace, 1947).

William Empson, *Seven Types of Ambiguity* (London: Chatto & Windus, 1930).

John Fekete, *The Critical Twilight: Explorations in the Ideology of Anglo-American Literary Theory from Eliot to McLuhan* (London: Routledge & Kegan Paul, 1977).

F. R. Leavis, *New Bearings in English Poetry* (London: Chatto & Windus, 1933).

F. R. Leavis, *The Great Tradition* (London: Chatto & Windus, 1948).

Francis Mulhern, *The Moment of 'Scrutiny'* (London: New Left Books, 1979).

Christopher Norris, *William Empson and the Philosophy of Literary Criticism* (London: 1978).

D. J. Palmer, *The Rise of English Studies* (London: Oxford University Press, 1965).

I. A. Richards, *Principles of Literary Criticism* (London: Kegan Paul, Trench, Trubner, 1924).

I. A. Richards, *Practical Criticism* (London: Routledge & Kegan Paul, 1929).

John Crowe Ransom, *The New Criticism* (Norfolk: New Directions, 1941).

From Russian Formalism to structuralism

Tony Bennett, *Formalism and Marxism* (London: Methuen, 1979).

Victor Erlich, *Russian Formalism: History – Doctrine* (The Hague: Mouton, 1955).

Northrop Frye, *Anatomy of Criticism* (Princeton: Princeton University Press, 1957).

Frederic Jameson, *The Prison-House of Language* (Princeton: Princeton University Press, Mouton, 1972).

Lee T. Lemon and Marion J. Reis (eds), *Russian Formalist Criticism: Four Essays* (Lincoln: University of Nebraska Press, 1965).

Christopher Pike (ed.), *The Futurists, the Formalists and the Marxist Critique* (London: Ink Links, 1979).

Jonathan Culler, *Saussure* (Glasgow: Collins, 1976).

Ewa M. Thompson, *Russian Formalism and Anglo-American New Criticism: A Comparative Study* (The Hague: Mouton, 1971).

Structuralism

Jonathan Culler, *Structuralist Poetics* (London: Routledge & Kegan Paul, 1975).

Umberto Eco, *A Theory of Semiotics* (London: Macmillan, 1976).

Terence Hawkes, *Structuralism and Semiotics* (London: Methuen, 1977).

Edmund Leach, *Lévi-Strauss* (London: Fontana, 1970).

Claude Lévi-Strauss, *The Savage Mind* (London: Weidenfeld & Nicolson, 1966).

David Robey (ed.), *Structuralism: An Introduction* (Oxford: Clarendon Press, 1973).

Tzvetan Todorov, *The Poetics of Prose* (Oxford: Basil Blackwell, 1977).

Post-structuralism and deconstruction

Roland Barthes, *S/Z* (London: Jonathan Cape, 1975).

Catherine Belsey, *Critical Practice* (London: Methuen, 1980).

Jonathan Culler, *On Deconstruction: Theory and Criticism After Structuralism* (London: Routledge & Kegan Paul, 1983).

Jonathan Culler, *Framing the Sign: Criticism and its Institutions* (Oxford: Basil Blackwell, 1988).

Paul de Man, *Allegories of Reading* (New Haven: Yale University Press, 1979).

Jacques Derrida, *Of Grammatology* (Baltimore: Johns Hopkins University Press, 1976).

Jacques Derrida, *Writing and Difference* (London: Routledge & Kegan Paul, 1978).

Geoffrey Hartman (ed.), *Deconstruction and Criticism* (London: Routledge & Kegan Paul, 1979).

J. Hillis Miller, *Fiction and Repetition: Seven English Novels* (Oxford: Basil Blackwell, 1982).

Frank Lentricchia, *After the New Criticism* (Chicago: University of Chicago Press, 1980).

Christopher Norris, *Deconstruction: Theory and Practice* (London: Methuen, 1982).

Christopher Norris, *Derrida* (London: Fontana, 1987).

Christopher Norris, *Deconstruction and the Interests of Theory* (New York: Routledge, 1988; London: Frances Pinter, 1988).

Feminism

Catherine Belsey and Jane Moore (eds), *The Feminist Reader: Essays in Gender and the Politics of Literary Criticism* (London: Macmillan, 1989).

Barbara Christian, *Black Feminist Criticism: Perspectives on Black Women Writers* (New York: Pergamon Press, 1985).

Hélène Cixous, *'Coming to Writing' and Other Essays* (Cambridge: Harvard University Press, 1991).

Mary Eagleton (ed.), *Feminist Literary Criticism* (London: Longman, 1991).

Jane Gallop, *Feminism and Psychoanalysis: The Daughter's Seduction* (Ithaca: Cornell University Press, 1982).

Sandra Gilbert and Susan Gubar, *The Madwoman in the Attic: The Woman Writer and the Nineteenth Century Literary Imagination* (New Haven: Yale University Press, 1979).

Mary Jacobus, *Women Writing and Writing about Women* (London: Croom Helm, 1979).

Julia Kristeva, *Desire in Language: A Semiotic Approach to Literature and Art* (New York: Columbia University Press, 1980).

Julia Kristeva, *Revolution in Poetic Language* (New York: Columbia University Press, 1984).

Elaine Marks and Isabelle de Courtivron, *New French Feminisms* (Brighton: Harvester, 1981).

Nancy K. Miller (ed.), *The Poetics of Gender* (New York: Columbia University Press, 1986).

Kate Millett, *Sexual Politics* (London: Virago, 1969).

Toril Moi, *Sexual/Textual Politics: Feminist Literary Theory* (London: Methuen, 1985).

Mary Poovey, *Uneven Developments: The Ideological Work of Gender in Mid-Victorian England* (London: Virago, 1988).

Marjorie Pryse and Hortense J. Spillers, *Conjuring: Black Women, Fiction, and Literary Tradition* (Bloomington: Indiana University Press, 1985).

Jacqueline Rose, *Sexuality in the Field of Vision* (London: Verso, 1986).

Morag Shiach, *Hélène Cixous: A Politics of Writing* (London: Routledge, 1991).

Elaine Showalter, *A Literature of Their Own: British Women Novelists from Brontë to Lessing* (Princeton: Princeton University Press, 1977).

Elaine Showalter (ed.), *Speaking of Gender* (London: Routledge, 1989).

Janet Todd, *Feminist Literary History* (Oxford: Polity Press, 1988).

Cheryl A. Wall (ed.), *Changing Our Own Words: Essays on Criticism, Theory and Writing by Black Women* (New Brunswick: Rutgers University Press, 1989).

Virginia Woolf, *A Room of One's Own* (London: Hogarth Press, 1929).

Virginia Woolf, *Women and Writing* (London: The Women's Press, 1979).

Marxism

Walter Benjamin, *Illuminations* (New York: Schocken, 1969).

Terry Eagleton, *Marxism and Literary Criticism* (London: Methuen, 1976).

John Frow, *Marxism and Literary History* (Oxford: Basil Blackwell, 1986).

Frederic Jameson, *Marxism and Form* (Princeton: Princeton University Press, 1971).

Frederic Jameson, *The Political Unconscious* (London: Methuen, 1981).

Georg Lukács, *The Historical Novel* (Harmondsworth: Penguin, 1974).

Pierre Macherey, *A Theory of Literary Production* (London: Routledge & Kegan Paul, 1978).

Michael Ryan, *Marxism and Deconstruction* (Baltimore: Johns Hopkins University Press, 1982).

Raymond Williams, *Marxism and Literature* (Oxford: Oxford University Press, 1977).

Narratology and reader-response criticism

M. M. Bakhtin, *The Dialogic Imagination* (Austin: University of Texas Press, 1981).

Umberto Eco, *The Role of the Reader: Explorations in the Semiotics of Texts* (London: Hutchinson, 1981).

Stanley Fish, *Is There a Text in This Class? The Authority of Interpretive Communities* (Cambridge: Harvard University Press, 1979).

Elizabeth Freund, *The Return of the Reader: Reader-Response Criticism* (London: Methuen, 1987).

Gérard Genette, *Narrative Discourse* (Oxford: Basil Blackwell, 1980).

Robert C. Holub, *Reception Theory* (London: Methuen, 1984).

Wolfgang Iser, *The Implied Reader* (Baltimore: Johns Hopkins University Press, 1974).

D. A. Miller, *Narrative and its Discontents: Problems of Closure in the Traditional Novel* (Princeton: Princeton University Press, 1981).

Vladimir Propp, *The Morphology of the Folktale* (Austin: University of Texas Press, 1968).

S. Rimmon-Kenan, *Narrative Fiction: Contemporary Poetics* (London: Methuen, 1983).

Jane P. Tompkins (ed.), *Reader-Response Criticism* (Baltimore: Johns Hopkins University Press, 1980).

New Historicism

Jonathan Dollimore and Alan Sinfied (eds), *Political Shakespeare: New Essays in Cultural Materialism* (London: Methuen, 1985).

Michel Foucault, *The Archaeology of Knowledge* (London: Tavistock, 1972).

Michel Foucault, *Madness and Civilization* (London: Tavistock, 1976).

Michel Foucault, *Discipline and Punish* (London: Allen Lane, 1977).

Michel Foucault, *The History of Sexuality* (London: Allen Lane, 1979).

Henry Louis Gates, Jr (ed.), *Race, Writing and Difference* (Chicago, University of Chicago Press, 1985).

Jonathan Goldberg, *James I and the Politics of Literature* (Baltimore: Johns Hopkins University Press, 1983).

Stephen Greenblatt, *Renaissance Self-Fashioning* (Chicago: Chicago University Press, 1980).

Stephen Greenblatt, *Representing the English Renaissance* (Berkeley: University of California Press, 1988).

Thomas Healy, *New Latitudes: Theory and English Renaissance Literature* (London: Edward Arnold, 1992).

Edward Said, *The World, the Text, and the Critic* (Cambridge: Harvard University Press, 1983).

Gayatri Chakravorty Spivak, *In Other Worlds: Essays in Cultural Politics* (London: Methuen, 1987).

Leonard Tennenhouse, *Power on Display: The Politics of Shakespeare's Genres* (New York: Methuen, 1986).

Harold A. Veeser (ed.), *The New Historicism* (London: Routledge, 1989).

Psychoanalysis and literature

Maud Bodkin, *Archetypal Patterns in Poetry* (London: Oxford University Press, 1934).

Marie Bonaparte, *The Life and Works of Edgar Allan Poe* (London: Imago, 1949).

Gilles Deleuze and Félix Guattari, *Anti-Oedipus: Capitalism and Schizophrenia* (Minneapolis: University of Minnesota Press, 1983).

Shoshana Felman, *Jacques Lacan and the Adventure of Insight: Psychoanalysis and Contemporary Culture* (Cambridge: Harvard University Press, 1987).

Jane Gallop, *Reading Lacan* (Ithaca: Cornell University Press, 1985).

Jacques Lacan, *Écrits: A Selection* (London: Tavistock, 1977).

Toril Moi (ed.), *The Kristeva Reader* (Oxford: Basil Blackwell, 1986).

Elizabeth Wright, *Psychoanalytic Criticism: Theory in Practice* (London: Methuen, 1984).

7.   Guides to literary terms

M. H. Abrams, *A Glossary of Literary Terms* (5th edn) (London: Holt, Rinehart & Winston, 1988).

Roger Fowler (ed.), *A Dictionary of Modern Critical Terms* (revised and enlarged edition) (London: Routledge & Kegan Paul, 1987).

Author index

This index lists the authors (with their dates in brackets) and critics discussed in the guide as well as titles of anonymous works, but not the Further Reading section. Page numbers in **bold type** identify the main discussion of an author.

Achebe, Chinua (*b.* 1930), 9
Adcock, Fleur (*b.* 1934), 75
Althusser, Louis, 147, 161, 169, 177
Anglo-Saxon Chronicles, 2
Arden, John (*b.* 1930), 103
Armstrong, Nancy, 172, 178
Arnold Matthew (1822–88), 42–3
Ashbery, John (*b.* 1927), 8, 73
Atwood, Margaret (*b.* 1939), 75, 130
Auden, W. H. (1907–73), 7, **71–2**
Austen, Jane (1775–1817), 4, 109, 111, 117, 118, **119–20**, 174
Ayckbourn, Alan (*b.* 1939), 103

Bakhtin, Mikhail, 137–8, 178–9, 190
Baldwin, James (1924–87), 10
Barthes, Roland, 157, 158, 159, 163, 169, 191, 194
Battle of Maldon, 2
Beardsley, Monroe, 132, 147
Beauvoir, Simone de (1908–86), 171
Beckett, Samuel (1906–89), 86, 92–3, 101, **103**
Beer, Gillian, 172
Bellow, Saul (*b.* 1915), 8, 127
Bennett, Arnold (1867–1931), 127
Beowulf, 2, 52
Berryman, John (1914–72), 8, 72, 73
Blackmur, R. P., 180
Blake, William (1757–1827), 5, **62–3**, 68–9, 70
Bloom, Harold, 163–4
Bodkin, Maud, 186

Bonaparte, Marie, 186
Bond, Edward (*b.* 1935), 103, 104
Brecht, Bertolt (1898–1956), 92, **102–3**, 105
Brenton, Howard (*b.* 1942), 103, 104
Brontë, Charlotte (1816–55), 124, **127**, 138, 171, 179
Brontë, Emily (1818–48), 75
Brooke, Rupert (1887–1915), 70
Brooks, Cleanth, 154–5, 180
Browning, Elizabeth Barrett (1806–61), 75
Browning, Robert (1812–89), 5, **26–7**, 35, 52, 68
Bunyan, John (1828–88), 133
Byron, Lord (1788–1824), 5, 35, 52, 62

Carpentier, Alejo (1904–80), 129
Carter, Angela (1940–92), 130
Castle of Perseverance, 90
Cervantes, Miguel de (1547–1616), **114**, 123
Chaucer, Geoffrey (*c.* 1340–1400), 2–3, 25–6, 27–8, 35, **52**, 57, 142
Chekhov, Anton (1860–1904), **85–6**, 91, 101
Churchill, Caryl (*b.* 1938), 7, 99, 101, **104–5**
Cixous, Hélène, 157, 171, 172
Coleridge, Samuel Taylor (1772–1834), 5, 17–18, 22, 28, 43, 52, 53, 62, **64–5**, 69, 143–4, 155, 159
Congreve, William (1670–1729), 93

Conrad, Joseph (1857–1924), 6, 117, **122**, 128, 149, 174
Crane, Stephen (1871–1900), 120
Crashaw, Richard (1612–49), 44

Defoe, Daniel (1660–1731), 107, **112–13**
Deleuze, Gilles, 188
Derrida, Jacques, 139, 169, 171, 183, 194, 195, 196
Dickens, Charles (1812–70), 5–6, 112, 116, **118**, 119, 122, 158–9, 161, 186
Dickinson, Emily (1830–86), 6, 75, **76**
Donne, John (1572–1631), 3, 15, 17, 24–5, 32, 35, 41–2, **44–6**, 57, 60, 148, 153, 154–5, 180
Douglas, Keith (1920–44), 72
Dream of the Rood, 2
Dreiser, Theodore (1871–1945), 120
Dryden, John (1631–1700), 4, 32, 35, 49, **50**, 58, 148, 159
Duffy, Carol Ann (b. 1955), 75

Eagleton, Terry, 178
Eliot, George (1819–80), 5–6, 109, 110, 111, **118**, 119, 121, 122, 126, 128, 158, 174, 196
Eliot, T. S. (1888–1965), 6, 7, 15, 24, 27, 34, **50–1**, 70, 71–2, 73, 180
Ellison, Ralph (b. 1914), 10
Emerson, Ralph Waldo (1803–82), 6
Empson, William, 134, 138, 181
Everyman, 90

Faulkner, William (1897–1962), 7, **125**
Fielding, Henry (1707–54), 4, 112, **113–14**, 121
Fish, Stanley, 189
Fitzgerald, F. Scott (1896–1940), 7, **122–3**
Forster, E. M. (1879–1970), 115, 117, 120
Foucault, Michel, 142, 170, 172, 183
Fowles, John (b. 1926), 121
Freud, Sigmund (1856–1939), 140, 186, 187
Frost, Robert (1875–1963), 27, 52, 73
Frye, Northrop, 136, 192
Fugard, Athol (b. 1932), 9

Gallagher, Catharine, 172
Galsworthy, John (1867–1933), 127
García Márquez, Gabriel (b. 1928), 129
Gems, Pam (b. 1925), 104
Genette, Gérard, 178
Gilbert, Sandra, 171
Golding, William (b. 1911), 7
Goldmann, Lucien, 169
Goldsmith, Oliver (1730–74), 85, **93–4**
Gray, Thomas (1716–71), 46–7
Greenblatt, Stephen, 182, 183–4
Greene, Graham (1904–91), 7, 117, 127
Griffiths, Trevor (b. 1953), 7, 103
Guattari, Félix, 188
Gubar, Susan, 171
Gunn, Thom (b. 1929), 72

Hardy, Thomas (1840–1928)
    novels, 6, **117–19**, 126, 186
    poetry, 36–7, 60, 73
Hare, David (b. 1948), 7, 103
Harrison, Tony (b. 1937), 73
Hartman, Geoffrey, 197
Hawthorne, Nathaniel (1804–64), 7
Heaney, Seamus (b. 1939), 7, 73
Hemingway, Ernest (1898–1961), 127
Herbert, George (1593–1633), 41, 42, 44, **45**, 67
Herrick, Robert (1591–1674), 32
Hopkins, Gerard Manley (1844–89), 18, **48–9**, 68
Housman, A. E. (1859–1936), 70
Hughes, Ted (b. 1930), 72
Hume, Keri (b. 1947), 9
Hurston, Zora Neale (1901–60), 10
Husserl, Edmund, 185

Ibsen, Henrik (1828–1906), 86–7, **91**, 99, 100, 105
Irigaray, Luce, 171, 172
Iser, Wolfgang, 188

Jacobus, Mary, 172
Jakobson, Roman, 153–4
James, Henry (1843–1916), 7, 120, 123, 124, 127, **128**, 174
Jameson, Frederic, 178
Jardine, Alice, 172
Jauss, Hans Robert, 188

Johnson, Samuel (1709–84), 29, 148
Jonson, Ben (1572–1637)
    drama, 3, 85, 87, **88–9**, 159
    poetry, 25, 28–9, 32, **41**
Joyce, James (1882–1941), 6, 7, 121–2,
    124, 128–9, 157, 159, 196

Keats, John (1795–1821), 5, 16, 19, 20,
    22, 35, 38, 42, 48, 52, 53, 55, 61–2,
    65, 70, 143, 144, 155, 159
Kipling, Rudyard (1865–1936), 27
Klein, Melanie, 186
Kristeva, Julia, 141, 171, 172
Kundera, Milan (*b.* 1929), 130
Kyd, Thomas (1558–95), 88

Lacan, Jacques, 140, 141, 161, 169, 171,
    172, 187
Lane, Carla, 105
Langland, William (*c.* 1330–1400), 28
Larkin, Philip (1922–85), 7, **43**, 72
Lawrence, D. H. (1885–1930), 6, 34, 120,
    125–7, **127–8**, 150–1, 174
Leavis, F. R., 167, 168, **173–6**, 177, 181,
    182
Lessing, Doris (*b.* 1919), 9, 127
Lévi-Strauss, Claude, 169, 191
Lewis, C. Day (1898–1963), 71
Lodge, David, 154
Lowell, Robert (1917–77), 8, 72, 73
Lukács, Georg, 169, 176

McEwan, Ian (*b.* 1948), 8
MacNeice, Louis (1907–63), 71
Macherey, Pierre, 169, 177
Mare, Walter de la (1873–1956), 70
Marlowe, Christopher (1564–93), 3, 82,
    87, **88**, 90, 184
Márquez, *see* García Márquez
Marvell, Andrew (1621–78), 32, 44, **54**,
    58–9, 154
Masefield, John (1878–1967), 70
Melville, Herman (1819–91), 7, 109, 122
Middleton, Thomas (1580–1627), 87, **89**
Miller, Arthur (*b.* 1915), 8, 100, 101
Miller, D. A., 179
Miller, J. Hillis, 139, 179, 185–6, 195,
    196
Millett, Kate, 155, 171

Milton, John (1608–74), 4, 19, 23, 26,
    30, **31–2**, 47, 50, 54, 56, 57, 66, 162
Morris, William (1834–96), 123
Morrison, Toni (*b.* 1931), 10, 130
Murdoch, Iris (*b.* 1919), 127

Nabokov, Vladimir (1899–1977), 129
Naipaul, V. S. (*b.* 1932), 9–10
Ngugi wa Thiong'o (*b.* 1938), 10

O'Casey, Sean (1884–1964), 102
O'Neill, Eugene (1888–1953), 8, 100,
    101
Orwell, George (1903–50), 133
Osborne, John (*b.* 1929), 7, 91, **102**
Owen, Wilfred (1893–1918), 20–1, 70

Peacock, Thomas Love (1785–1866),
    111, 159
Pinter, Harold (*b.* 1930), 7, **82**, 101, 103
Plath, Sylvia (1932–63), 72, 73, 75
Poe, Edgar Allan (1809–49), 122
Poovey, Mary, 138, 172, 178
Pope, Alexander (1688–1744), 4, 28,
    29–30, 35–6, 49, 52, 58, **73–5**, 144,
    147–8, 159, 162
Poulet, Georges, 185
Pound, Ezra (1885–1974), 7, 34, **39–40**,
    50, 70, 71–2, 73
Propp, Vladimir, 178
Pynchon, Thomas (*b.* 1937), 8, 129

Raine, Craig (*b.* 1944), 73
Ransom, John Crowe, 180
Rich, Adrienne (*b.* 1929), 8, 73, 75,
    76–7
Richards, I. A., 150, 174, 180
Richardson, Dorothy (1873–1957), 125
Richardson, Samuel (1689–1761), 4,
    113, 120, 124
Robbe-Grillet, Alain (*b.* 1922), 129
Rose, Jacqueline, 172
Rossetti, Christina Georgina (1830–94),
    75
Rushdie, Salman (*b.* 1947), 8, 129
Ruskin, John (1819–1900), 155

Said, Edward, 130
Sassoon, Siegfried (1886–1967), 70

Saussure, Ferdinand de, 139, 169, 190–1

Scott, Sir Walter (1771–1832), 123

Scribe, Eugène (1791–1861), 91

Sexton, Anne (1928–74), 73

Shakespeare, William (1564–1616)·
  drama, 3–4, 23, 33, 78, 80, 81, 83, 84–5, 87, 90, 92, **94–9**, 99–100, 134, 135, 137, 143, 146, 152, 154, 156, 183, 184
  poetry, 17, 26, 35, 42, 56–7, **66–7**, 163

Shaw, George Bernard (1856–1950), 85, 91, **101**, 102, 104

Shelley, Percy Bysshe (1792–1822), 5, 32, 62, **65**, 139

Sheridan, Richard Brinsley (1751–1816), 85, **93–4**

Shklovsky, Victor, 189

Sidney, Sir Philip, (1554–86), 26, 32, 37–8, 66

Sir Gawain and the Green Knight, 2–3, 52, 61

Smith, Stevie (1902–71), 75

Smollet, Tobias (1721–71), 114

Soyinka, Wole (b. 1934), 9

Spender, Stephen (b. 1909), 71

Spenser, Edmund (1552–99), 3, 18, 19, 23, 26, 31, **32–3**, 35, 55–6, 57, 58, 61–2, 66, 133

Spivak, Gayatri, 173, 180

Sterne, Laurence (1713–68), 114, **121**, 189

Stevens, Wallace (1879–1955), 8, 34, 51, 65, 73

Stoppard, Tom (b. 1937), 7, **87**, 101, 103

Strindberg, August (1849–1912), 99, 100–1

Swift, Jonathan (1667–1745), 133, **148**, 149, 159

Synge, John Millington (1871–1909), 86, 101–2

Tate, Allen, 180

Tennyson, Alfred, Lord (1809–92), 5, 27, **30**, 32, 42, 52, 60–1

Terry, Megan (b. 1932), 104

Thackeray, William Makepeace (1811–63), 112, 117, 141

Thomas, D. M. (b. 1935), 8

Thomas, Dylan (1914–53), 72

Thomas, R. S. (b. 1913), 72

Tillyard, E. M. W., 182

Tolkien, J. R. R. (1892–1973), 107

Tomlinson, Charles (b. 1927), 73

Trollope, Anthony (1815–82), 120

Twain, Mark (1835–1910), 7, 122

Updike, John (b. 1932), 127

Vargas Llosa, Mario (b. 1936), 129

Vaughan, Henry (1622–95), 44

Walker, Alice (b. 1944), 10, 124, 130

Wandor, Michelene (b. 1940), 104

Webster, John (1580–1625), **83**, 87, 89

Wesker, Arnold (b. 1932), 103

White, Patrick (1912–90), 9

Whitman, Walt (1819–92), 6, **34–5**

Wilde, Oscar (1856–1900), 80, **85**, 91

Williams, Raymond, 169, 177, 178, 183

Williams, William Carlos (1883–1963), 8, 34, 40, 73

Wimsatt, W. K., 132, 147

Winterson, Jeanette (b. 1959), 130

Wollstonecraft, Mary (1759–97), 170

Women's Theatre Group, 104

Woolf, Virginia (1882–1941), 6, **125**, 128–9, 130–1, 171

Wordsworth, William (1770–1850), 5, 12, 15, 16, 19, 22, 23, 42, **43–4**, 52, 53–4, 55, 56, 62, 63–4, 65, 144, 151, 159, 192, 197

Wright, Richard (1908–60), 10

Wycherley, William (1640–1716), 93

Yeats, W. B. (1865–1939), 6, 37, 43, **51**, 58, 59, 65, 70, 71, 73

Zola, Émile (1840–1902), 120

Subject index

This index lists the terms and topics discussed in the guide. Page numbers in **bold type** identify the main discussion of a term.

absurd, theatre of, 86, 92–3, **103**
act, 81
affective fallacy, 132–3
African literature, 9
African-American literature, 10
alexandrine, 48
alienation, 92, **102–3**
allegory, 28, 32, 56, 57, 61–2, **133–4**
alliteration, 17–18
alliterative poetry, 48
allusion, 134
ambiguity, **134–5**, 138
American literature, **6–7**, 8, 10–11, 73, 122–3
Anglo-Saxon literature, 2
anisochrony, 178
antagonist, 83
anti-hero, 101
anxiety of influence, 163
aporia, **135–6**, 138
archaism, 19–20
archetype, 113, 136, 192
assonance, 20–1
Augustan, 29

ballad, **21–2**, 43, 52
binary opposition, **136–7**, 139, 143, 195, 198
black comedy, 86
Black studies, 173
blank verse, **22–3**, 47
British criticism, 173–6

caesura, 49
canon, the, 131, 156, 157, 176

canto, 68
carnival, **137–8**, 179
carpe diem motif, 154
character
  in drama, 78–80, **83–4**
  in novels, 107–8, **110–11**
closed couplets, 35
comedy
  drama, 81, **84–6**, 93–4, 94–5, 160
  novels, *see* comic novels
  satire, *difference from,* 158–9
comedy of manners, 84, **85**, 93
comic novels, **111–12**, 113
complication *in* drama, **79**, 86, 160
conceit, **24–5**, 45, 153, 154
consonance, **20–1**, 59
content, 144–5
context, 1–2
contradiction, **138–9**, 164, 167, 177
conventions, 139–40
couplet, 29, 35–6, **68**
courtesy rhymes, 59
courtly-love code, 25
courtly-love poetry, 25–6
critical appreciation, 145
critical concepts, **132–64**
  see affective fallacy, allegory, allusion, ambiguity, aporia, archetype, binary opposition, carnival, content, contradiction, conventions, desire, didactic, discourse, empathy, fancy, form, hermeneutics, ideology, imagination, interpretation, intentional fallacy, irony, language, metaphor, motif, para-

dox, pathetic fallacy, patriarchy, readerly, satire, semiotics, structure, style, subject, syntax, text, theme, writerly.

critical positions and perspectives, **165–99**

    see British criticism, deconstruction, feminist criticism, Marxist criticism, narratology, New Criticism, New Historicism, phenomenological criticism, post-structuralism, psychoanalytic criticism, reader-response criticism, Russian Formalism, structuralism

critical theory, 168–70

criticism, 165–70

    guidelines, 1–2, 135, 141–2, 144–5, 147, 151, 160, **165–8**

    of drama, 78–81

    of novels, 107–9

    of poetry, 12–17

critique, 166

cultural materialism, 183, 184

curtal sonnet, 68

Czech Formalism, *see* Prague school

death of the author, 163, 166

deconstruction, 135, 136, 137, 138, 139, 163, 169–70, 171, 172, 178, 183, 187, 189, 190, **195–9**

defamiliarisation, **153**, 189

dénouement, 86

desire, 140–1

dialogic, 137

didactic, 141–2

différance, 139, 194

discourse, 53, 108, **142–3**, 183

drama, **78–106**

    see act, character, comedy, dramatic structure, Elizabethan and Jacobean drama, feminist theatre, film, medieval drama, nineteenth-century drama, plot, Restoration comedy, scene, Shakespeare, television, tragedy, twentieth-century drama

dramatic form, 87

dramatic irony, 149

dramatic monologue, 26–7

dramatic structure, **86–7**, 105

dream poetry, 27–8

écriture féminine, 157, 172

education novel, 115

eighteenth-century literature, 4

    see also eighteenth-century novels, eighteenth-century poetry, irony, Restoration comedy, satire

eighteenth-century novels, 112–14

eighteenth-century poetry, **28–9**, 35–6, 74–5

elegy, 30

Elizabethan and Jacobean drama, 3–4, 22, 84–5, **87–9**, 90, 99, 100

    see also Shakespeare, 94–9

empathy, 143

end rhymes, 59

end-stopped rhymes, 49

English sonnet, 65–7

enjambement, 49

epic, 23, **31–2**, 57–8

epic simile, 31–2

epic theatre, 92, **102–3**

epistolary novel, 113

epithalamion, 32–3

Eurocentrism, 10, **130**

exposition *in* drama, **79**, 86, 160

expressive criticism, **166**, 167, 175

eye rhymes, 59

fallacy, **132–3**, 147

fancy, 143–4

fantasy literature, 124

farce, 86

feminine, the, 156

feminine rhymes, 59

feminist criticism, 75, 131, 137, 138, 140, 155, 156, 169, **170–3**, 178, 183, 187, 190, 198

    French feminist criticism, 171–2

feminist novelists, 130–1

feminist theatre, 104–5

figurative imagery, **37–9**, 126–7, 151–2

film, 105

first-person narrative, 116

foot, 47–8

foregrounding, 189
form, 13, **144–5**, 159–60
formal analysis, 145
free verse, **33–5**, 49
Freudian criticism, 186

gay criticism, 173
gender, 156, **172–3**, 187
gender studies, 156
generic context, 1–2
Geneva school, 185
genre, **1–2**, 144
Georgian poets, 70
Gothic novels, 124
gynocriticism, 157

half-rhyme, 21, **59**, 70
hegemony, 146
hermeneutics, 145–6
hero, **83**, 99
heroic couplet, 29, **35–6**, 68
heroine, 83
hexameter, 48
historical context, 1, 2
history play, 96–7
hypotactic sentences, 162

iambic pentameter, 22, 35, **46–8**
ideology, 105, 106, **146–7**, 161, 177
imagery, **36–9**, 69, 151–2
imaginary, the, 140
imagination, 5, 63–5, **143–4**
imagism, 39–40
imperfect rhymes, 59
imposed form, 159
incremental repetition, 22
intentional fallacy, **147**, 164
internal rhyme, 58
interpretation, 145, 165
intertextuality, 163
intrusive narrator, 113–14, **117**
ironic persona, 148
irony, **147–50**, 159, 180
    see also satire
Italian sonnet, 65

Jacobean drama, *see* Elizabethan and
    Jacobean drama

Jungian criticism, 186

language, 10, 36–9, 125–7, 136, 138, 140,
    141, 142, **150–1**, 151–4, 157,
    160–1, 171, 189, 190, 191–2, 194,
    195
language and poetry, **151–3**, 154–5
    see also alliteration, assonance, im-
        agery, rhyme, rhythm, symbol
langue, 191
Law of the Father, 140
lesbian criticism, 173
liberal humanism, **175**, 176, 183
lisible, 157
literary ballads, 22
literary criticism, 165–70
    see also criticism
literary terms, 139–40
logocentrism, 139
lyric, 40–3
    introduction to, 14–17
    see also elegy, ode, sonnet
lyrical ballad, 43–4

magical realism, **129–30**, 131
main plot, 92
manque-à-être, 141
marginal, 156
Marxist criticism, 138, 146–7, 161, 169,
    173, 175, **176–8**, 179, 183, 187, 198
masculine, the, 156
masculine rhymes, 59
media studies, 105–6
medieval drama, 79, **89–90**
medieval literature, **2–3**, 4
    see also allegory, courtly-love poetry,
        dream poetry, medieval drama,
        romance
melodrama, 90–1
metaphor, 23–5, 37, 126–7, **151–4**
metaphysical poetry, 24–5, **44–6**, 153,
    154
metonymy, 153–4
metre, 46–9
Middle English literature, *see* medieval
    literature
miracle plays, 79, **89–90**
misprision, 164

mock-heroic, 49–50
  see also heroic couplet, irony, satire
mode, 1
modern poetry, 6–8, **50–2**, 70–1
  see also free verse, imagism, symbol, twentieth-century poetry
modernist, 6
morality plays, 79, 88, **90**
motif, 154
Movement, the, 72

narrative poetry, 52–4
  see also ballad, epic, romance
narrative structure, 115–16
narratology, 178–80
narrator
  in novels, **116–17**, 148–9
  in poetry, 52–3
naturalism, 91, **120**
near rhymes, 59
neoclassic, 29
New Criticism, 148, 151, 155, 167, 168, 175, 177, **180–2**, 197
New Historicism, 169–70, 172, 173, 178, **182–5**, 190, 198
New Poetry, the, 72
nineteenth-century drama, 85–6, **90–1**, 99, 100–1
nineteenth-century literature, *see* Victorian literature
nineteenth-century novels, 118–19
nineteenth-century poetry, *see* Victorian poetry
nouveau roman, 19⁰
novel, the, **107–31**
  see character, comic novels, dialogic, eighteenth-century novels, narrative structure, narratology, narrator, nineteenth-century novels, realism, reflexive novels, romance, stream of consciousness, style, twentieth-century novels

octava rima, 68
octave, 66
ode, **54–5**, 160
Oedipus complex, 140

off-rhymes, 59
Old English literature, **2**, 48
omniscient narrator, 116
open couplets, 35
organic form, **159–60**, 181
Other, the, 141, 143

paradox, 45, 46, **154–5**, 180
paratactic sentences, 162
parole, 191
partial rhymes, 59
pastoral, 55–6
pathetic fallacy, 155
patriarchy, 76, 77, 137, **155–7**, 170, 172, 173
periods of English literature, 2–8
personification, 155
Petrarchan sonnet, **65–6**, 67
phallocentricism, **156**, 172, 187
phenomenological criticism, 185–6
picaresque novels, 114
plot
  in drama, 92–3
  in novels, 115
pluralist criticism, 175
poetic diction, 19
poetry, **12–77**
  see alliteration, archaism, assonance, ballad, blank verse, conceit, courtly-love poetry, dramatic monologue, dream poetry, eighteenth-century poetry, elegy, epic, epithalamion, free verse, heroic couplet, imagery, imagism, lyric, lyrical ballad, metaphysical poetry, metre, mock-heroic, modern poetry, narrative poetry, ode, pastoral, Renaissance poetry, rhyme, rhythm, romance, romantic poetry, sonnet, stanza, symbol, twentieth-century poetry, verse epistle, women's poetry
point-of-view, 116
political criticism, 138, 146, 175, 190
  see also feminist criticism, Marxist criticism
polyphonic, 137, 179, 190
post-colonial literature, 8–11

post-modernist, 8, 72–3
post-structuralism, 138, 140, 141, 142, 151, 157, 160–1, 164, 169, 189, **194–9**
    see also deconstruction, structuralism
power, **142**, 146, 172, 184
practical criticism, 145, **174**
Prague school, **169**, 190
presence, 139
problem play, 91
prosody, 49
protagonist, 83
psychoanalytic criticism, 140, 161, 172, **186–8**, 198
psychobiography, 186
psychological novels, 113, **124–5**
pure-stress metre, 48–9

quatrain, 67, **68**

reader, the, 165, 167, 168
reader-response criticism, 188–9
readerly, 157–8
realism, 119–21
realistic novels, 5–6, 108–9, 111, 112–13, 114, 116–17, **119–21**, 127
reception theory, 188
reflexive novels, 109, 114, **121–2**
Renaissance drama, *see* Elizabethan and Jacobean drama
Renaissance literature, **3–4**, 182, 183–4
    see also Elizabethan and Jacobean drama, Renaissance poetry, Shakespeare
Renaissance poetry, 3–4, 41–2, **56–8**
    see also conceit, courtly love poetry, epic, metaphysical poetry, pastoral, sonnet
resolution *in* drama, 79, 81, 86, 160
Restoration comedy, 85, **93–4**
revenge tragedy, 88
rhyme, 58–60
rhyme royal, 68
rhythm, 60–1
romance
    drama, 98–9
    novels, 7, 109, **122–4**
    poetry, 61–2

romantic comedy, **84–5**, 94
romantic literature, **4–5**, 62
romantic poetry, 4–5, 43, **62–6**, 143–4, 159–60
    see also dream poetry, lyrical ballad, ode
run-on lines, 49
Russian Formalism, 169, 178, **189–90**

satire, 111, 148, **158–9**
    see also eighteenth-century poetry, heroic couplet, irony, satiric comedy, verse epistle
satiric comedy, 84, **85**, 88–9, 93
scene, 80, **81–2**, 92
science fiction, 124
scriptible, 157
semiotic, the, 141
semiotics, 159
sentimental comedy, 93–4
sestet, 66
seventeenth-century literature, *see* Renaissance literature
sexual politics, 155
Shakespearean sonnet, **65–7**, 163
signified, 191–2
signifier, 191–2
simile, 37, 152
site of struggle, 138
situational irony, 149
slant rhymes, 59
social poetry, *see* eighteenth-century poetry
soliloquy, **95**, 143, 152
sonnet, 14, 22, **65–7**, 68, 139, 144, 145, 163
sonnet sequence, **26**, 57, 66
sound *in* poetry, 17–18, 20–1, **36–7**, 58–60
South African literature, 9
South American literature, 8, 129, 130
Spenserian stanza, 32, **68**
spondee, 48
sprung rhythm, 49
stanza, 13, **67–8**
stereotype, 75, 104, 105, **156**
story
    in drama, 92

in novels, 107–8, 114, **114–16**
in poetry, 14, **52–4**
stream of consciousness, **124–5**, 128
stress, 46–9
stressed syllables, 46–8
strong-stress metre, 48–9
strong rhymes, 59
structuralism, 136–7, 139, 151, 157, 159,
    167, 169, 175, 177, 183, 187, 188,
    189, **190–4**, 197, 198
    see also deconstruction, post-structur-
    alism
structure, 159–60
    of drama, **78–81**, 105
    of novels, 107–9, *114–16*
    of poetry, 13–17
style, 150–1
    in novels, 125–7
subject, the, 140, 141, 142, 147, **160–1**,
    186, 187, 188
subject (tenor) *in* metaphor, 152
subplot, 92
symbol, 55, **68–70**, 134
Symbolic Order, the, **140–1**, 161, 171
sympathy, 143
syntax, 36, **161–3**

television, 105–6
tenor *in* metaphor, 152
tercet, 68
tetrameter, 48
text, 163–4
theatre of the absurd, 86, 92–3, **103**
theme, 154
thesis play, 91
tragedy, 79, 81, 92, 97–8, **99–101**, 160
tragicomedy, **84–5**, 95
tragic hero, 83, 88, **99–100**, 101
transcendental signified, 139

triplet, 68
trochaic foot, 48
trochee, 48
twentieth-century criticism, 167–70
twentieth-century drama, 7–8, 82, 86,
    100–1, **101–6**
twentieth-century literature, 6–11
    see also modern poetry, twentieth-
    century drama, twentieth-century
    novels, twentieth-century poetry
twentieth-century novels, 6, 7, 8–10,
    124–5, **127–31**
twentieth-century poetry, 70–4
    see also imagism, modern poetry,
    symbol, women's poetry

unintrusive narrator, 116
unreliable narrator, 117
unstressed syllables, 46–8
utopian novels, 123

vehicle *in* metaphor, 152
verse epistle, 40, 42, **73–5**
verse paragraph, 23
Vice, the, 90
Victorian literature, 5–6
    see also nineteenth-century drama,
    nineteenth-century novels, Vic-
    torian poetry
Victorian poetry, **5**, 26–7, 42
villain, 83

weak rhymes, 59
well-made play, **91**, 101
wit, 46
women's poetry, 157–8
writerly, 157–8

Yale school, 196

SYNTAGMATICCHAN

SHEDHUT

SEEN IN RELATION

FLAT BUNGALOW HOUSE Mansion

Have to be seen

in relation